THE HEAD BHOYS

THE HEAD BHOYS

Celtic's Managers

Graham McColl

MAINSTREAM
PUBLISHING

EDINBURGH AND LONDON

First published in Great Britain in 2002 by
MAINSTREAM PUBLISHING COMPANY (EDINBURGH) LTD
7 Albany Street
Edinburgh EH1 3UG

ISBN 1 84018 620 8

A catalogue record for this book is available from the British Library

Typeset in Franklin and Janson
Printed and bound in Great Britain by
Creative Print and Design, Wales

Contents

Acknowledgements

I would like to thank the following, all of whose help was indispensable in my work on this book: John Barnes, Eric Black, Alec Boden, Liam Brady, Davie Brown, Jock Brown, Willie Buchan, Tommy Burns, Gordon Cowans, John Divers, Tommy Gemmell, David Hay, John Hughes, Ally Hunter, Jim Huskie, www.icons.com, Paul Lagan, David Low, Eugene MacBride, Jim McColl, Jack McGinn, Fiona MacLean, Murdo MacLeod, Billy McNeill, Lou Macari, Lubo Moravcik, Betty Murray, George Sheridan, Gillian Snowden, Iain Spragg, Billy Stark, Diana van Bunnens, Dr Jozef Venglos, Dr Juraj Venglos, Adam Ward, Paul Ward, Jackie Watters, John Wilson, Johnnie Wilson.

Special thanks also to all at Mainstream, especially Bill Campbell for giving my idea for this book the go-ahead, Tina Hudson for her work on the cover design, and Graeme Blaikie and Jess Thompson for editorial coordination.

This book is dedicated to my wife, Jackie, whose patience, support and help made everything easier.

Introduction

The manager has always been the most important person at Celtic Football Club. That is as true today as it was in 1897 when Willie Maley became the first of 13 men to hold the position. The exact nature of the job has fluctuated in tandem with football fashion throughout each decade of the club's existence but the strength and personality of each manager has always been the key element in the club's fortunes.

Willie Maley's official title was secretary-manager but the next eight men in charge of team matters were given the streamlined title of manager, although each approached the job in a very different manner. Then, during the late 1990s, the title of manager was abolished and Wim Jansen, Doctor Jozef Venglos and John Barnes were titled head coach. Martin O'Neill, on his arrival at Celtic Park in 2000, insisted on his title reverting to that of manager, which confers on its holder the authority of the man who solely selects the team and has a hands-on involvement in all the major decisions in connection with transfers and playing matters. It is, ultimately, such decisions that decide the direction in which the club travels.

Sixty thousand pairs of eyes pick out the figure of Martin O'Neill as he hovers on the touchline at Celtic Park on match days. It is the type of scrutiny that would undo anyone susceptible to pressure but the Irishman appears to thrive on the responsibility of being solely to account for every aspect of the team's performance. His concentration on the job in hand and his uncluttered approach to his work ensures that no one in his charge is in any doubt as to what he requires from his players individually and as a team. The characteristics that have brought such success to him as Celtic manager are described here through inside insights and in minute detail in the chapter that tells his story as Celtic manager.

Martin O'Neill's earliest predecessor, Willie Maley, was, literally, 'in with the bricks' at Celtic Park. His appointment as the club's first manager allowed him to devote his time fully to keeping a permanently watchful eye on the players at a crucial time, when the club was switching from being a charitable institution to a limited company. The Celtic committee had previously selected the team. Maley ruled by fear and, through sheer strength of will in tandem with iron discipline, he made Celtic the most attractive and successful club in Scotland. Former players Willie Buchan, Johnnie Wilson and Jackie Watters provide lively descriptions of the doings of this intimidating figure. His chapter describes how, despite his exceptional service, he left the club in acrimonious circumstances. He would not be the last Celtic manager to leave on such terms.

Maley's successors, Jimmy McStay and Jimmy McGrory, mimicked his aloof, authoritarian style but neither had the bark nor the bite to carry it off with the players and during their eras as manager Celtic plunged into serious decline. Both men were manipulated wilfully by the Celtic board, almost as if they were puppets, and Celtic were directionless for years as a consequence. No one could manipulate the man who followed them, Jock Stein, an individual of enormous presence, vision and charisma. His achievements in winning numerous trophies, nine championships in a row and, in particular, the European Cup, elevated him to near-sainthood in the eyes of many Celtic supporters. His chapter will look closely at the sophisticated methods that Stein employed to achieve his great successes. His ability to achieve excellence with players whose careers had been frittering away under Jimmy McGrory emphasises the massive difference the right manager can make.

Jock Stein's captain during the club's most glorious years of the 1960s and 1970s, Billy McNeill, was an obvious successor to Stein when Stein left the club in 1978. A natural leader on the field, McNeill's teams were never short of spirit. McNeill's greatest managerial victories were do-or-die affairs but after five trophies in five years a clash with the Celtic board saw him walk out on the club he genuinely loves to take up the offer of a job with Manchester City. He makes the reasons for his dissatisfaction clear in his chapter. A more reserved individual, David Hay, took his place but he was sometimes perceived by the more excitable elements amongst Celtic's support as someone who was less than committed to the cause. That was far from the truth, as he explains. He also recounts how he became the first Celtic manager to be sacked rather than to resign.

The composition of the Celtic board had changed sufficiently by 1987 to enable an approach to be made to Billy McNeill to return as manager. Following the death of Desmond White in 1985, it seemed almost as though other board members were now re-recruiting McNeill as the best possible apology for the shabby treatment he had received at the hands of the White-dominated board four years previously. McNeill's punchy style of leadership made for a fantastic first year back as Celtic won the League and Scottish Cup double in their centenary year. He later paid for two successive trophyless seasons with his job.

The summer of 1991 saw the Celtic board, now under pressure from the support due to their inefficient running of the club, go to extremes to show that they were ushering in a new era. Instead of the old 'nod and a wink' approach to appointing a former player as manager, they drew up a shortlist of four candidates who were interviewed amidst great publicity. Liam Brady, a newcomer to management who had had no previous connection with Celtic, was given the job. He relates how he coped with the pressures surrounding the post during a problem-riddled period in the club's history.

Lou Macari's appointment in 1993 was, in one way, a return to tradition in that he was a former Celtic player and although he made a good start he had been in the job for only four months when Fergus McCann took control of Celtic. McCann sacked Macari in the summer of 1994, an action that resulted in Macari launching a lengthy but unsuccessful court action against the club's new owner.

Tommy Burns restored flair to the Celtic team and went desperately close to taking the Scottish League title with a team that departed from tradition by featuring star foreigners, such as Paolo Di Canio, Jorge Cadete and Pierre van Hooijdonk. Their introduction, which is discussed in detail by Burns in his chapter, caused as many problems as pleasures for their manager and Burns followed them out of Celtic Park after three years.

The first continental European to manage Celtic was a Dutchman, Wim Jansen. His appointment heralded a new era in which a head coach would work with a general manager in a continental-type system but friction led to Jansen quitting the club after just ten months in charge of the team. He was succeeded by Slovakian Dr Jozef Venglos, who was whisked into position at Celtic on the eve of the 1998–99 season and as he points out it was not surprising that he struggled initially. The Scottish press were confused by Venglos' gentlemanly demeanour and intelligent approach to management and responded by ridiculing him. Despite these trying circumstances, during the second half of the 1998–99 season Celtic rallied to considerable effect, playing superb football and almost pipping Rangers to the title. Venglos deserves to have his tarnished reputation reassessed – his chapter shows how he introduced the skilful Lubomir Moravcik and harnessed the talents of others to create a dynamic team. John Barnes, Venglos' successor, was forced to quit after a shocking home defeat by Inverness Caledonian Thistle, just seven months into the job. As he reveals, he now regrets taking the job on with such a lack of experience. Lubo Moravcik helps to discuss this era in entertaining fashion.

From Maley to O'Neill, every manager of Celtic has influenced, to a greater or lesser degree, the progress of the club. Even those who have lacked success have cleared the way for a more illustrious successor. Others have failed to land a trophy but have brought key players to the club. This book portrays in fine detail the character of each manager of Celtic and, with the use of intricate interview material with players and the former managers themselves, takes you inside the dressing-room at Celtic Park to bring alive the style and substance of each one of the Head Bhoys.

ONE

Willie Maley – The Iron Man

Willie Maley turned on his heel and strode out of Celtic Park, leaving behind him a football club whose adventurous, attacking style he had done much to shape. It was 1939 and Maley was divorcing himself, deeply reluctantly, from the club to which he had devoted 52 years of painstaking work. As he moved off from the ground and looked across the east end of Glasgow, wearing his habitual grimace, he could reflect on how he, more than any other individual, had branded Celtic as a club whose teams would win with style. Brother Walfrid had founded Celtic Football Club for charitable purposes back in 1888 but it was Maley who had quickly taken up the baton and had done much to develop it into a hugely entertaining enterprise.

On emerging into the light that December day, having been propelled firmly into retirement by the Celtic board, Maley could also reflect on how he had been initially as reluctant to join the club as he was now reluctant to leave. He had signed for the club almost by accident in its earliest days. A party of Celtic committee men, featuring the club's first chairman John Glass, and Brother Walfrid, had visited Maley's father's house in Cathcart, Glasgow, in December 1887, purposefully seeking the signature of Tom Maley, Willie's brother. Tom was out seeing his girlfriend but Willie was at home and got into conversation with the visitors. At that time he had played a few games for Third Lanark, a club on the south side of Glasgow, but he was actually much more involved in athletics than in football. He considered himself a footballing 'second-rater' and told the visitors that he was actually on the point of giving up the game entirely to concentrate on cross-country running. The persuasive powers of the Celtic men eventually convinced him to join their new club along with his brother and five months later, on 28 May 1888, he was at right-half in the side that defeated Rangers 5–2 in Celtic's first-ever match.

Tom Maley, a winger, was also in that team and the brothers were relied upon heavily by the Celtic committee in those early days to seek out players and to advise on team selection. Half a dozen players arrived at Celtic Park from Hibernian prior to the club's first competitive fixture, a Scottish Cup tie in September 1888. They had been poached from the Edinburgh club by Tom Maley, a former Hibernian player. Tom was, in common with others who ran Celtic in its earliest days, quite determined and sometimes ruthless in his methods. His Celtic playing career was short – he made just nine competitive appearances – but in 1897 he was made a director of the club in recognition of his knowledge of football and ability to advise other directors on the game. Willie, meanwhile, had been a regular performer during the club's opening decade, making close to 100 appearances in the team. Tireless in his duties as a midfielder, he could never stand accused of giving anything less than his all for the Celtic cause. During the 1893 Scottish Cup final with Queen's Park, which ended in a 2–1 defeat for Celtic, Maley took a ferocious kick in the face from an opponent's boot that saw him removed from the action to have four teeth extracted. Happier days with the club had seen him win a Cup medal in 1892 and he was a key member of the side that won League championships in 1893, 1894 and 1896.

The young Willie Maley, in common with his late-Victorian team-mates, followed the fashion of wearing a moustache but any indication of vivaciousness ended there. Alongside such players as the somewhat rakish centre-forward Johnny Campbell and the dreamy-looking inside-left Sandy McMahon, nicknamed 'the Duke', Maley was stern in appearance. The possessor of a bold, challenging stare, he was a man who looked the world in the eye and saw it for what it was worth. He had been Celtic's first match secretary at the club's inception and his work in developing the club in its earliest years had been rewarded in 1893 when he was promoted to club secretary, a job that it was felt suited him in that he was an accountant by profession.

His credentials as an organiser and an establishment man were strengthened greatly three years later when he spearheaded action to break a strike that had been perpetrated by three players: Barney Battles, John Divers and Peter Meechan. They refused to take the field for a League match with Hibernian in late 1896 because they were unhappy about the way the *Glasgow Evening News* and the *Scottish Referee* had reported Celtic's conduct in a match with Rangers a week previously. Both papers had condemned Celtic players for taking an ultra-physical approach and, as the minutes ticked away before kick-off in the Hibs match, Battles, Divers and Meechan insisted they would not take the pitch unless those papers' correspondents were removed from the Celtic Park press box.

Maley sprang into life. Although he had retired as a Celtic player at the end of the 1895–96 season he decided to make a comeback to thwart the strikers. A green-and-white striped jersey was supplied and, as Maley got stripped, Celtic brought in a reserve player, Barney Crossan, and started the match with ten men. Another full-back, Tom Dunbar, was sent for and he rushed from Hampden Park, where he had been playing for the reserves, to join the first-team for the second half of the Hibs game. Celtic managed to end the match with a 1–1 draw. The strike had been crushed and the three individuals responsible were swiftly shown the door at Celtic Park. At the end of that season, Maley's loyalty was rewarded when he was appointed the club's first secretary-manager on 3 April 1897 with a salary of £150 per year. He was a mere 29 years old but he was already a worldly man and had a brisk, businesslike approach that was to prove vitally important at a club that had been converted into a limited company only a month previously. Celtic's charitable roots were not to be ignored entirely, but Maley's appointment coincided with a new dawn: the club now had to be run more along business lines, and to this end Maley would work in tandem with the new chairman, a finance-driven individual called John McLaughlin.

It did not take long for Maley to make his mark in management. He led Celtic to the Scottish League title in his first full season as manager, 1897–98, and then to the Scottish Cup in each of the following two seasons. His active intervention in the strike of November 1896 had marked him out as a manager who would not be messed with and, having swapped his football equipment for a bow tie, hat and suit, he now looked more stern and authoritarian than ever.

The team had been selected and run by the Celtic committee during the nine years prior to Willie Maley becoming Celtic's first manager and from them he had inherited an ageing side, some of whom had been at Celtic since the club's earliest days. Dan Doyle, the star full-back, was in his mid-30s, and others such as forward Sandy McMahon, goalkeeper Dan McArthur and centre-forward Johnny Campbell had had a decade's worth of knocks in the highly physical game of the late-Victorian era. It was time for reconstruction and although Celtic went from 1900 to 1904 without winning any of the national trophies, Maley was given full backing to build a new team. When it eventually took shape, it became clear that Maley had sculpted into existence one of the finest footballing sides in Celtic's history. That team won six League championship titles in succession from 1905 to 1910, a run that included the club's first two Cup and League Doubles, in 1907 and 1908.

It had taken Maley several years of hard labour to assemble that team, and no player had proved more difficult for him to net than its leading man, Jimmy Quinn, the centre-forward. Quinn had been hunted down in Junior football by Maley, but the player was a quiet, self-effacing type and had initially been reluctant to sign despite a personal visit from the Celtic manager to his home in Croy. 'Father, mother, brother Peter and Jimmy himself received me,' Maley was to recall years later. 'I joined them in a cup of tea. Then, fingering my registration form, I asked Quinn if he would not sign for Celtic. Quick and curt was his reply, "No, Mr Maley. I don't want to leave the Juniors."' Quinn reiterated to Maley several times that he was quite content to play in the Juniors but Maley simply refused to take no for an answer. The manager knew that a number of leading English clubs were after Quinn's signature and was determined not to leave Croy without a result.

After hours of discussion with the player and his family, he persuaded Quinn to sign a registration form with Celtic but promised not to lodge it with the Scottish Football Association (SFA) unless he was given the player's express permission. Feeling secure in the knowledge that he had what amounted to a pledge from the player and that no one else could now sign Quinn, Maley came away from Croy knowing that he had bought himself time. Weeks later, after Maley had carefully cultivated the player's trust during a number of practice games and training sessions with Celtic, Jimmy Quinn finally put Smithston Albion behind him and signed for Maley. The manager's perseverance and guile would be amply rewarded – Quinn went on to score 216 goals for the club in a 14-year career at Celtic Park.

Willie Maley's keen decisiveness was well illustrated by his handling of his team selection for the 1904 Scottish Cup final. Alec Bennett had been centre-forward in the run-up to the final but Maley was aware that the player was being tapped by Rangers, Celtic's opponents. In the days prior to the match Maley ruminated over whether to continue with Bennett but eventually opted to drop the player even though Bennett had been in fine goalscoring form throughout the season. Having decided that he could not be 100 per cent sure of Bennett against the team that was currently seeking the player's services, the manager put out the story that Bennett was suffering from the flu and took a gamble on Jimmy Quinn, moving him from his habitual left-wing position to centre-forward specifically for that match. Maley's men went 2–0 down within 12 minutes and, with no substitutes allowed in those days, he had no way of altering his experimental forward line. By half-time his faith in Quinn had been rewarded. The converted centre-forward had scored the two goals that had cancelled Rangers' lead and seven minutes from time he became the first scorer of a Scottish Cup final hat-trick when he slipped the winning goal into the net.

Maley's gamble had been handsomely rewarded. It had brought him Celtic's first trophy for four years, the first for his newly constructed team, and had revealed a hidden talent in Quinn as a principal goalscorer. It was a move on Maley's part that required nerve, self-belief and courage; the hallmarks of all great managers in whichever era. Maley must have perceived something in Quinn that convinced him, rightly, that his faith in the player's ability to score goals would be rewarded.

Quinn was typical of the new set of Celtic signings in the opening decade of the twentieth century. Maley had transformed the club from being one that purchased ready-made senior professionals at high prices to one that smoked out untapped talent from the Junior ranks and found bargain signings elsewhere. This reliance on unproven players was a high-risk policy for the club and its failure could have set Celtic back years. Maley agonised long, hard and often during those years as to whether he was doing the right thing, but his determination and eye for talent eventually saw those misgivings entirely erased. The team that won Celtic the club's first Double by beating Hearts 3–0 in the 1907 Scottish Cup final included six players who had been signed from Junior clubs: goalkeeper Davy Adams, outside-right Alec Bennett, left-half Jimmy Hay, inside-right Jimmy McMenemy, centre-half Alec McNair, and Quinn. Two players had arrived from minor Scottish clubs: right-back Donald McLeod from Stenhousemuir and inside-left Peter Somers from Hamilton Accies. Right-half 'Sunny Jim' Young had arrived on a free transfer from Bristol Rovers while outside-left Bobby Templeton had been recruited in 1904 from the then cash-strapped Woolwich Arsenal. Willie Orr, the left-back who had been at the club since 1897, was the oddity in that side in that he had been a costly recruit from a leading English club, Preston North End, at a time when, shortly after having become a limited company, Celtic were splashing out cash.

The recruitment of young, inexperienced players as twentieth-century Bhoys enabled Maley to enforce iron discipline on his players. These youngsters would be unlikely to step out of line – unlike more experienced, hardened professionals – and Maley was able to mould them into Celtic men and exercise close to complete control over them. A lack of big-name individuals among the players also held the team together. Maley's methods were effective: as their six-in-a-row run progressed, this selection of surprise stars from small-time origins were soon being described as the greatest team in the world. For the manager, the team's success consolidated his own position at the club and his organisational skills and knowledge of football made him close to irreplaceable. He also had several key allies alongside him on the Celtic board of directors. Mick Dunbar and James Kelly had been in the very first Celtic team back in 1888 alongside Maley and he could confide in them and, when he so desired, discuss football matters with them in the knowledge that these were directors who had opinions on football to which it would be worth listening. John McLaughlin, whose appointment as chairman had coincided with Maley becoming secretary-manager, was still in position in the opening decade of the twentieth century and continuity would be guaranteed when McLaughlin was succeeded by Kelly in 1909.

As Maley celebrated his 40th birthday in April 1908 with a second successive Double for Celtic he could reflect on two full and fruitful decades in football during which he had grown into the role of manager. He now projected an image of authority and respectability. He was always impeccably dressed and his good clothes, his confident, challenging expression and his powerful physique emphasised the prosperity and financial security that he had gained from his association with Celtic. This was a man with whom you would meddle at your peril.

Once his six-times champions began to age, Maley revamped his side once again and his remodelled outfit went on another long championship-winning run, taking four titles in succession between 1914 and 1917 and winning the title again in 1919. Although a disciplinarian, Maley was not a fanatic when it came to training his players. At Celtic, as with the majority of other clubs in the first half of the twentieth century, training involved little ballwork and for Maley the purpose of training was to maintain players at their fighting weight. Heavyweights such as Quinn would be trained hard because they would require work to stay in shape. Others, such as the lightweight Patsy Gallacher, who joined Celtic in 1911, would be allowed the least demanding of training regimes and would be actively encouraged to save their efforts for the Saturday's match. In its way, this approach was quite progressive in that the manager accepted the different requirements of individuals and did not employ hard training as a means of battering players into submission, an approach that always contains inbuilt flaws.

Money was a different matter. Numerous disputes arose between Maley and star players over wages and bonuses, often leading to the departure of aggrieved individuals from the club. Throughout the

1920s a steady stream of talented players were moved on from Celtic Park after daring to challenge Maley with regard to financial matters. In 1928 Maley attempted to sell the club's leading star of the time and the team's top scorer, the smiling, effervescent Jimmy McGrory, to Arsenal. It was an unpleasant episode in Maley's managerial career. McGrory, a humble man whose love of Celtic was deep and genuine, was a devoted Catholic. That year he accompanied Maley on a visit to Lourdes. The manager, with the approval of the Celtic board of directors, opportunistically used the trip to make a diversion and meet Arsenal's manager Herbert Chapman in an attempt to arrange Maley's transfer from Celtic. Arsenal were willing to pay a British record fee of £10,000 for McGrory but the player refused the offer made by Chapman, Arsenal's hugely successful manager. Maley would not accept that this was the end of the matter. On the way back from their pilgrimage to the grotto in the south-west of France, Maley once again took McGrory to see Chapman in another attempt to sell off Celtic's prize asset. This time, McGrory, tiring of the entire business, brought matters to a swift conclusion by stating that he would only join Arsenal if they paid him a monstrous signing-on fee of £2,000, a fee so high that McGrory, Maley and Chapman all knew it to be impossible.

The deal was off and McGrory returned to Glasgow with Maley. McGrory would remain with the club for the rest of his career, finishing it as Celtic's greatest-ever goalscorer. Off the field, the tawdry conclusion to his refusal to move to Arsenal was that Maley, in collusion with the Celtic board, decided that they would pay McGrory less than his due. The player, unknown to him, would receive less money than his team-mates for the remainder of his Celtic career, quiet vengeance by Maley and the Celtic board of directors for McGrory's refusal to help add to the Celtic coffers through the sale of his talents. It was not quite what might have been expected as the result of a visit to one of the most famous Catholic shrines.

Throughout the 1920s Maley's grip on managerial matters at Celtic appeared as strong as ever, but it was a decade in which Celtic won just two League championships and three Scottish Cups. Rangers, who had appointed a new, progressive manager – Bill Struth

– in 1920, won the other eight championships and one Scottish Cup, making this the first decade in which the Ibrox club had been the dominant force in Scottish football. Celtic even found themselves eclipsed by Airdrieonians during the early 1920s. For three seasons in succession, from 1922–23 to 1924–25, Airdrie rather than Celtic were Rangers' chief title challengers. Airdrie were now managed by ex-Celt Willie Orr, and perhaps an injection of fresh, modern managerial talent in the shape of Orr might have done much for Celtic. Instead, he was allowed to move south in 1926 to take over as manager at Leicester City and during his six impressive years at Filbert Street he led Leicester to their highest-ever League finish, when they ended the 1928–29 season second in the First Division, just one point behind champions Sheffield Wednesday.

Rangers' – and Airdrie's – cause was undoubtedly aided by the constant flow of talent out of Celtic Park as a result of disputes over money with Maley who was still, literally, Celtic's Mr Moneybags. Visitors to his Bank restaurant at the foot of Queen Street in the centre of Glasgow would be treated to the sight of Maley, after a home match, carrying bags of coins and notes containing the turnstile takings into the vaults of his appropriately named establishment. 'East, West, hame's best,' said Maley to journalists as he sat ensconced in the Bank once again after Celtic's two-month tour of North America in the summer of 1931 – and no wonder he felt pleased to be surrounded by those particular home comforts. 'He must have made millions – and I mean millions – out of the Bank restaurant,' says Willie Buchan, who joined Celtic in the early 1930s, when Maley was the indisputable, unchallengeable authority figure at Celtic.

'He was very stern, like a major in the army,' adds Buchan. 'That's how he seemed to the younger players. Willie Maley used to make the younger players tremble. He was a disciplinarian: his general attitude had the younger players, like myself, Paterson and Delaney and the others, more or less afraid of him, afraid to go in and ask him for a ten-bob rise or something like that. Any young boy there would be scared for his job. I remember I was getting four pounds and ten shillings and he promised me a ten-bob rise if I got a game in the first team. So I got in the first-team but I didn't get my ten bob. So I asked him for my ten bob. Maley said to me, in his very loud voice, "I didn't promise you a ten-shilling rise if you played in the first-team!" I said, "Excuse me, Mr Maley, you did." He said, "If I promised you it, it will be in your wages this week." Ten bob! You wouldn't pick it up if it was lying on the floor nowadays!'

Buchan was a typical Maley signing. He had been playing for Grange Rovers, one of three Junior sides in his native Grangemouth, when he turned out for a Junior select at Firhill. This parade of talent was attended by both Willie Maley and the Rangers manager, Bill Struth. After the game both managers visited Grangemouth to offer Buchan the opportunity to join their respective clubs. It is a sign of those times that Buchan, who was 18, had seen neither Celtic nor Rangers play and was unaware of which club was which. Buchan's decision to join Celtic was unrelated to Maley. The player's friend and fellow inside-right, Archie MacAulay, who had also participated in that match at Firhill, had joined Rangers from Camelon Juniors. Not wishing to compete with MacAulay, whom he considered a 'smashing' player, for an inside-forward's jersey at Ibrox, Buchan joined Celtic and soon found that everyone now thought he was a Catholic, even though the only chapel he had seen was the one he passed on the way to his local public park.

'You didn't argue with Willie Maley or anything like that: what he said went – oh aye,' says Buchan. Nor did the manager need to do a great deal of shouting at his players to get them to do his will. In the hungry '30s, when the Great Depression was settling over the land, it was not a time for arguing strenuously with the man who controlled your employment. 'We just treated him like a boss at a workplace,' remembers Buchan. 'Willie Maley was your boss. If he said you should do something, you had to do it. I wouldn't say I liked him but I quite admired him as a boss. He wasn't a person that you would go out with or anything like that, you know, you'd never think of spending a night out with him, at least I wouldn't, but his heart and soul was in Celtic – I wouldn't grudge him that. Jimmy McMenemy, an ex-player, took the training; he was our trainer. You never actually saw Maley as such unless you were going in to talk to him about wages or something like that. So you wouldn't see him during the week; he took nothing at all to do with the training.'

These were hard but simple times. Celtic bought Buchan a season-ticket for his local bus company and along with fellow Celts George Paterson and Charlie Napier he would take the bus through to Glasgow from central Scotland before jumping on the tram from London Road to Celtic Park. Eleven players used to travel through on the bus to Queen Street; a mixture of Celtic, Rangers and Partick Thistle players, all enjoying each other's company. 'When it came to the team selection,' explains Buchan of life at Celtic, 'you more or less got it off the papers! So you did! Before a match we wouldn't get any instructions as such from Willie Maley. You just went out and played your game. You knew your position, do you know what I mean? I played inside-right or inside-left and the reason I did that is because you are never out of position. You can attack and you can defend. If you were a left-back you were a left-back; if you were a right-back you were a right-back! That's why I liked the inside-forward position. You were up attacking or back defending.'

Jackie Watters was a schoolboy at St Aloysius' College in Glasgow and part of the school's all-conquering football team. During the early 1930s he would see Maley at nine o'clock mass in the baroque grandeur of St Aloysius' chapel in Garnethill almost every morning in life. Watters was 15 years old when he caught the eye of Celtic and has vivid memories of how Maley and the club supported him financially even before he became a professional at Celtic Park in the late 1930s. 'He was manager of one of the best teams in the world, then, that's number one,' says Watters of Maley. 'I played at Fulham's ground for Glasgow secondary schools against London secondary schools – there were three or four boys from St Aloysius in that team. I came back and the Celtic chief scout wanted me to sign provisionally. Well, I was then going to study physiotherapy, you see, and anyway I signed on provisionally and I used to go down to the Bank restaurant and get my wee bawbees. The money would be in an envelope when I got that. They were very good to me. It helped to pay for my education and I had a young brother who did veterinary medicine so I assisted him as well.'

Those brown envelopes passed across the counter of the Bank helped persuade Watters to commit himself to Celtic and after having been farmed out to Glasgow Junior side St Roch's for a season, he signed as a professional for Celtic. He then began to see a bit more of Maley. 'You would sometimes see Willie Maley in the background when you went into the Bank restaurant,' he says. 'Then when I signed on as a professional the reserve team and the full team used always to go into the Bank restaurant and he was always there. He was a very imposing man. You would look at him twice and when he spoke you would listen to him. He was Mr Celtic, that's for certain. He was a big man, well over six feet, although when I was a youngster he was an old manager. He was always immaculately dressed, always with a soft hat on; he was a big, powerful man. As soon as he walked into the dressing-room there would be silence. He didn't need to ask for it – he got it automatically.

'The Bank was not particularly nicely decorated,' Watters points out. 'It wasn't a salubrious place. It was very, very ordinary. In fact, I have been back there a few times recently and it is exactly the same as it was in the '30s, when we went into it. The food was great – you sometimes lost count of how many courses you would be given. We would be starving and we used to go there for our pre-match meal and it was mutton. When we were in the restaurant Mr Maley would not come and speak to the players. He left the players alone although he would be around and about – but not in the dining-room as it was. You see, nowadays you go in and there are people having a drink and they can have their meal there but in the '30s there was an alleyway right through and that was for Celtic. Other people didn't get in there. It was a haven for sportsmen. You'd get boxers in and theatrical types and celebrities would go in there.'

Benny Lynch, the hugely popular Glasgow boxer, was one of the most celebrated habitués of the Bank. Johnny Crum, Celtic's charismatic centre-forward, could often be found belting out a tune on the house piano whilst waiting for the team bus to pick up the players to take them to a match. Other players could be seen studiously scrutinising the football coupons to put bets on matches, an illegal practice at the time. The Bank would also be crammed with people keen to rub shoulders with the Celtic players, sometimes in the strangest ways. If a player left his table to pay a visit to the toilet he would often find himself being followed there by supporters looking for a chat or hoping to discover news about the team.

The magnetic attraction of Celtic made the Bank restaurant a busy place. It doubled as Maley's headquarters and a most profitable leisure enterprise, as Willie Buchan noticed. 'When you did extra training – morning and afternoon – you went to the Bank restaurant for your meals. If it was Friday you got fish, guaranteed! You got good meals in there; he made sure of that, and I suppose he would charge Celtic for it too. He must have made a fortune off the Bank restaurant with Celtic. It was a goldmine. The money he was collecting and the number of people he was getting into it meant that you would damn near need a season ticket to get in. So you would! It had several bars as well as the restaurant.'

Maley, as Jackie Watters testifies, had a seemingly detached role with regard to team matters. 'He was aloof. You never saw him. When I was in the first-team he would come in but there were no team-talks, nothing like that. He didn't give any team-talks. He might pass through the dressing-room before a game but his input to the first-team was simply picking them. Nowadays, with the managers, it's verbosity plus-plus-plus. At that time, the team picked itself. I got into the team because Malcolm MacDonald went down with an appendix. Now that was important: who was going to go in and take his place? I had played against Motherwell reserves at Fir Park the week before and the team was picked on a Thursday and was in the *Daily Record* on a Friday. So my father came in with the newspaper like a Cheshire cat and that was how I knew that I was in the team for my debut. That's how I got to know: I saw it in the paper. Willie Maley said nothing to me; there was no taking you into the office and telling you.'

The manager was always extremely careful to keep his emotions in check in front of his players, as Willie Buchan remembers. 'Even if you played well, Maley never actually congratulated you, as such, even if the team had had an outstanding game, like the game against Motherwell when we were getting beaten 4–1 and drew 4–4 – and we went on to win the Cup after that. Even after that game he would not even come and shake your hand or anything like that. He stood like a statue and you expected to see him there, just standing there like a statue, in the changing-room after the match. I never, ever heard him congratulating anybody. I think his idea was that you were a team and if you had played well, then that was what you were supposed to do. If it was your day today it would be somebody else's day tomorrow. I don't think I ever heard him say, "Well done, boys." Older players like McGonagle didn't give a damn about Maley. Kennaway, the Canadian, didn't care a hoot about Maley, whether he was pleased or displeased. He never bothered me; to me he was Celtic, just like a sort of statue. You never had any conversation with him, as such. He would say to you, "Just go out there and play your own game." When you came in at time-up he didn't say, "Well played" or "You played badly". To me it was more of a ball game in those days and you enjoyed yourself. If a match was put off you were disappointed. I enjoyed my days at Celtic Park, right enough.'

The Cup run that included that comeback to 4–4 with Motherwell concluded with a 2–1 victory for Celtic over Aberdeen in the 1937 Scottish Cup final in front of the record crowd for any European club match. The official attendance was given as 146,433 but it was estimated that approximately 5,000 others 'broke in' to the ground on the day, taking the crowd above 150,000. Before the match, Maley told his players that it would be an honour for Aberdeen to win the trophy but that it would not be an honour for Celtic to do so. He told his players that it would simply be what was expected of them – he told them it was their job to win trophies for Celtic and that they should just get out there and do their duty by the club.

Willie Buchan was Celtic's key man on that famous occasion. His magnificent passing created a whole range of openings for Celtic and it was an intervention from Buchan that led to the opening goal after 11 minutes: Johnny Crum put the ball in the net after the Aberdeen goalkeeper had been unable to hold Buchan's shot. Aberdeen equalised within a minute but 20 minutes from the end of the match Buchan burst into the penalty area and sent a low shot goalwards that struck the inside of a post, rolled along the line and then into the net. 'It took ages to get across the line,' says Buchan, 'I missed a heartbeat!' It proved to be the winner. After the match, goalscorers Crum and Buchan stood smiling on the Hampden pitch, each holding an arm of the Cup as seagulls scavenged on the deserted terraces. The team then celebrated victory at a Bank restaurant crammed wall-to-wall with Celtic supporters.

Willie Buchan was on top of his game and had excellent team-mates in that Celtic forward line, such as Crum, Jimmy Delaney and Jimmy McGrory. Buchan started the following season in style and had scored 12 goals from the inside-forward position by the November of the 1937–38 season. He was completely content at Celtic Park and had no thoughts about leaving until the idea was firmly inserted into his mind by Willie Maley in a typically brusque, brief, gruff meeting. 'I didn't want to leave Celtic, no,' says Buchan, 'I was quite happy playing away, playing my football and I had never even considered moving but I never got a chance to say anything about it. I always remember getting this message to go to the Bank restaurant, where he held all his meetings. I sat down and Maley said to me, "Blackpool want to give us £10,000 for you." I was only a laddie, you know, so I didn't have the sense to say, "Well, I want such-and-such and such-and-such." I suppose I had a choice but I was, what, 23? That was me on my way – I had never even seen Blackpool. I didn't get a house to move to or anything like that; changed days from today! You didn't think about asking for transfers in those days. I got transferred to Blackpool for £10,000 and I got a pittance out of that. I got £250 and bought a car, a split-new Ford 10. You wouldn't get a tyre for that nowadays!'

That dour send-off for a star player was entirely in character with Maley. 'I can't actually remember him smiling,' says Buchan. 'As for bursting out laughing . . . He was well-dressed, of course, he should have been. You always expected to see him well-dressed with the soft hat, you know.' The move to Blackpool opened Buchan's eyes as to how Maley's regime at Celtic Park was becoming somewhat outdated. At training with Celtic the players would be told by the trainer to do a few laps of the track or to sprint the length of the field. At Blackpool it was different. Players were encouraged to carry out a training programme that suited their individual requirements. 'Stanley Matthews was my outside-right,' says Buchan, 'and he just used to stand, then walk along, then do a short sprint over ten yards or so. When I told him about the sprint training we had had to do at Celtic he said, "What football player runs 100 yards flat-out? That's a waste of time." He said, "If you did that twice in a match you'd be exhausted!" Stan was some player. I think he was the best outside-right I ever saw.'

27

On the same day as Willie Buchan was told he was on his way to Blackpool, Maley was fixing up a potential replacement from the Junior ranks. Johnnie Wilson, a 21 year old, had been approached the previous Sunday by Steve Callaghan, a Celtic scout, who got the Lochgelly Albert inside-forward to sign a form committing himself to Celtic. This was a similar move to the one Maley had used on Jimmy Quinn nearly four decades previously but it was an illegality, both because it took place on a Sunday and because there were no Lochgelly Albert officials present. The reason for Callaghan's action was that he was aware that Arsenal and Lochgelly Albert were already discussing a transfer for Wilson to Highbury although the two clubs had not bothered to notify Wilson of their negotiations.

Callaghan told Wilson to report to Celtic Park the following Thursday, where the player took part in the match between Celtic's first-team and reserves that was a fixture on every Thursday afternoon in the season. Wilson played in the first-team and after the game went to the Bank restaurant, which proudly displayed Willie Maley's name on its facade, for a meeting with the Celtic manager. A representative of Lochgelly Albert had also been summoned to Maley's headquarters, having been informed that Wilson was playing a trial for Celtic. 'Willie Maley told me I had played really well alongside McGrory and had fitted in to Willie Buchan's position,' remembers Johnnie Wilson. 'Old Maley then put the form in front of me,' says Wilson, 'and said to the Lochgelly Albert official, "I am signing on your inside-forward. He had a really good game today and he played so well that I can do nothing else bar sign him." This was all lies because I had already signed! That was it. The Albert official never knew that I had signed on the Sunday. When I went outside it was on the billboard, "Celtic sign Fife Junior." It was there when I went out!' Maley, it seems, wrote the football headlines even before the news had been made. It was only later that Wilson learned Arsenal had been interested in him, long after Maley had moved swiftly and surely for his signature.

'You never saw Maley much,' remembers Wilson. 'The only time you saw him was on a Thursday when he would be sitting in the stand with the soft hat on, watching the first-team against the reserves. He would be sitting there on his own; what was in his mind all the time,

I don't know. Colonel Shaughnessy looked after us in the reserves; he never missed a match. He was a great person; he would come and ask you about your family, your parents, your holidays. Any time I met Willie Maley I found him to be an intimidating man. He could make people afraid of him just by looking at them. I think everybody was afraid of Willie Maley. He was law, he was the boss, an iron-fisted man.

'On a Thursday we trained in the morning and then we walked back to the Bank restaurant for a bit of lunch then back to the ground for the match. That was the only time I would see him – in the Bank restaurant. He was never out on the training field. I never once saw him on the training ground.'

Wilson and his team-mates in the reserve team would not receive any coaching as such but when they faced the first-team on a Thursday they would scrutinise the play of their opponents to try to glean information about how to play the game at the top level. They would receive encouragement from Colonel Shaughnessy and reserve-team trainer Joe Dodds but if players encountered Maley he would walk past, stone-faced. The team's training consisted almost entirely of laps of the park and exercises. The ball would be produced only rarely and then chiefly to practise free-kicks and corner-kicks. 'You never saw much of the ball, really,' says Wilson, 'except on a Thursday. That was the only time you got wired in; for a full game, an hour and a half. The idea at the time was that we would be hungry for it on a Saturday, which we were, of course.

'I remember MacDonald, Crum and Divers got nicknamed the Terrible Trio,' continues Johnnie Wilson. Those three forwards spearheaded the Celtic attack in the late 1930s and blinded the opposition through their ability to work in tandem. Johnny Crum was the Celtic centre-forward, with Malcolm MacDonald at inside-right and John Divers at inside-left and each of the three could switch position with their striking partners effortlessly, at high speed and to stunning effect. It was an early form of total football at which the Celtic forward line excelled and they soon became famous for this innovative approach to the game. 'I can remember old Maley got up in the Bank restaurant and told all the press that he was the instigator of the Terrible Trio and the three players said he was a liar!' says

Wilson. 'They didn't say that to Maley, of course, or they would have been out the door! MacDonald, Crum and Divers said it was rubbish. They had worked out all that interchanging themselves. He never egged them on, he never suggested what to do. They just made it up themselves.'

The practice that Maley pursued of never praising players was not one that met the approval of Johnnie Wilson, who witnessed the manager's curt style at close quarters. 'I think you should give credit where it's due,' he says, 'to tell someone they are doing well. You were never doing well with Willie Maley; you were never doing all right. I think he was a hard, hard man.' Shortly after Wilson joined Celtic, an incident occurred that underlined the autocratic behaviour of Maley. Alex Millar, the centre-half in an excellent Celtic reserve team that won the Reserve League in 1937–38, had got his hands on a second-hand car and used to park it at Alexandra Parade before walking across to Celtic Park for training. Maley heard about this, called Millar into his office and told Millar, who was 26 years old at the time, to get rid of the car because he wasn't capable of looking after it. Millar asked Maley why George Paterson, the first-team left-half, was allowed to bring his new car to Celtic Park and leave it next to the main door. Maley responded that Paterson was an officer with the YMCA and a responsible man, and therefore the right type of person to have a car. There was no option for Millar but to relinquish ownership of his car, but it prompted him to ask for a move from Celtic and in 1938 he was transferred to Preston North End.

Another player, outside-left Frank Murphy, was receiving only £6 as his weekly wage at a time when the other first-team players were receiving £8. Murphy had become a first-team regular in the mid-'30s and was part of the team that won the League title in 1936 and 1938 and the Scottish Cup in 1937. The other players told him he should go in to see the manager to ask why he was receiving £2 less than his team-mates, so he plucked up the courage to go to see the manager, knocked on the door and went in. Maley rattled out the greeting, 'What do you want?' Faced with the stern features of his manager at close quarters, the terrified player lost his nerve and instead of asking for more money he blurted out, 'I want to know if I can get two tickets for the match on Saturday for a couple of my friends.' Maley gave him the tickets but told him to think long and hard before making such a request again. He sent Murphy on his way with a pertinent piece of advice: 'If your own friends won't pay to see you, how can you expect other people to do so?'

Jackie Watters can recall a rare face-to-face meeting with Willie Maley, when the manager's approach wrong-footed the then teenage Watters. 'I played in a reserve game against Clyde at Shawfield,' says Watters. 'Clyde had signed two South Africans; Wallace and Milligan. They were all-in wrestlers and a whole lot of other things besides. To cut a long story short, I got ordered off through this Wallace. I was only a boy and he was trying to intimidate me and in the second half he clicked my heels and I went down. I put my leg out and he fell over it, you know, and I put my knee into his stomach as hard as I could. I was only a baby and on the Saturday night, as I say, the reserves used to come into the Bank restaurant, the same as the first-team, and get the old nosh. I remember Crum, Kennaway and Morrison, all the prima donnas, saying I would "get it" because there was no Celtic player ever ordered off. I had now had that ignominy and I was petrified as to what Mr Maley's reaction would be.

'At the time, I was doing my physiotherapy course but I plunked my classes on the Monday and went up to face the music, and when I went up I met someone who worked at the club. "Oh," he says, "the boss is looking for you. He wants to see you." I started shaking so much I thought I had Parkinson's. I was frightened. To cut a long story short, eventually I went in. Anyway, he cawed the feet away from under me. The first thing he said to me was, "I've heard all about it from the Colonel." Colonel Shaughnessy was one of the directors who always went with the reserve team. "I've heard all about it," he said. "Forget all about it." His reaction was the exact opposite of what I had expected. I had expected him to give me a bollocking. So eventually I had to go to Carlton Place – that was where all the bad boys went – and I got fined £2 by the Scottish Football Association and severely censured but the thing is I was frightened to go in to see him. I never paid the £2, I don't know who did.'

There was to be a grand finale to the 1937–38 season when Celtic competed in the Empire Exhibition Cup, an eight-club tournament held in Glasgow for top names in British football that also featured Aberdeen, Hearts, Rangers, Brentford, Chelsea, Everton and Sunderland. It was a prestigious trophy to celebrate the Empire Exhibition that was being held at Bellahouston Park and Celtic defeated Everton 1–0 in a dramatic final watched by an 82,000 crowd at Ibrox Park. It would prove to be Maley's final major trophy as Celtic manager. Johnnie Wilson was one of five reserve players who accompanied the first-team to Govan for that match and he remembers watching Maley as the action took place on the field. 'I never heard him shouting. Even that day at that Cup final with Everton, he was sitting in the stand and he was quiet all the time. He was sitting beside all the reserve players. He was never down on the field or on the touchline; he was always up in the stand in the directors' box on his own.'

At the time of the Exhibition Cup, Jackie Watters was an 18-year-old Celtic player and he remembers the final with affection. 'What a game that was!' he says. 'After 90 minutes there was no score and then in extra-time Johnny Crum, who was the centre-forward, nutmegged the centre-half and scored a goal. Every one of those players were great: Kennaway, Hogg, Morrison, Geatons, Lyon, Paterson, Delaney, MacDonald, Crum, Divers and Murphy. So we won the game and then we went to the Bank restaurant. I was one of four or five reserves who had travelled to that match with the team, another of whom was Joe Carruth, who was a very nice man and a great friend of mine as well. I always remember the tables were all set and at our table was Johnny Crum and the goalkeeper Joe Kennaway, who was a Canadian. On the table there were two bottles of champagne. So we sat down and after about ten minutes, Johnny Crum says, "Well, boys," referring to Carruth and I, "you're too young. So I'm taking that home for Mrs Crum – okay?" So then he took the champagne away off the table. Then Kennaway said exactly the same thing: "I'm taking that home for Mrs Kennaway – okay?" So we didn't get any champagne to celebrate the victory!'

Watters had made his debut in late 1938 for a Celtic team that had become champions of Scotland for the 19th time the previous year. He was still in the team when they travelled to Kirkcaldy in January 1939 to face a Raith Rovers side who had been promoted as Second

Division champions the previous spring but who were finding it tough in the First Division and were now plummeting towards relegation. Celtic had suffered two debilitating defeats in succession in their previous matches, away to Rangers and at home to Queen's Park, and the team's decline was underlined when they reached rock bottom at Stark's Park. A 4–0 defeat for the champions left them reeling in the race for the 1938–39 League title and in the dressing-room afterwards there was much debate about the shambolic Celtic performance until Maley walked in and commanded complete silence. 'He didn't do anything next,' says Watters. 'All he said was, "Tomorrow morning, everybody report to the Bank restaurant to go to Seamill for a week." That was because of the result; it was a terrible result against Raith Rovers. So we did our training down at Seamill for a week. We didn't really get any extra training, that wasn't what it was for. I don't know if there were any drinkers at Celtic at the time – I don't suppose there were – but if there were any then it meant that he would have had control over them for that week. He was down there as well even though he did not take any active part in training. He would not watch the training either. He was an old, old man by then and his trainer McMenemy would be an old man then, as well. He had been a great player for Celtic but I'm thinking he would be in his late 50s by then.'

In common with Watters, Johnnie Wilson found himself disoriented on the only occasion on which he had a meeting with Maley in the manager's office. 'I remember I scored four goals for the reserves against Motherwell,' he says, 'and on the Tuesday at training Mr Maley sent for me to go to the office. When I went to the office, I got a row. I walked in, he looked up and he said, "I've got a letter here saying that you are never out of the public houses. If you don't stay out of the pubs, you will be away from here. We're not having it." That wasn't true. He also said that in the match against Motherwell I had deliberately kept the ball off of the outside-left, Jimmy Birrell. So he said, "That'll have to stop." That wasn't true either; I hadn't kept the ball from Jimmy Birrell.'

Wilson, a dedicated man to whom his football was everything, answered the more serious of Maley's charges by explaining to him that he was never inside pubs for the simple reason that he did not drink alcohol. The manager refused to listen. He stated that the letter was from a person who was, in his eyes, a reliable individual. Wilson knew that the letter was malicious and suspected strongly that it had been sent to Maley by the secretary of his local side, Blairhall Juniors, who had been discomfited by Wilson having left that club for Lochgelly Albert prior to his signing for Celtic.

That meeting left Wilson disillusioned and distraught. In his defence, he told Maley that the local priest would confirm that Wilson was indeed teetotal and no frequenter of pubs. Maley threw that offer out; he refused to countenance meeting the priest. Hugh O'Neill and Jimmy Birrell, two other Celtic players who lived alongside Wilson in the same Fife mining village of Blairhall, were amazed at the allegations that had been repeated to Wilson by Maley and offered to testify to Wilson's innocence of the alleged offence. Maley threw out their offer as well – he was uninterested in their proposal. It was the end for Wilson at Celtic – he was a fanatical Celtic man but now no longer wished to play for a club managed by Maley and one month later he left Celtic Park. The manager's intransigence in that situation hints at an alternative agenda. Within days Wilson learned that Maley had arranged a move for him to Chelsea but the player insisted on switching instead to Chesterfield.

'I remember Matt Lynch saying to me that old Maley would never give you praise,' says Johnnie Wilson, 'no matter how well you played. He was a strange, strange man. He wasn't a man that you would want to meet. You would want to get away from him altogether. It wasn't interesting meeting him. I had thought the world of Willie Maley, simply because he was manager of Celtic, but when I left the club I thought he was a very unfair man.'

Great Britain declared war on Germany in September 1939 and Jackie Watters was immediately called up to the navy, in which he served for six-and-a-half years. Like many other players who were called up to serve in the armed forces, he lost contact with Celtic even though they still held his registration. Johnnie Wilson, who had been at Chesterfield for only a few weeks, returned to Scotland to work in the pits as part of the war effort. Within a few months, Maley joined those who had been cast adrift from Celtic.

The manager's overbearing manner and his insistence on sole control of team affairs had long rankled with the Celtic directors but his dictatorial style had been acceptable as long as Celtic were gathering trophies. The 1930s, however, had been a predominantly unsuccessful decade for Celtic. They had won the Scottish Cup three times and the League twice but as the decade ended, Rangers could look back on much more sustained success, having won seven League titles and five Scottish Cups during those ten years. Celtic's best side of that era had shone between 1936 and 1938 but by late 1939 there were signs of serious decline – the team had made an atrocious start to their fixtures at the beginning of the 1939–40 season. Fingers began pointing in Maley's direction and murmurs grew in volume about the way in which he ran so much club business from within the raucous confines of the Bank restaurant. It was also widely known that Desmond White, son of Celtic chairman Tom White, coveted the position of club secretary; Maley was still, officially, the club's secretary-manager and responsible for the corresponding administrative duties as well as team matters. To certain directors, Maley was also a man with too tight a grip on the club's transfer dealings.

It would, finally, be the stubbornness and egocentricity that had characterised Maley's managerial methods that would provide an opportunity for the directors to sever ties with him once and for all. The June of 1938 had seen Tom White present Maley with a gift of 2,500 guineas to mark the Golden Jubilee of the club's existence. That token of gratitude met with a suitably humble public response from Maley at the time, but a row rumbled on for the following 18 months between Maley and the board over which of the two parties should pay the tax due on the gift. White, a businessman, had become a Celtic director in 1906 and club chairman in 1914. He did not have the emotional connection with Maley that White's immediate predecessors Kelly and McLaughlin had done; unlike them, White did not share with Maley an involvement with the club that went back to its founding days. Relations between Maley and the board dipped lower and lower until, just a few days prior to Christmas 1939, he was pressurised to resign from his position. It was the type of unpleasant exit that Maley had inflicted on countless players, and now the biter had been bitten. An unsuspecting public was informed of Maley's departure from Celtic on New Year's Day 1940. Celtic were now looking for a new manager for the first time in more than half a century.

TWO

Jimmy McStay – A Casualty of War

Life at Celtic was never easy for Jimmy McStay. He was a seasoned player when taken on trial by the club at the age of 25 in 1920, but performed extremely poorly when fielded in a midfield position in several practice matches. His passing was so bad, so inaccurate, that club chairman Tom White made clear his opinion that McStay did not have the necessary talent to be a useful addition to the playing staff at Celtic Park. It was only the direct intervention of manager Willie Maley that saved the player from rejection. Maley asked for McStay to be given one more chance to impress. The player did so and went on to make 472 Scottish League and Cup appearances for Celtic's first team in a 12-year career, at centre-half, that stretched from his debut in 1922 to 1934.

Those were tough times for Celtic – they won just one Scottish League title during McStay's dozen years as a first-team regular at Celtic Park. He was a steady rather than spectacular central defender and that steadiness saw him made team captain in 1929. Jimmy, then 34, was older in years than his team-mates and his tightly drawn, almost haggard, features made him look much more elderly, much more careworn, than the lads he played alongside. Smiles came easily to the other, more talented Celts of the late 1920s and early 1930s, such as genial goalscorer Jimmy McGrory, the fantastically two-footed inside-forward Charlie 'Happy Feet' Napier or the winger Bertie Thomson, whose feckless socialising reflected his freewheeling approach to his football. Jimmy McStay was different – he was no 'natural' footballer. Every appearance he made for Celtic demanded rock-hard concentration and adherence to his specific role of stopping the opposing centre-forward from playing. He was too aware of how close he had come to missing out on playing for his beloved Celtic, and of how hard he had had to work to earn his modicum of success, to take matters lightly.

Jimmy was the Celtic captain at Ibrox on 5 September 1931 when tragedy befell the club with the death of goalkeeper John Thomson in a League match with Rangers. The Celtic captain was the first on the scene as Thomson lay prone, with blood gushing from his head. He walked ahead of the funeral cortege as Thomson's body was carried to its grave in Cardenden, Fife. Within weeks, inside-forward Peter Scarff complained of feeling short of breath during a match and was soon diagnosed with tuberculosis, a condition that claimed his life at the age of 25. The serious side of life, and football, had once again been graphically emphasised at close quarters to McStay to whom, as captain, it fell to guide his team-mates through their mournful farewells to their fellow players.

That seriousness of manner made McStay suitable to become a manager after his playing career had drawn gently to a close at Hamilton Academicals. Alloa Athletic recruited him to be their besuited figurehead in April 1938. McStay was given full control of all team matters at Alloa and in his first season as manager he led the tiny Clackmannanshire club to promotion from the Second to the First Division. It was a rare opportunity for Second Division regulars Alloa to get a bite at the big-time and McStay's instantaneous success at Recreation Park had attracted the attention of the Celtic directors. McStay was 44 years old when, in February 1940, he accepted their invitation to become the second manager of Celtic.

It proved even more difficult for McStay to establish himself at Celtic as manager than it had been for him to make it at the club as a player. The directors were extremely pleased not to have to deal with the fearsome Maley any longer, and delightedly meddled in McStay's team selections and signings. Maley had been a team-mate of men such as James Kelly and Michael Dunbar, who later became directors of the club. He could justifiably feel on the same level as them when he took over as Celtic team manager. Jimmy's relationship with the directors was never that close. Celtic was now firmly established as a business with a rigid directorial hierarchy.

Jimmy McStay was very much their employee, and they were very much his bosses. Jimmy was well aware of the powers they held. Tom White, the man who had proposed ditching him as a player, was still the Celtic chairman, an everyday reminder of how close Jimmy had come to missing out on his eventual odyssey with the club.

McStay faced equally troublesome circumstances in his efforts to build a useful Celtic team. Football had been briefly suspended by the Government after Britain had declared war on Germany in September 1939 and when league football resumed within a few weeks it was on a restricted basis. Teams were grouped in regional leagues so that the amount of travelling done by clubs was reduced and valuable resources were saved for more vital purposes. Celtic, when McStay joined as manager, were playing in the Western Regional League. Then, from mid-1940 to 1946, they competed in the Southern League. The Scottish Cup was suspended. Most of the young, fit men who had brought success to the club in the second half of the 1930s were now required for the war effort and footballers' wages were reduced to £2 a week, an encouragement to players to help out with wartime production as a means of earning a living wage. Some players, such as winger Frank Murphy and half-backs George Paterson and Willie Lyon, enlisted in the armed services. Others, such as Chic Geatons and Jock Morrison, helped the war effort with shifts in factories and in mines. Jimmy Delaney had suffered a complicated fracture of the arm at Arbroath in April 1939, which denied the new manager the influential winger's services entirely until the beginning of the 1941–42 season. It meant that numerous quality players were unavailable to McStay at various times and that others, when they did turn up for their football, were often in a state of exhaustion because of their wartime work.

The Celtic directors, viewing all these circumstances, ran up the white flag of surrender to the effects of war and decided to restrict the amount of resources they afforded the team. The result was that McStay's teams trundled through the war years in mediocre fashion. It is to McStay's great credit that, despite these various handicaps, he made strenuous attempts to sign up the best young talent available in the hope of constructing his own, new side for whenever peace might break out. The gifted midfielder Bobby Evans, impressively brave goalkeeper Willie Miller and the powerful centre-forward John McPhail were among the players signed as teenagers by Jimmy McStay during the years of the Second World War. They and others would bud brightly and colourfully with Celtic.

Alec Boden was another of the teenagers signed by McStay during the first half of the 1940s. He had come to the attention of Celtic in 1943 through being part of a highly successful Duntocher St Mary's Boys' Guild team. Boden, then 17, had also attracted an offer from Wolverhampton Wanderers, who had sent high-profile representatives to Glasgow to offer him terms. He had been considering a career as a golf professional so he asked Wolves to give him time to think over their offer. It was at that point that Celtic came calling and he was asked to meet manager McStay at a private house in Boden's native Hardgate. Boden's recollections of that encounter reveal that McStay was not averse to employing craftiness and pressure to sign young players. 'The local priest, wee Father Cassidy, was there,' recounts Boden, 'as were various other people, including Johnny Gibbons, an outside-right from the Boys' Guild team. When we got down to business McStay said to me, "I understand you're nearly set to go to Wolverhampton. Why not come to Parkhead? There's a place there for you immediately because Bobby Hogg is ready to retire and although you play centre-half down here we think you'll make a right-back." So I said, "Mr McStay, if I go to Wolverhampton I'm going to be exempt from the army because they're going to put me into a pit job and the pit job consists of being in a big shed counting the trucks going past the window." He said, "Don't worry about that. We'll get you in beside Jimmy Delaney and Malky MacDonald, and all the others who are exempt from the army."

'Then wee Father Cassidy said, "Look Alec, you're going away from your mother and father, away down to England and you'll not see your mother and father except for a couple of times in the year. You'll be staying in a house with just a landlady and another two or three players." I thought I was going to hell because of the way he said it to me in a sort of gloomy, warning tone. Up to then, I had been excited about it! Then Jimmy McStay said to me that he would show me some foolscaps and on them were more than 300 names. He said, "That's all the people who are on Wolverhampton's books. They've got 340 players on their books." I said, "Three hundred and forty?" So that put me right off because I started wondering how I was going to make it down there if there were 340 English guys also looking to get in the team! It was just a wee bit of kidology on his part because all those names included the names of people from things like works teams that Wolverhampton sent their coaches out to work with. In reality I would have gone into their second or third team.

'I took a while to discuss different things with them and then McStay went away into a room with Johnny Gibbons and Johnny Gibbons' father and he came out and said, "Come on now, Alec, and sign for the Celtic. Johnny has just signed for the Celtic." So I went in and haggled a wee bit and at the end of the day I signed because of the fact that he had promised me a job that was free of the army. Needless to say – and I'll never forgive Jimmy McStay for it – I got my call-up papers, had my medical and was off in the army three months later. It was 12 December 1943 when I went up to Fort George, about 40 miles west of Inverness, where there was 11 inches of snow, and I was in the army for three years.'

McStay was not the only manager to promise a player that he would be able to find a way of exempting them from military service only to discover that the demands of government could over-rule even the most wily manager. Matt Busby, even in peacetime, was among the many managers who would have to concede defeat in a similar situation. It is a more unforgivable matter that Boden soon found that with his entry into the armed forces he seemed to become, as far as Jimmy McStay and Celtic were concerned, a forgotten man. 'In the three years I was in the army,' remembers Boden, 'I was only home for one period of leave because in the approach to D-Day all leave had been cancelled and you couldn't get home on leave. Do you know what I never, ever got? In those three years I never got a Christmas card from Celtic or a letter asking how I was getting on or a couple of bob at Christmas. So from December '43 until I was demobbed I never heard a word from the manager or anyone else at Celtic Park.

'In the few months I had been with Celtic before I went into the army, nobody said a word of advice to me other than Alex Dowdells, the trainer. It was Alex Dowdells that kept McStay in business. McStay didn't coach or take you out and lead the training. Alex Dowdells was a smashing fellow and he did all that at that time. Alex was a trained physiotherapist and what he didn't know about muscles and bones was not worth knowing. You practically wouldn't see McStay. He would be in his wee office.'

McStay, having brought some keen young talent to the club, expected to be given a chance to prove himself as the Celtic manager once peace and normal league football was restored to Europe in 1945 but, within weeks of the war drawing to a close in May 1945, his connection with the club was severed with the swiftness and mercilessness of a guillotine execution. McStay's account of the matter provides a flavour of his duties at the time and of the casual manner in which the directors felt it was their right to remove their manager. 'I must confess I was deeply hurt over the whole thing,' said McStay in July 1945. 'No hint of a change had been given me when I prepared to leave for two weeks' holiday. I made up the groundsmen's wages just before I left and went down to Ayr with my family. You can imagine my feelings when, a few days later, I picked up a paper and read that I was likely to lose my job. It was obviously not just a rumour so when I returned I called on the chairman, Mr White, who asked me to hand in my resignation. I did so, of course, but the whole affair has caused me much unjustified embarrassment.'

The directors had conveniently and callously retained McStay's services whilst simultaneously plotting to replace him as soon as the war ended and league and cup football began to return to normal. McStay did return to Celtic in 1951 to become the club's chief scout, a position he was to hold for ten years – although by then, Celtic had a new chairman, which may have made it easier for McStay to return. Robert Kelly had taken over that role after the death of Tom White in 1947. McStay's successor was Jimmy McGrory, a legendary name in the club's history for his mammoth goalscoring feats in the 1920s and '30s. As with McStay, he would soon feel the heavy hand of his chairman on his shoulders.

THREE

Jimmy McGrory – A Marginal Manager

Football managers of the 1940s and '50s did not have the iconic status that they were to achieve in the latter decades of the twentieth century. The man in the mac who watched from the sidelines was expected to deal with the players and keep them in line off the field but he was not yet credited with the power to control a match or change its course in midstream. Those powers would only be accredited to managers in the latter decades of the century. There were good reasons why managers in the post-war years had a lower profile than in modern times. Substitutions were not yet allowed so if a player was struggling, either for form or through injury, the manager did not have the option of making a change during a match. Dugouts had only just begun to appear pitchside at some but not all football stadiums in those post-war years. That meant that most managers retained a remote presence in the stand.

British football was also fairly rigid tactically. Teams lined up in a 2–3–5 formation, with two full-backs; a right-half, a centre-half and a left-half in midfield; and five forwards, consisting of a right- and left-winger, a centre-forward and two inside-forwards. Players were expected to know how to play in their position and to stick to their task. The opposition would line up in the same way so the contest would be down to how the 11 men on the field measured up to their opponents. The manager chose the 11 players for the match, signed players and dealt with their contracts on behalf of the management. He then put them on the park and let them express themselves.

Jimmy McGrory, who took over as Celtic manager from Jimmy McStay in July 1945, was a hat-and-coat manager, as McStay and

Willie Maley had been before him. He dressed formally, like a boss in an office or factory, and he would not get his hands dirty in terms of working with the players on the training field. It was the traditional British approach to management but cracks were beginning to appear in that particular edifice. Jimmy Hogan, the manager of Aston Villa in the late 1930s, had taken to the training field in boots, shorts and football shirt, an idea that was revolutionary in British football at the time. He emphasised ball-work in training and his approach brought considerable success to Villa before the experiment was cut short by the intervention of the war. Matt Busby, who became manager of Manchester United after being demobbed in 1945, took part in training matches with his players and, in tandem with his right-hand man Jimmy Murphy, drilled his players relentlessly for the challenges that awaited them on the field of play. United's training was thorough and meticulous. During games, players would remember practical pieces of advice that the manager and his coach had planted in their heads.

One Celtic star would be lucky enough to experience Busby's methods first-hand: Jimmy Delaney joined Manchester United in February 1946 and helped United win the FA Cup in 1948 as part of Busby's first great team. Busby rated Delaney as his most important signing of all. The player's departure from Celtic had resulted from a dispute over money. Wartime wages had been restricted to £2 a week – the same as in the First World War – and Delaney, who had carried the team throughout the war years, expected a suitable increase in his terms once peace had broken out. The Celtic board had no wish to accommodate such a wish and when his increase failed to materialise, Delaney headed south, graciously declining the heartfelt offer of Celtic supporters to club together to make up the type of wages he expected.

The appointment of Jimmy McGrory as Celtic manager had been a popular one. He had set an all-time Celtic goalscoring record of 472 goals in 445 Scottish League and Cup appearances during the 1920s and '30s and his ebullient excellence in leading the forward line had endeared him to the support. He was 41 years old on his return to Celtic Park and had been manager of Kilmarnock since his retirement as a Celtic player in the autumn of 1937, taking

Kilmarnock to the 1938 Scottish Cup final, where they lost to East Fife after a replay. Through marriage, McGrory had also become better off financially than most footballers of the era. He had married Eva Green, a member of the family that owned the popular Green's Playhouse in Glasgow's Renfield Street. He was given a cinema as a wedding present and on a Saturday evening after the match McGrory could be found in his bow tie outside his picture house, greeting the queue of filmgoers warmly.

McGrory was a humble man and had been a well-liked figure among his Celtic Park team-mates. 'I thought he was going to be a good manager,' says Johnnie Wilson, who was on the Celtic playing staff alongside McGrory during the late 1930s. 'When you played alongside him in a training match he seemed to be coaxing you and telling you what to do. He would be giving you tips and advice all the time. He told me I was doing as well as Willie Buchan as a ball-player.' Jackie Watters, another former Celtic team-mate, was less sure that McGrory was the right man to be Celtic manager. McGrory had always been a quiet, modest individual and, away from the game, not the most assertive of people.

Alec Boden had returned from military service after having left the army late in 1946. 'When I was demobbed,' he says, 'on the second day I was back in Hardgate, I went up to Parkhead to see what was happening. I knew I was still a player because I got a receipt every year on the same day to say that I was registered with Celtic FC – that happened for '43–44, '44–45 and '45–46.' He found a new manager in charge at Celtic but one who was less than inspirational. 'All the time I was there,' he says, 'Jimmy McGrory never had a tracksuit on or came and said anything to you in terms of encouragement or tactically. He used to come in on a Saturday for the game and stand up at the massage table in the middle of the floor. He had this wee smoker's cough because he was always smoking, although he didn't smoke in the dressing-room. He would say, "Come on then, lads. Are we all ready now? Now, we've got to win here today! Let's go then! Come on boys!" And out we'd go. Honestly, it was diabolical.'

At the end of the first peacetime season in which full Scottish League competition was restored – 1946–47 – a young, largely inexperienced Celtic side, badly missing Jimmy Delaney, finished in mid-table. Celtic then went into a tailspin and the team travelled to Dens Park, Dundee, on the final day of the 1947–48 season needing to win to be sure of avoiding relegation. It was the first time in the club's history that Celtic had been involved in such a scenario and at one point in the match Dundee were 2–1 ahead. Goals from outside-right Jock Weir gave Celtic a 3–2 victory. McGrory had been prepared to resign if Celtic had dropped down a division and it had been such a close thing that the directors were forced to act. They kept McGrory in place but recruited Jimmy Hogan, the former Aston Villa manager, as coach that summer of 1948. It was an imaginative attempt by the board, now led by a new chairman, Robert Kelly, to liven up the team. Hogan, who was originally from the north-west of England, was 66 years old but he was still something of a livewire and his experience in football was exceptional. Prior to joining Villa in 1936 his coaching skills had been in demand throughout Europe and he had worked in Austria, France, Germany, Holland, Hungary, Italy and Switzerland. Those were then young footballing nations and Hogan's work had done much to develop the game on the continent. Most notably, he and the Austrian Hugo Meisl had, in partnership, created the legendary Austrian 'wunderteam' of the '20s and early '30s, one of the finest national teams in Europe at the time. Their style of football had been based on an intricate passing game designed by Hogan and they had come tantalisingly close to winning the 1934 World Cup. Hogan would also later be credited with inspiring the playing style of the famous Hungarian national team of the 1950s that doled out England's first defeat on home soil by continental opposition and reached the 1954 World Cup final.

'With Jimmy Hogan, now you're talking about a guy,' enthuses Alec Boden. 'By God, did Jimmy Hogan know the game and he knew the exercises and training routines and all that. He was over 60 but he was out there every day and neither McGrory nor McStay were ever out in a tracksuit. McGrory would occasionally stand out at the end of the players' tunnel with his hands in his pockets, smoking, just watching us training. He wouldn't watch the whole session. He would just come out for a bit. McGrory never held coaching meetings or took players aside. Even if something had gone wrong on a Saturday and a player had made an obvious mistake, McGrory would never come across and speak to the guy during the week. We never got an ounce of coaching from either McStay or McGrory.

'On the day Jimmy Hogan joined, we went for dinner out to the golf course in Uddingston – a bus used to take the first-team players out to Uddingston on a Monday and we would play a couple of rounds of golf. They wouldn't tolerate golf during the rest of the week – quite rightly – but it was all right on a Monday because we only played on Saturdays then. So that was where we were introduced to Jimmy and the next day he got us all together just outside the dressing-room on the halfway line at Celtic Park. There would have been about 30 of us and he introduced himself and spoke about the great Celtic and how he was hoping to be part of the resurrection of this great club. He would insert wee bits of poetry into his speech and he had great wee sayings and bits of advice for you to remember.

'He used to say things like, "See if you're inside the 18-yard box and you've got nobody to give it to, just stick it in the back of the net." Or he would say, "Keep the high balls low" or "Get the ball on the deck – it won't hurt the grass if we move it about on the deck."' Those simple nuggets of information made a lot of sense to the players, and were easy to remember because they were so idiosyncratic. Hogan preached a passing game and introduced new ideas such as making runs on the blind side of the defence. He would work on the technical aspects of football, such as how to trap a ball on the run, how to trap it using the outside or inside of the foot, and how to head the ball properly. This was genuine coaching and as such it was a refreshing, radical change for the players, who were generally receptive to Hogan's ideas. The new coach also stressed the need for a good physique and encouraged the players to develop upper-body strength, another fresh idea for the time.

The only disconcerting element in Hogan's make-up was his approach to his Catholic religion, which was as evangelical as his coaching. Players would be preparing for the match on the Saturday and would see Hogan making the sign of the cross above goalkeeper Willie Miller's hands. They would be bending down to tie their bootlaces or adjust their shinguards and would feel a small cross being made lightly by Hogan on their forehead. 'I was a Catholic,' says Boden, 'but I didn't like it because of the other fellows who weren't. Let's face it, before a game you always hope that you can keep your end up and play well enough and you may say a wee prayer yourself. Players of all sorts of religions would do that, I suppose, but I didn't like it to be so obvious.'

Hogan's coaching perked up the players in the two years in which he was at the club. His work was supplemented by that of Alex Dowdells, the trainer. 'Alex Dowdells was still there to take the training and keep us fit,' says Boden. 'He would do a wee bit of coaching but not what you would really call coaching nowadays, but he kept us fit and he did a lot to keep us going. I remember that on the first Tuesday of every month he used to give us a tumbler full of this foul-tasting, jet-black draught. It came out of a huge big bottle – it was cascara sagrada to ensure that the players' bowels were moving!' McGrory remained firmly in the background. 'I guarantee you,' continues Boden, 'that when McGrory left the house on a Saturday to go up to Parkhead he wouldn't know one player that was playing that afternoon. It was Bob Kelly that was selecting the team and Kelly would tell Alex Dowdells the team well in advance of the match so that Alex could get each player's boots out and attend to anyone who needed to have an ankle strapped up or any other preparations before taking the field. Kelly would come to the park every morning before he went into his office in the town and he would stand at the end of the tunnel for five or ten minutes to watch the players. On a Saturday Alex Dowdells would be running the dressing-room, strapping up players and getting them ready for the match.'

Dowdells would also take a personal interest in the players – if a player's wife gave birth to a new baby Dowdells would present the player with a box full of gifts such as baby powder. Alex Dowdells worked night and day with the players and would even have players up to his house, where he had installed physiotherapy equipment, for extra treatment. The trainer was also the man the players consulted first on any problem they might have.

It was a strange set-up, with the players being given expert coaching, guidance and physical conditioning by Hogan and Dowdells only for the vital matter of team selection to be in the inexpert hands of the chairman, and the passive manager having little to do with team matters. Unsurprisingly, Celtic spent the late 1940s and early '50s rooted in mid-table of the Scottish League's top division although they did win the Scottish Cup in 1951, John McPhail scoring the only goal of the game against Motherwell, which was Celtic's sole major triumph in a 15-year period.

Later in 1951, Jock Stein arrived at the club. He was initially recruited from Llanelli as a reserve centre-half but a string of injuries saw him make his first-team debut on 8 December 1951, just four days after his arrival at Celtic. Stein never looked back; he retained his place in the team and one year later he was made captain of Celtic, where his on-field influence was felt increasingly strongly as he marshalled the players around him.

Stein was central to Celtic's impressive feat of capturing the Coronation Cup in the summer of 1953. The tournament was held in Glasgow to celebrate the accession to the British throne of Queen Elizabeth II and featured eight of the top English and Scottish clubs of the day: Celtic defeated Arsenal, Manchester United and Hibernian to take the trophy. Prior to that competition, the Celtic players had rebelled because they were to be paid reduced, close-season wages for the matches, which took place after the end of the League season but which were guaranteed massive crowds at the two venues of Hampden Park and Ibrox. Kelly intervened personally to end the dispute, picking off the players one-by-one through a series of head-to-head meetings and making it clear to them that those who failed to play in the Coronation Cup would find their futures at the club under severe threat. McGrory remained firmly in the background throughout this dispute. The Celtic players had had the full backing of the players' union and had held numerous well-attended meetings to build their own resolve but their resistance simply crumbled in the face of pressure from Kelly, whose iron grip on the club had been reinforced yet again.

A surprise spurt of success saw Stein lead the team to the Scottish League and Cup Double during the 1953–54 season, the first time they had done the Double for four decades. The team came close to mirroring that performance during the subsequent 1954–55 season, finishing just three points behind Aberdeen in the League and reaching the Scottish Cup final with Clyde. The match at Hampden ended in a 1–1 draw but the skilled, driving midfielder Bobby Collins was dropped for the replay. Chairman Kelly had disliked seeing some heavy challenges that the aggressive Collins had made on the Clyde goalkeeper during the first game and omitted him from the team. Minus Collins, one of their most outstanding players, Celtic tumbled to a 1–0 defeat.

The chairman would clamp down on the activities of some players while favouring others. Sean Fallon, who possessed a fraction of Collins' talent, was exceptionally close to Robert Kelly, acting as chauffeur to drive home Mr and Mrs Kelly after matches, staying at the chairman's house, dining with him, even walking his dog. His team-mates, back in the 1950s, would clam up in his presence, aware that anything they said could quickly be conveyed to the chairman. It made for an uneasy atmosphere inside the dressing-room at times, with players aware they could not speak freely in front of Fallon. At one stage in that 1954–55 season Fallon was fielded at centre-forward by Kelly and went 11 games without scoring a goal. 'Kelly would never have stood for that from any other player – if anyone else had gone three games without scoring he would have been wanting to change it,' says Alec Boden.

Jock Stein suffered a severe ankle injury in an Old Firm match in August 1955 that kept him out of the team for most of the remainder of that season and without his influence on the field Celtic finished fifth in the League. They did reach the 1956 Scottish Cup final to play Hearts. Again Kelly would intervene to the detriment of the team. Jim Sharkey, the centre-forward who had scored one of the goals in the 2–1 semi-final victory over Clyde, was dropped by Kelly as a result of an indiscretion on the part of the player whilst the team was preparing for the cup final at Seamill. Most bizarrely, Kelly replaced Sharkey in the forward line with right-back Mike Haughney. He was partnered on the right side of the Celtic attacking five by 19-year-old Billy Craig, a surprise selection who had only appeared in five previous League games. Although Haughney did manage to score in one of his team's few attacks, Celtic were entirely outplayed on the day and lost the final 3–1. Those successive Cup final defeats were the most obviously costly instances of Kelly's unpredictable team selections, but he was apt to chop and change the Celtic team at will from week to week, creating an unstable, unpredictable environment inside the club.

McGrory was still, nominally, the manager during the late '50s but the influence of Robert Kelly on playing matters was implicitly understood by everyone at the club. Another man, however, was bringing his gigantic personality to bear on the young players at Celtic. Jock Stein, after his ankle injury had finished his career, began coaching the reserve team in 1957. 'Jimmy McGrory had very little, in actual fact, to do with my signing for the club,' recalls Billy McNeill, who joined the club shortly after Stein's appointment to the coaching staff. 'I would have followed the same route as so many Scottish boys – I would have been down in England somewhere – had it not been for the fact that Jock Stein, who had been injured, saw me playing for Scottish Schoolboys against English Schoolboys and he impressed upon Bob Kelly, who was a big influence at Celtic Park in those days, that he should sign me – and that's what happened. Mr McGrory was involved in the actual signing but it was big Jock who had actually seen me. His influence was the important thing and he took a big interest in me, as he did with all of the youngsters.

'Mr McGrory was the manager but Bob Kelly was the dominating influence and, basically, more or less what Bob Kelly said, went. Mr McGrory was a lovely man, a very, very nice man, different, the old style of manager. I cannot recollect seeing him in a tracksuit or out on the training field,' continues McNeill. 'Mr McGrory was a really nice man. He would talk to you and he would announce the team and would be in the dressing-room but there was no doubt whatsoever that the dominating influence was Bob Kelly. You knew that if he didn't like the team, the team got changed. It was as simple as that. That's why the club struggled for so long. It was hopeless. Jimmy McGrory did not have any real day-to-day contact with you. He was there but, as I say, I never, ever saw him out of a suit or anything like that. He was a lovely man, don't get me wrong, he was a superb man but he must have had a hell of a difficult job. I think the chairman would be a real handful for him.

'As young players you didn't know what to expect. People had totally different ideas about all aspects of football to those that they have today. You knew that if you crossed Bob Kelly or even if Bob Kelly just took a dislike to you then you wouldn't be in the team. We were lucky because big Jock took a great interest in the youngsters. The Lanarkshire boys were particularly fortunate because the club gave big Jock a car at one time and we used to get a lift home, predominantly myself and John Clark and a lad called Jim Conway who left the club and went elsewhere. Before he got the car, the three of us used to walk big Jock up to the bus stop at Tollcross Road. Big Jock's bus was different to ours because it went towards Hamilton and we all went towards Motherwell but if big Jock's bus didn't come first we had to wait until his bus came. He just wouldn't let you go.'

McNeill was one of a talented group of young players who were given the nickname the Kelly Kids. It carries the silent implication that these youngsters were hand-picked and reared by the chairman, but McNeill is quick to quash any such idea. 'I think it was just a glib title. He was the chairman but he never had any involvement with anything like that; you never, ever saw him. Celtic had this reputation of selling whenever the opportunity came; they talked about youth development but there was never any scale plan about it. You really had to find your own way and your only source of education was the senior players and big Jock.'

Stein had been co-opted on to the coaching staff after five years as a player in which he had had a huge influence on the team, cajoling and urging his team-mates on during matches from his position of centre-half. It was no coincidence that his time as captain had dovetailed with Celtic's major trophy-winning run of the 1950s. His serious ankle injury in August 1955 had put Stein out of action and during the subsequent 17 months he had impressed Robert Kelly with his ideas on the game and his influence behind the scenes. Kelly had had no wish to lose such a man and when Stein was finally forced to retire as a player in January 1957 Kelly had given him a job as a scout; Stein would learn about football management from Jimmy McGrory and that, in Kelly's words, would 'stand him in good stead for the future'.

Six months later, in the summer of 1957 Stein had been promoted to reserve team coach and during the following season, 1957–58, Stein's charges carved out an eye-opening victory in the final of the Scottish Second XI Cup final when they defeated a Rangers team that included several experienced players in an 8–2 aggregate victory, watched by 40,000 over two legs at Celtic Park and Ibrox. 'Reserve football was far better supported at that time than it is now,' explains John Divers, who was one of the youngsters who excelled on those two occasions. 'That Celtic reserve team contained a lot of players who were to be very successful later in their careers but Rangers had a lot of big names playing for them. We were a lot of boys. I do remember the crowd: there were 22,000 people at Celtic Park to see us win the first game of that final by 3–1. Under floodlights at Ibrox, the Celtic reserves won 5–1 and that was quite a media event – the doing of all these boys, these 18 and 19 year olds.'

Stein had given his players a taste of the pleasures they could enjoy if they worked to his remit. He was making things happen, creating excitement, showing the way. At the time he was drafted on to the coaching staff he was still only 35 years old, still sharp-featured through exercise, close enough to the players in age to be more like a good friend than the father figure he later became. He put the stress on enjoyment laced with hard work and his charges responded eagerly to his methods. Stein was genuinely curious about his players, curious about what made each of them react to situations in their own individual way, curious about how their lives were progressing away from the football club. He improved their material conditions, obtaining for them better gear and ensuring that it was washed after each training session. This had not previously been the case and reserve-team players prior to Stein's time had had to go out and train in gear that was stiff with dirt because it had not been cleaned for weeks on end. He was also prepared to sit down and talk to the players for hours about his experiences in football, such as travelling to the World Cup in 1954, his memories of the great players he had seen and his own time as a player at Celtic, Albion Rovers and Llanelli.

'It was interesting,' remembers Billy McNeill, who was then an exuberant teenager. 'We were youngsters and nobody with the reputation and status that big Jock had as a player had ever really taken the time to talk to you and to blether to you. He planted a seed of enthusiasm in everybody at an early stage. So big Jock was a big, powerful influence and, to be fair, so were the rest of the senior players. They were excellent – players such as Bertie Peacock, Neilly Mochan, Bobby Collins and Willie Fernie were super because they took an interest in the younger players and gave us the benefit of their experience and their attitude and their appetite for things. I was lucky in that I broke into the team at 18 and when I think about it, it was terrific. It made life very, very exciting; it was great. The disappointing thing was that not all that long into his involvement with the reserve team big Jock disappeared and went to Dunfermline and the club just careered on without ever looking as if it was going in one direction.'

A lack of guidance at first-team level meant that Celtic Football Club was hurtling towards crisis as it entered the 1960s. Celtic had won the League Cup in successive seasons in 1956 and in 1957 – the latter thanks to a stunning 7–1 victory over Rangers – but between then and the middle of the 1960s no trophies had arrived at Celtic Park. Jimmy McGrory turned 60 years of age in 1964 and after two decades as manager was still subordinate to Robert Kelly in all important matters. Sean Fallon had been appointed first-team coach in 1961 and assistant to McGrory in 1962 but training was still monotonous and unimaginative. Players were forced to run laps around the pitch and were given little opportunity to practise with the ball. Fallon's friendship with Kelly had seen the Irishman rewarded with staff positions after the end of Fallon's playing career, but his influence was not proving effective.

Even those who were most committed to the club could not see much of a future for Celtic in such uninspiring circumstances, as Billy McNeill recalls. 'It was quite interesting because by season 1964–65 a lot of the boys with whom I had gone to Celtic had disappeared. Lots and lots of good players had left: Bobby Collins, Willie Fernie, Bobby Evans; you saw a catalogue of good-quality players leaving. I had made up my mind I was going as well. I was ready to go in the summer of 1965, probably to Tottenham. I had resisted a variety of overtures from good-quality clubs in England to go earlier on – Celtic were my heart and Celtic were my club – but I had made up my mind. I had had enough; the club was going nowhere.'

FOUR

Jock Stein – Glorious Genius

The din is dying down at Celtic Park as the supporters head home happily after the match to all points north, south, east and west of the ground. It is the late 1960s and inside the dressing-room there is hustle and bustle as Jock Stein enters. Exhausted players, their strips dirty with toil, sit side by side along the narrow bench, and the manager goes to the first man to his left, ruffles his hair, gives him an affectionate pat and some words of encouragement, and thanks him for a good performance. He proceeds steadily round the dressing-room, repeating these actions from player to player until he comes to a man whose performance has disappointed Stein. As his team-mates watch, Stein pointedly ignores the player, blanking him completely, and moves on to encourage the next man. He continues all round the room, congratulating those who have pleased him, ignoring completely the one or two whom he feels have let him down. Stein's hands-on approach to management is at work, building up the confidence of players who have done their duty by him whilst simultaneously showing them their hurtful, humiliating fate if they should become too pleased with themselves and consider easing off.

Stein's departure from the Celtic coaching staff in March 1960 had created a vacuum at the club and those who had enjoyed his football tuition at Celtic Park were unsurprised at how his massive presence had bulked out the fortunes of Dunfermline Athletic. His first match as a fully-fledged manager had, strangely enough, pitted his team against Celtic and there were 10,000 at East End Park to see the Pars, despite being reduced to ten men through injury, push on to a 3–2 victory. Stein spent his first few weeks at Dunfermline saving them from what had seemed almost certain relegation and, astonishingly, in the following season, 1960–61, he led Dunfermline to the first major trophy in their history, the Scottish Cup, which they took after a 2–0 replay victory over Celtic in the final. He also brought European football to Fife for the first time, delivering that treat to the club in three of the four seasons in which he was manager at East End Park.

Those successes were achieved through Jock Stein's determined, driven, thorough approach to management. Nothing was left to chance and a sloppy attitude was never tolerated. At a Dunfermline training session one day, Jackie Sinclair, who was a bit of a joker, called the manager 'Jock'. Stein said, 'Listen, come here. I am the boss, not Jock. So remember that.' Thoroughness was one of Stein's special qualities and, not satisfied with telling the player directly, he broached the matter with Sinclair's father, telling Sinclair senior to drive the message home to his son that he was to avoid any familiarity with the manager. Stein's thoroughness would be shown when he brought local Junior sides in to play against his Dunfermline team. He would stop the game at certain stages to analyse what players were doing or to suddenly practise taking free-kicks and work out particular moves. Four enjoyable, rewarding years for Stein and Dunfermline came to a close when Stein was offered the manager's job at Hibernian in 1964. Hibs had been idling in mid-table but with Stein at the helm they were soon speeding in the direction of the top of the League.

The ability of Stein to transform teams with instantaneous effect had alerted clubs throughout Britain to his magisterial, almost magical, managerial powers. Wolverhampton Wanderers were floundering in the lower reaches of England's top division in the middle of the 1964–65 season and early in 1965 the Midlands club's directors approached Stein with the proposal that he join them as manager. Stein promised them he would mull it over and as part of that process asked the Celtic chairman Robert Kelly to meet him for lunch. That appointment would allow Stein to talk over the details of the Wolves offer with Kelly and would also, Stein knew, alert Kelly to the possibility that Stein could be lost to England forever at a time when it was becoming entirely clear that Celtic required the type of inspiration Stein could bring to the club.

Robert Kelly was a traditionalist and although Celtic had always been a non-sectarian club, it was a club permeated by Catholicism; all the directors and managers up to that point had been Catholics. Appointing Stein manager would make him the first non-Catholic person in the club's 77-year history to hold such a senior position. It was a difficult decision for the chairman to make but Kelly chose the purely football-based option over the traditional one and gave Jock Stein the job. Stein's appointment was announced on the final day of January 1965 but an agreement with Hibs meant he would remain manager at Easter Road until the Edinburgh club had found a successor to Stein. That process took five weeks and, by another happy coincidence, Stein's final match in charge of Hibs saw them defeat Rangers 2–1 in the Scottish Cup.

Stein was now free to take control at Celtic Park although one further hurdle had still to be overcome. Robert Kelly had, during the early 1960s, been giving Sean Fallon more and more responsibility with regard to playing matters and fully intended to make him the next Celtic manager. Despite the director's patronage, Fallon had failed to show a trace of the management potential of Stein. It would have been sheer folly for Kelly to have continued to pursue his plans for Fallon to take over as manager but he did request of Stein that Fallon should work with him as joint manager. Stein, who had played alongside Fallon for Celtic during the early 1950s, immediately dismissed the idea – he demanded sole power to make decisions as manager of the club without interference from anyone, including directors. He did, however, allow Kelly to keep Fallon on as assistant manager. 'Jock got on with Sean to a degree,' says Alec Boden, 'but Jock knew him, as I did, and knew that you could not say too much in front of him because Sean was so well-in with Kelly. Jock tolerated Fallon being assistant to him because he would never have stepped out of line with Jock or Jock would have nipped that in the bud. Jock wouldn't have stood for any tales being carried to the boss.' Fallon would gradually grow into the role of Stein's assistant and would, over the years, carry out a considerable amount of valuable legwork to relieve the burden on Stein.

When Stein finally quit Easter Road, Hibs were third in the League, two points behind leaders Hearts. Celtic were in seventh position. The return of Stein to Celtic in March 1965 contrasted sharply with his initial arrival at the club as a player 14 years previously. He had joined Celtic in December 1951 without fuss and without any flurry in the press, having been recruited as a centre-half to strengthen the reserve team. It was to prove the high point in a career that had seen him move from Junior football to Albion Rovers, then on to Llanelli in Wales. 'He was never a good player,' says Johnnie Wilson, who played alongside Stein at Blantyre Vics during the Second World War. 'He was just a big strong player. He admitted himself he was never a player because he couldn't get his place at Blantyre Vics when I was there. He was a reserve at that time.' Determination and drive had seen Stein push his playing career as far as it could go, but when he had joined Celtic from Llanelli in early December 1951 he had still been a virtual unknown. 'I thought he felt a bit inferior at that time because he had been playing non-League down in Wales and now here he was at Celtic,' says Alec Boden, a team-mate in the 1950s and a member of Stein's coaching staff in the 1960s, 'but what a lift that must have been for his confidence. I thought he was quite a humble man and he remained quite humble throughout his life – he always gave people their place and their views.'

Stein's return to the club in 1965 received widespread acclaim and was enough in itself for several players to shelve their plans to move on from Celtic. 'Along came '65 and big Jock returned,' says Billy McNeill. 'The rest is history. When big Jock did come that just put any thoughts I had of leaving out of my head. I think we would probably still have won the Scottish Cup that year – I think that sometimes things are predestined – but what wouldn't have happened was the incredible record of success big Jock had after that. It wasn't until big Jock came that any thoughts or ideas developed.'

A 6–0 League victory over Airdrie at Broomfield on 10 March 1965 heralded Stein's arrival as the working Celtic manager but the team's form fluctuated wildly over the remainder of the 1964–65 season. With the League out of Celtic's reach, Stein was using League games almost as friendlies, matches in which he was experimenting with his players' positions. There were few among the Celtic team who did not find Stein telling them to try another position on the field – sometimes during a game – or asking them to try something different in the way they approached their tasks during the game. Most notably, he pulled Bobby Murdoch back from the inside-right position to right-half. As inside-right, Murdoch had been expected to fetch and carry between midfield and the forward line. Now he could see the play laid out before him and use his exceptional passing skills to greatest effect, prompting and prodding Celtic's attacks. Once he had moved back into that deep midfield position at Stein's behest, it seemed so natural for Murdoch to be there that it was difficult to understand how anyone could have played him in any other position. Jimmy Johnstone had been lingering in the reserves at the time of Stein's arrival but his wing trickery was required by Stein and he was soon pushed into the first-team. The lithe, alert Stevie Chalmers moved to Murdoch's inside-right position, where his speedy reflexes could be best employed both to link the play and to score goals.

The rejuvenating process on the field of play was complemented by Stein's approach to training. Jimmy McGrory's soft hat and coat were consigned to the cloakroom of the past as Stein bounded around the training pitch in a green tracksuit, joining in training games, pulling players aside to dole out advice from time to time and pitching in with jokes and banter to inject an element of fun into proceedings. It worked. Celtic's reinvigorated side swept through a replayed Scottish Cup semi-final with Motherwell, winning 3–0 to set up a final with Dunfermline, most of whose players had grown greatly in stature under Stein. Dunfermline had finished third in the League and Stein's team faced a formidable task in that 1965 final. As the match approached and Celtic prepared for the game at Largs, Stein put the players through light training sessions to keep them supple enough for the final without taxing them too much. He even named his team in advance and then sent them home to relax for a couple of days prior to the match, secure in the knowledge that they were in his starting 11.

The final, on 24 April 1965, was watched by 109,000 supporters and the favourites Dunfermline grabbed hold of the game in the first half, gaining a 2–1 lead by half-time. Stein sharpened the senses of his players at the break and they took hold of the match in the second half. The manager had implanted small nuggets of advice in their minds. Bobby Lennox had been reminded by Stein to run hard at the Dunfermline defence and when one such run took him deep into the Dunfermline half he zipped the ball into the penalty area for Bertie Auld to poke it home and make the score 2–2. Nine minutes from the end, another powerful run saw Lennox sear another hole in the Dunfermline defence – it was ended only by Dunfermline desperately conceding a corner. Charlie Gallagher's floated kick drifted beautifully into the central section of the Dunfermline penalty area, from where the ball was rammed home by the head of Billy McNeill. The Cup belonged to Celtic and Jock Stein had won the first trophy for which he had competed as Celtic manager; it was also the first trophy the club had captured for eight years. The combination of his charismatic presence and intelligence had ended the careworn era in which Celtic had perennially straggled behind those clubs who had the organisation and the zest to win trophies. Under Stein, still only 42, there was a new youthfulness about Celtic.

Stein knew the importance of that victory but he was never one for dwelling too long on his achievements. The following month was a busy one for him. He travelled to Dublin early that May of 1965 to watch Spain take on Ireland in a friendly international and chatted to an agent with regard to the possibility of signing up a couple of the Spanish players. Nothing came of it, but the importation of two top-class continental internationals would have been a radical move for a Scottish side in the mid-'60s. The Spanish national team then visited Glasgow and in the aftermath of a drab 0–0 friendly with Scotland at Hampden Park, the Scottish international team manager, Ian McColl, resigned. Stein, ever energetic, agreed to the request of the SFA to take over as Scotland manager for two World Cup qualifying ties in late May 1965. A 1–1 draw with Poland in Chorzow and a 2–1 victory over Finland in Helsinki were useful results for Scotland and Stein was asked by the SFA to continue as manager for the World Cup ties that were due to take place in the 1965–66 season. It would be a part-time agreement; Stein's duties would extend only as far as joining up with the squad prior to each match to guide them through the game. Stein also found time to break the Celtic transfer record when he signed Joe McBride from Motherwell for a £22,500 fee.

That busy summer of 1965 then saw Stein arrange for four young Brazilian players to spend a month on trial at the club and although none of them were eventually signed by the club, it was another indication of Stein's open-mindedness and willingness to explore new options.

David Hay was one of a mass of young players who were training at Celtic Park on Tuesday and Thursday nights when Stein arrived at the club. The manager was soon holding trials to look more closely at the numbers in an effort to deplete them. Hay caught Stein's eye and early in 1965 Hay became one of Stein's first signings. He began training full-time with the club as a 17-year-old in the pre-season of 1965. 'This was at the start of Jock's first full season,' Hay remembers. 'Listening to the experienced players, his type of training was new at that particular time. It was very much a lot of work being done with the ball and circuit training. He got you exceptionally fit. You could see – from a distance, watching him with the first-team – that he was more involved tactically than managers had been before. You could almost at that early stage see how good he was going to be. They had beaten Dunfermline in the Cup so he became a winner quickly and from then on he was always a winner. He brought success back to Celtic that early and the style of the play, with Billy scoring the winner, epitomised what happened with Jock in ensuing years. He had an exceptional group of players and he got the best out of them. Tactically he had a knowledge of the game second to none. There was an element of fear with him. There was always a bit of trepidation that you wouldn't want to do anything wrong . . . that's not to say it didn't happen sometimes. The simplest way to analyse it is that I felt he got the best out of me individually and within the system of the team. Accordingly, he got the best out of the team.'

Pre-season training that balmy summer of 1965 was entirely different from anything the Celtic players had previously experienced. Every single member of the squad was provided with a football on their first day back, in mid-July 1965; in previous years the players had been made to sweat off their summer excesses on cross-country runs after returning from their summer break. The players loved the joyful release of working with the ball all the time from the opening day of pre-season onwards. Certain senior players were also given a degree of responsibility themselves to supervise mini-groups of men as the training began.

It had been a refreshing, radical change for the players but when the season's fixtures began, the old inconsistency that had dogged Celtic for so many years surfaced again. They lost two of their three opening fixtures and in the third of those – all of which were ties in a four-team League Cup group – they lost 2–0 at home to Dundee in front of 34,000 at Celtic Park. As the match wore on and Celtic struggled to score, a slow handclap crackled round the crowd.

Those early setbacks would prove to be only temporary faults and they were swiftly forgotten as Stein's team clicked into top gear and powered on to achieve a marvellous consistency of performance that saw them lose just once more – 2–1 in a League encounter with Rangers at Ibrox – before facing their major rivals at Hampden Park in the final of the League Cup on 23 October 1965. Two first-half penalties, converted in style by John Hughes, gave Celtic a 2–1 victory over Rangers and one that meant a great deal to Stein. 'He thought that was the result that mattered most,' says John Divers. 'There was the final of a national trophy and Celtic had beaten Rangers. That was a real boost – he thought that was very important.' Heartened by that victory, Celtic stepped on the gas and by New Year 1966 they were level on points with Rangers. The annual Old Firm derby resulted in a 5–1 victory for Stein's men, Celtic's first New Year Old Firm victory since, significantly, their last championship-winning year of 1954. Celtic had gained a decisive advantage over their opponents on the day by wearing training shoes instead of boots on the frozen-hard playing surface. It provided them with the impetus to take the 1965–66 title, even though they faltered nervously once or twice along the way. They also reached the semi-finals of the European Cup-Winners' Cup, where they were unluckily eliminated on a 2–1 aggregate by Liverpool and lost the replayed 1966 Scottish Cup final 1–0 to Rangers.

Celtic had been transformed into a powerful force in every competition that season thanks to Stein's all-pervasive influence. The manager seemed to know instinctively how to motivate each player. Players felt that he understood them intrinsically because Stein could always be relied upon to press the right buttons to get them working productively. He knew all their moods and habits, on and off the pitch. Glasgow also seemed to teem with a network of informers who could advise Stein as to the movements of each one of his players away from Celtic Park.

John Divers, a thinking player who observed Stein closely over the manager's opening season at Celtic Park, expands on Stein's methods: 'He was terrific at getting people to play in the position he thought they were best suited for and to do it at 100 per cent of their ability for themselves, for Jock Stein and for the support. People had specific roles. He would say, "You have a role and it might not be appreciated by the supporters on the terracing but it's what I want you to do and if you do it the way I want you to do it that's fine. He would tell people to do things which would not be glamorous but if someone did that type of job properly he would make a point of congratulating them after the game. They might get four out of ten in the newspaper but they'd have done what big Jock wanted them to do.'

Stein had resigned as Scotland manager in late 1965. A defeat in Italy had meant the Scottish team could not qualify for the 1966 World Cup and Stein had become frustrated by the constrictions presented by working with the national team. He had been even more frustrated at Anfield during the second leg of the 1966 Cup-Winners' Cup semi-final with Liverpool when a Bobby Lennox goal was disallowed for offside. Lennox was so quick at running past defenders on to a ball that he often put the ball in the net only to find the goal had been disallowed – linesmen could not believe that anyone could get behind a defence so quickly and still be onside, but that was actually one of Lennox's specialities. His team-mates and Stein were convinced that the goal against Liverpool should have stood, which would have kept Celtic alive in the tie and taken them closer to a final against Borussia Dortmund in Glasgow.

Instead, it made Stein and his players even hungrier for success in Europe as they anticipated the 1966–67 season, which would see Celtic's first-ever participation in the European Cup. 'It is up to us,' said Stein after Celtic had captured the 1965–66 Scottish League title, 'to everyone at Celtic Park now, to build up our own legends.

We don't want to live with history, to be compared with legends from the past. We must make new legends and our League Championship win is the first step towards doing that. The greatness of a club in modern football will be judged on performances in Europe. It is only in the major European tournaments that you can really get a chance to rate yourself alongside the great teams.'

The summer of 1966 saw Celtic embark on a five-and-a-half-week, 11-game tour of Bermuda, Canada and the USA. Stein used the trip to increase team spirit, as Tommy Gemmell remembers fondly: 'We were always creating laughs and doing wind-ups on each other. Jock was trying to make us one big family and he succeeded. We were also hungry for success. We'd never had success so we wanted to win things. Once you start winning things it becomes a habit and you don't want to stop winning. It was all about guidance and leadership. The players were there. They just needed to be moulded into a team and that's basically what he did. We were one big happy family with players that could play and that makes a big difference. You get a lot of players with good ability in different sides but the actual players don't play as a team. They play as individual units. You've got to get the whole team playing as one single unit before you can get success and that's what happened with us.'

The opening European Cup tie was at Celtic Park on 28 September 1966 and the opposition was FC Zurich, the champions of Switzerland. It was a nervous, tense occasion and the Swiss proved durable opponents until, just after the hour, Gemmell intervened by streaking on to the ball 35 yards from goal to send a stunning shot past the Swiss goalkeeper. A Joe McBride goal made the final score a comfortable 2–0. Gemmell comments, 'I was told by the management people before Jock Stein came that if I crossed the halfway line I wouldn't be in the team. I'd heard that Jock liked attacking full-backs so when he came I thought, "This is going to suit me." When he arrived at first I went crazy and did too much attacking and not enough defending and he gave me a wee fright in the early weeks and left me out of a couple of games.'

The transformation of Gemmell from a traditional left-back who stayed planted on his own defensive patch into a streamlined, auxiliary attacker – almost like a modern wing-back – when the team was going forward was typical of the way Stein had shifted the approach to the game at Celtic Park. The tall, well-built John Hughes had been a powerful centre-forward until the arrival of Stein, who imaginatively transformed him into an outside-left, a position in which the player, who had been concentrating on athletics before joining Celtic, could make better use of his power and pace. Bertie Auld switched from the left wing to midfield, where his incisive passing could be put to better use. The team that had trotted out for the tie with Zurich had contained only one player – Joe McBride – whom Stein had not inherited from Jimmy McGrory but although the names had stayed the same they were now playing a different game. Every member of the team was kept sharp by Stein in the knowledge that he would ruthlessly replace them if they lost form. His forwards, in particular, could never feel assured of their place – the manager would 'freshen up' the forward line frequently to ensure the Celtic attack never became stale.

A 3–0 victory in the return with Zurich, which included another 35-yarder from Gemmell, led to a tie with Nantes, which Celtic negotiated safely with a 6–2 aggregate victory to put them into the quarter-finals of the European Cup. Those ties were typical of a season in which Celtic developed into an unstoppable force. In between those two European Cup ties, Rangers had tried to restrain Stein's team in the League Cup final but a wonderful reverse header from McBride set up Lennox to clip home the only goal of the game. Celtic's progress in the Scottish League was equally smooth and by the time Christmas 1966 arrived, Celtic had played a total of 30 fixtures in European and domestic competition and were still unbeaten. They would lose only twice in the Scottish League all season – both defeats to Dundee United – and would take their second successive title by a three-point margin from close pursuers Rangers. The Scottish Cup, too, would fall to Celtic, a 2–0 victory over Aberdeen in April 1967 securing the first Treble in Celtic's history.

The European Cup quarter-final was the trickiest test Celtic faced in that year's competition. Their opponents, Yugoslavian champions Vojvodina, possessed a formidable blend of toughness, tactical awareness and skill. Each of their players was ultra-comfortable on the ball and they played well as a team. It led to Vojvodina taking a 1–0 lead in the tie after the first leg and in the return at Celtic Park in March 1967 the Yugoslavs constructed a seemingly impenetrable wall of defence. Celtic consequently failed to score in the first half. Stein now came into his own. He was always a good reader of the game and would make numerous detailed adjustments to the way the players were playing as the game was progressing and if he had to attend to something major, he would do so during the half-time interval. Against Vojvodina, this was when Stein worked one of his smart tactical changes. For the second period, Hughes was switched from the left wing to the right while Johnstone remained on the right wing. With both wingers picking away at the left side of the Yugoslavs' defence, Vojvodina's rearguard was unbalanced and undermined, and under incessant Celtic pressure the Yugoslavs finally cracked. A 2–0 victory took Celtic into the semis, where they faced Czechoslovakian champions Dukla Prague. At half-time in the first leg at Celtic Park, with the score 1–1, Stein told his men to press up hard against the Czechs' defence and a 3–1 win followed. Celtic defended in depth in the return at the Juliska Stadium and 90 nerve-racking minutes yielded a 0–0 draw that meant they became the first British club to reach the European Cup final. 'Prague,' states Tommy Gemmell, 'was the one and only time we were ever asked to play defensively by Jock Stein. We put the shutters up. Stevie Chalmers played on his own up front and everybody else played at the back of midfield. Ronnie Simpson had a tremendous match in goal. Big Jock, hands up to him, said afterwards, "We'll never play defensively ever again." We had got the result but it was fingernails stuff.'

Celtic had uncharacteristically indulged in time-wasting, spoiling tactics in Prague as a means of holding on to their first-leg lead. Stein promised there would be no repeat of that display in the European Cup final against Internazionale of Milan in the National Stadium, Lisbon, on 25 May 1967. The final also afforded Stein the opportunity to renew his acquaintance with the manager of Inter, Helenio Herrera, who had allowed Stein to visit Milan in the early 1960s to observe his methods. That trip had yielded much tactical knowledge for Stein and had resulted in his adoption of the use of overlapping full-backs as a means of supplementing the attack without sacrificing too much from defence. The Celtic team that Stein would field for the final featured the athletic Tommy Gemmell and Jim Craig, each of whom was free to power forward on their flank although Stein's strict instruction was that only one of those full-backs could go forward at a time. The other had to remain in defence as cover.

Ronnie Simpson, the 36-year-old goalkeeper, was enjoying a new lease of life at Celtic as his career drew to a close. He had been transferred to Celtic from Hibernian by Stein in late 1964 and, consequently, had been sure there would be no future for him at Celtic when Stein arrived as manager in early 1965. Instead, Stein's open-mindedness had allowed Simpson a second chance to prove himself to the manager and it was one he had taken with aplomb. Central defenders John Clark and Billy McNeill, both Lanarkshire boys, had been groomed by Stein at the club in the late-'50s, as had forward Stevie Chalmers. Midfielders Bertie Auld and Bobby Murdoch were enjoying the new roles Stein had found for them. Wingers Jimmy Johnstone and Bobby Lennox were encouraged by Stein to show the full range of their talents freely. Willie Wallace had been signed by Stein from Hearts in late 1966, just in time to replace Joe McBride after the high-scoring centre-forward had sustained a severe knee injury at Aberdeen on Christmas Eve. There was a tightly-bound closeness between the manager and this group of players that ensured communication between the boss and his men was smooth and easy.

The sumptuous, ornate Hotel Palacio in the palm-tree-lined resort of Estoril, on the Portuguese Riviera, a few miles west of Lisbon, was to be the Celtic team's base in the run-up to the final. Billy McNeill has good memories of that time. 'When we got to Estoril,' he says, 'the hotel was absolutely magnificent. It was perfect, with a beautiful swimming pool and beautiful gardens, but the big fellow gave you half an hour or so in the swimming pool and then said, "Right, get out of the sun because the sun will tire you." Whether the sun would have tired us or not is another matter. I think what he was doing was always reminding you that you were here to do a job of work. It was extreme luxury at the hotel. So therefore he was showing us, "This is where you are now. You are at the top end of the market. We're here now but don't lose sight of the reason we're here. We're not here just to relax and enjoy ourselves. We're here to appreciate these luxuries because of the level at which we're playing but we've got here and we'll stay here through hard work and being diligent and remembering that we're here to play a game." He planned everything to perfection.'

Jock Stein was in his element on the day of the European Cup final, delighted to be exercising his wits at the highest level and looking almost Italianate in style with his choice of a dark suit and shades as he took his place on the bench. He looked the equal of Herrera and now his team would prove that they too could match the Italians for style. Fittingly, in light of Stein's pilgrimage to Milan several years earlier, the game would hinge on interventions by the Celtic full-backs. After seven minutes, right-back Jim Craig needlessly fouled Inter's Cappellini as the Italian swerved to his inside and Celtic conceded a penalty. The Celtic players protested but German referee Kurt Tschenscher stood firm and Sandro Mazzola stroked the ball into the net to give Inter the lead. It looked a deadly blow: the Italians would now employ their *catenaccio* system, by which they would bolt their defence tightly to try to protect their lead. This tactic involved the sweeper, Armando Picchi, augmenting a four-man defence to snuff out any opposition attacks through negativity and sheer weight of numbers, and Herrera was the world leader in its perfection. It was the major reason Inter had captured the European Cups of 1964 and 1965. Stein and Celtic were truly up against it.

The score remained 1–0 to Inter at half-time and the Celtic players were still raging at the penalty award as they made their way through the subterranean passage that links the pitch with the small yard that houses the two self-contained dressing-room buildings at the National Stadium. 'At half-time,' says Billy McNeill, 'it took big Jock a bit of time to settle us down because we were all having a go at the referee, giving him pelters. It took him time to calm us, which he did do and, of course, we went out and it went all right. He encouraged us to keep doing what we had been doing in the first half.' That meant Celtic were to continue their relentless, spirited attacking of the Inter goal – Stein was certain that if Celtic played to their biggest strength, inventiveness in attack, they would prevail over the Italians' deep defending.

After 63 minutes Stein's use of overlapping full-backs paid off in full when Craig drew the ball into Gemmell's path and Gemmell whacked a truly unstoppable shot from the edge of the penalty area into the roof of the Inter net. It was one of the most spectacular, inspirational goals in Celtic's history and it directly contravened Jock Stein's specific instructions to his players. 'I should actually have had my behind kicked for that,' says Gemmell, 'because I shouldn't have been there in the first place. The golden rule was that if one full-back was up, the other one should be round covering central defence and it was Jim Craig who cut the ball back for me. There was no need for me to be back because they only had one player in our half, as against our two defenders. If they'd had two, I would have had to have stayed back. If you look at the game on film you'll see there's an Italian defender comes out to attack the ball as Jim Craig squares it to me but he stops and half-turns two yards from me. If that guy had taken one more pace he could have changed the whole course of Celtic's history. They could have broken away and scored a goal and I would have been castigated because there was no way I should have been there in the first place. Sometimes rules are made to be broken.' The Italian who had wilted in the face of Celtic's force was Armando Picchi, the mainstay of Inter's defence.

Five minutes from time, one of Stein's moves from the training ground was executed to perfection when Gemmell cut the ball back for Bobby Murdoch to send a low, hard ball across the face of goal and Stevie Chalmers, as he had done so often in a training top and bib, diverted it past Giuliano Sarti in the Inter goal. 'That wasn't an accident,' says Gemmell. 'We did exactly the same thing in training every day of the week: players going down either side, cutting it back to midfield players supporting front players, hitting it and the front players always trying to deflect it. It was no fluke. Even if Bobby's shot had been going in, Stevie would still have deflected it.'

Afterwards Stein wore an expression of deep satisfaction and joy as he clutched the European Cup. He said, 'We won and we won on merit. This win gives us more satisfaction than anything. I can still hardly believe that it's true. To say I am proud of them is a complete understatement of the case.' The players had been exceptional. On a day of searing Lisbon heat, sweat seeped from every pore as they attacked the game and the Italians with brio from first to last. The Celtic players' desire to get forward at every opportunity had, on the day, overwhelmed Inter, who could easily have conceded a greater number of goals. The players deserve their accolades for their performances that day but the man behind the construction of the entire achievement, as all the players knew deep down, was Jock Stein.

'The more you look at that game against Inter,' says David Hay, 'Two–one wasn't a reflection of how well Celtic played. Each time I see it again I find it phenomenal how Celtic played that day. A lot of it was down to the players themselves, obviously, but I think the way that he had set them up for the game was vital. After winning every tournament and playing so many games, there wasn't an ounce of tiredness in their bones. They were playing in warm sunshine and having to take the game to Inter Milan, then going one behind. The more you think about it, the more phenomenal the result was. That's what puts him up there with the top managers and, you've got to say, that's what makes him the best Celtic manager of all time.'

The capturing of the European Cup instantly crowned Celtic with regal credentials for continued success in continental competition. Stein loved the cut and thrust of his jousts with sophisticated opposition coaches and over the next few years he would enjoy numerous other opportunities to measure his knowledge of football against that of European football's tactical grandmasters. The club's ongoing involvement in the European Cup arose from Celtic's domination of the Scottish League, where they were close to invincible between 1966 and 1974 as they won a Scottish record nine titles in succession. Stein had reinvigorated the club – even as the Lisbon Lions had been glorying in the aftermath of their success, he was bringing through a new set of players, cubs whom he was grooming to take, eventually, the places of the men who had won the European Cup.

David Hay, who made his Celtic debut in 1968, thinks back to the late 1960s and his days under Stein's tutelage with great affection. 'He trained us simply, although there was always an edge to the training. As kids we always trained with the Lisbon Lions at the time. Sean Fallon or Willie Fernie would take us for our wee bit of training and then we would come together. Your football was always geared to a two-touch game, which meant sharpness was required. It was almost as competitive as a game could be without having the same competitive edge. So your training was set at a high standard. Then what would happen in games was that most games would look after themselves on the basis that Celtic were superior to the other team. So there wasn't a need to go into it tactically but in the European games he would plot how the game would normally run. He would give you a background to the opposing team, individually, and how they played and, accordingly, how we would play collectively and what your individual task was. You knew, going out there, what to do and what your team-mates had to do and invariably he gave you the feeling that if you did it properly you would win. Normally, that was the case.'

Celtic's bonus system, which was geared towards achievement, helped Stein to make his players enjoy winning enormously. If the team was doing well the players would be rewarded handsomely. The bonus for capturing the European Cup in 1967 had been £1,500 per man, a reward that compared more than favourably with anything else on offer in Britain – the following year Manchester United's players were paid a lesser bonus of £1000 per man for winning the same trophy. The difference was that the United players were on a considerably higher basic wage. United first paid £100 per week to a player in 1966; that level of basic pay would not be reached at Celtic until the middle of the 1970s.

Stein always wanted to be as close to his players as possible during a match and he was the first Celtic manager to watch matches from a dugout; Jimmy McGrory and his predecessors had all watched proceedings from the stand. Stein would spend most of a match crouched on the bench, yelling instructions, and would occasionally leap up and out to the touchline to get across a particularly serious point. Tommy Gemmell can recall one European tie in which Stein bustled round the running track at Celtic Park to get as physically close as possible to the player and berate him for a piece of unnecessary over-elaboration. Stein's attentive promptings meant that the Celtic players were left in no doubt as to their precise duties, but his dugout duty was not without its humorous cameos. On one occasion during a big European game in the late 1960s, Ronnie Simpson sent a powerful throw-out spinning down the wing towards a team-mate who was hugging the touchline. The man in question lifted his leg to control the ball but it went flying under his foot and he stood stork-like, embarrassed, as the ball hurtled towards the Celtic dugout where it only narrowly missed whacking Stein full in the face. 'I don't know why I select him, the stupid so-and-so,' the manager was heard to mutter, shaking his head ruefully.

'Jock was fantastic,' says Lou Macari, who joined Celtic at the age of 17 in the summer of 1966. 'He was unbelievable. He trained you. He worked you. He knew how to get every single bit out of you. We used to run to the training ground at Barrowfield to go training every morning. He would come down in his car and if he saw you jogging or walking he would wind down his car window and shout, "Get a move on!" So you were always on your toes. Back in the '60s and '70s you didn't bother either. If I was to do now what he did then in management, there would be riots with the players. They wouldn't stand for it, which is the reason why we haven't got such good players now. All those that are coming through now, the supposed stars, are never going to be stars. We're telling them they're stars and they're getting paid like stars long before they've achieved anything. Going back to Jock, he was sharp. He was a smart operator. We used to go to Seamill for the big games and he didn't leave anything to chance, he didn't leave a stone unturned where he thought he could get an advantage or get more out of a player.

'With Jock, your preparation was every day of the week and that started before you were a Celtic player. It started when you went up to Celtic Park as a youngster. I used to leave St Michael's at four o'clock, jump on the train at Kilwinning, where I went to school, take the train to Glasgow, take the 263 Auchenshuggle bus and then another bus to Celtic Park. You would be terrified in case you were late even though you were at the mercy of the buses and the railways. You were still terrified because Jock would be waiting at the door, looking at his watch, to see who was late and who wasn't late.

'When you went in, the training was clever. You were young, so physical training was always required. At Celtic Park, the physical training meant you went straight on to the track. So you pounded the track and you would get a little bonus at the end of training when you played a little game behind the goals at the Celtic end because there was a massive area of grass behind the goals at the time and you used to have a little five-a-side there. It wasn't long since I had been travelling on the Celtic supporters' buses from Largs to watch Billy McNeill and wee Jimmy and all them and now it felt great to be involved with the club and to be allowed to play practice matches on the turf at the Park. That was the same every Tuesday and Thursday: running, running, running, up the terracing, back down the terracing, and then at the end of it, for 10 or 15 minutes, a game of football. Then it was back into the dressing-room, showered, back to Glasgow Central on the bus, home to Largs at about half-eleven at night. So, very early on in your career, work was instilled into you. That stood you in good stead when you became a player.'

A second Treble was captured in the 1968–69 season, during which Celtic were desperately unlucky to go out to AC Milan on a 1–0 aggregate defeat in the quarter-finals of the European Cup. The away leg had yielded a 0–0 draw and shown how Stein had grown in sophistication in European football since the away semi-final with Dukla Prague two years earlier. In the San Siro, Milan, he used the speedy Lennox at centre-forward with Hughes and Johnstone as deep-lying wingers who were prepared to support Lennox when Celtic had the ball, but who were also ready to defend when they were without it. The loss of an early goal in the return at Celtic Park was all it took to undo that good work; a reminder of the hair's-breadth between success and failure in the European arena. Celtic made up for that disappointment when, in the 1969–70 tournament, they knocked out an impressive collection of European champions – FC Basle, Benfica and Fiorentina – before defeating England's much-touted Leeds United in each leg of an epic semi-final. That took Celtic into their second European Cup final, in which they would face the Dutch club Feyenoord on 6 May 1970 in Milan. Celtic were peaking nicely – they had strolled away with the Scottish League title that 1969–70 season, separating themselves from their closest challengers, Rangers, by a 12-point margin, the most emphatic title triumph under Stein.

The 1969 European Cup final had seen Ajax Amsterdam, the first Dutch club to reach the final, defeated 4–1 by AC Milan. Many expected Feyenoord to suffer a fate similar to that of Ajax when they faced Celtic the following year but two days before the final Stein counselled against such loose talk. 'I cannot agree with the current impression that Celtic cannot be beaten,' he said. 'As far as I am concerned, it is certainly a problem and an attitude I don't fancy at all. Mind you, the occasion should bring out the best in our team. They won't be professionals if they are caught out by all this talk at this stage and I will be driving the point home to them in our discussions after training tomorrow.' Stein did, however, believe that Feyenoord were not used to teams attacking them fiercely in the way that he knew Celtic could. He believed that the key to the game could lie in how the Dutch defence coped with Celtic's pacy forwards. 'We must attack the game,' he stressed beforehand, 'and stretch the Dutch defence from the start. Our wingers may present Feyenoord with a situation they have never encountered in their previous rounds. No one knows exactly how they will react to our attacking style.'

It meant that Celtic lined up in a 4–2–4 formation on the night of the final, with midfielders Murdoch and Auld expected to service all-out attackers Johnstone, Hughes, Lennox and Wallace. Feyenoord went 4–3–3 and with an extra man in the middle had soon established a stranglehold on midfield. Celtic took the lead through a Gemmell free-kick but with Wim Jansen, Franz Hasil and Wim van Hanegem dominating the centre of the park, Feyenoord equalised quickly and three minutes from the end of extra-time Feyenoord forward Ove Kindvall prodded the ball past Celtic goalkeeper Evan Williams to give the Dutch club the trophy.

Stein had used a more defensive 4–4–2 formation in Italy previously that season: after a 3–0 first-leg victory over Fiorentina in the quarter-final he had used it to play safe in the away leg and had been content with a 1–0 defeat. He had used 4–3–3 both away to Leeds and in the return home leg and had been rewarded bountifully when the talented young central midfielder George Connelly scored the goal that gave Celtic their vital 1–0 first-leg win at Elland Road. Celtic had also used 4–3–3 in the San Siro the year before to obtain a 0–0 draw with AC Milan. It was Stein's sense of adventure and decision to go with an attacking 4–2–4 formation that had failed him in the final. It had served him well in Lisbon in 1967 but in Milan it flopped.

'We were unlucky in the sense that our season had basically finished whereas theirs was still going on,' says Billy McNeill as he recalls that final with Feyenoord. 'They were still much more battle-sharpened than we were but I think our whole preparation was far too relaxed and easy. There was too much thought given to what should happen afterwards – should we get an open-decked bus to travel through the streets of Glasgow and so on. There was no disgrace in losing to a team as good as Feyenoord but I would like to go back and have the preparations much more realistic and to the point than they were.'

David Hay was at right-back in that European Cup final side. He comments, 'The only one time when he probably failed in all his time – and we all played our part in that – was the European Cup final against Feyenoord where I think we all underestimated the opposition after doing so well against Leeds United. That was almost, probably, the final before the final. Strangely enough, despite the fact that we didn't play well we could almost have won that game against Feyenoord; not that we would have deserved it. If it had gone to a draw and a replay I think we would have beaten Feyenoord. I think we were all to blame for losing that game; it was maybe the one error in his long career but I wouldn't dwell on that because if you look back to how a team like Celtic had won the European Cup against the masters Inter Milan you have got to say that that was an exceptional feat.'

Stein was very much a hands-on manager, as Hay confirms. 'He was totally in control of training, every single day. He was the man in charge. There was no coaching manual. It was the Jock Stein way: I'd call it the "simple football" manual, which was the correct way. It was training done with an edge. It was never static, it was never boring. He would know when to train you hard, when to ease off. He was ahead of the game at that time. It was a simple form of training but very much enjoyable and always with an edge to it. Jokingly, we used to say to the Lisbon Lions, "What was your hardest game?" And they would say playing against us young fellows, the Quality Street Gang. There were one or two ding-dongs, you know! We probably never beat them, they wouldn't allow that, but it created an edge in training. You were never allowed to develop any bad habits or slackness in training or in the games. Slackness makes for mistakes so you were not allowed to take the wrong option or hit the wrong type of pass. You were always geared to do the right thing. Normally speaking in football, if you do the simple thing and you are a good player, it will be the correct thing to do. Wee Jimmy was different, he could over-elaborate on the ball, but for the rest of us it was stressed to us how important it was that we never unnecessarily over-elaborated on the ball.'

Ferrari's restaurant in central Glasgow had by the late 1960s taken over from the Bank restaurant as the most popular city-centre gathering place for Celtic players and staff. On a Saturday evening, Stein would go there to meet up with the coaches who were in charge of the second team and, in great detail, he would quiz his assistants about how the team and the players had played. It kept him fully abreast of the young players' progress and helped him to gauge when the time might be right to throw those players into the first team. Lou Macari, a contemporary of Hay at Celtic Park, was grateful for Stein's guidance. 'I think any of the younger ones who were there at the time,' he says, 'myself and Kenny Dalglish and Danny McGrain and David Hay, I could go on and on – I think if any of us later in our lives now look back and can't credit him with the fact that we played for a long, long time and the fact that we were fortunate to be involved in football for a long, long time, then there is something wrong with us. Knowing what I know now about football management and bringing players up and getting them into good habits, as compared to bad habits, what he instilled in us is, I believe, a major reason why I played for so long and also why I've been fortunate enough to go into management. It's all down to him.

'Discipline was the main thing he instilled in us. You know, when you're an up-and-coming player, or when you're young, I think it's definitely a major thing to have it instilled into you what is accepted and what isn't accepted. The great need for fitness was drummed into you. It was emphasised that although we were bringing to Celtic our ability to play football, once we were at the club it was a case of getting us fit and strong to the point where we could play for the club week-in and week-out for a number of years. Obviously that can't be achieved by having nights out and ending up in pubs and being sloshed half the time. Again, that was another part of his education. Drink was absolutely taboo. I've never had a drink in my life. That wasn't down to Jock although, in another way, it could have been. I'd never had a drink before I went to Celtic as a youngster. I'd never ever considered it, I didn't like it because of the taste. It was also something that he'd made perfectly clear wasn't going to be accepted so that may have influenced me to continue to avoid drink. He never had cause to tell me or any of the other young players about the perils of drink. We just learned from what we saw and how he reacted at certain times with the senior players. If there was any suggestion they might have had a drink he would let them know in no uncertain terms that he wasn't happy with it – and by a drink I mean half a lager somewhere. That's also why he used to tell you to get to your bed early when you were away preparing for a big match.

'When you were away preparing for a game, such as Celtic v. Rangers, he would be telling you when to get into your bed. If you weren't in your bed you would be in trouble then as well. If he went into your room and he found Coca-Cola or milk he would come in and pour it down the sink because he believed it wasn't good for you. Coca-Cola was too gassy. He wanted to control every step of your preparation for a big game and if you stepped out of line with that preparation he'd let you know. Us younger ones were so terrified of him that we never felt his tongue, really, because we saw his behaviour with the senior players. Again, that was good management because it was an indication of what he was going to stand for and he was spelling it out to you without actually spelling it out to you in your face what he was going to accept and not accept.

'I must say that at the time you would probably be rebelling and saying that it was a joke and all that sort of thing but I can look back, now that I am a lot wiser, and credit the success that I had with that bunch of players to Jock Stein's dedication and, as a result of his dedication, the other players' dedication. It carried the team on for year after year, season after season. No one could get near them in terms of beating them. I think when you are young you don't like or dislike a manager. If he told you something that you thought was stupid and you couldn't understand why he was doing it, I wouldn't say you would dislike him. You would just be a bit angry with him at that particular time. I couldn't say anything bad about Jock because, looking back on it, everything he did was right, everything he did was perfect. Those who didn't listen to him maybe later on in their careers fell by the wayside. It's a bit like the way Alex Ferguson, who worked under Jock, manages at Old Trafford. If you don't abide by his rules, then you go and most of those that go just fall by the wayside. They just disappear.

'When you went away for a big game,' continues Macari, 'from the minute you arrived at Seamill, Jock arranged everything so that the only spare time you had during the whole blooming day was half an hour. So if anybody wanted to nip up to the little pub up the road they had half an hour in which to do it. The rest of the time was filled by having a meeting or a massage or a sauna, things like that. My first big game was the Scottish Cup final in 1971. I was a sub on the Saturday and we had been at Seamill and done all the preparation. We were winning 1–0 when Rangers equalised three minutes from the end. We were sick but there was no messing – we went straight back to Seamill on the team bus. Nowadays players wouldn't stand for being away for seven days to prepare for a game during the season. Anyway, we would just go because we would expect it and we would want to do it and we realised the importance of it.

'So we got back there and we trained and he had no criticism of the team, which you wouldn't expect him to have. So we went through the routine and went back to Hampden on the Wednesday night. Right out of the blue, at seven o'clock, he tells me I'm playing. I think that was smart management. He didn't give me three days in which to panic; three days to be twisting and turning in bed. You got half an hour to prepare yourself to go out and play. That's how simple his management was and that's how simple management is.' Stein was rewarded by a sharp, clever goal from Macari as Celtic defeated Rangers 2–1 in the replay to complete a Scottish Cup and League Double at the end of that 1970–71 season.

One of the great perks that the Celtic players of the time used to enjoy was that on a Saturday after a game, if they wished, they could go into the Vesuvio, an Italian restaurant on St Vincent Street, just off George Square, and have a meal. The chance to enjoy a good meal on the club in well-appointed surroundings was deeply appreciated by the players. The younger ones especially would delight in the chance to experience a taste of good living. Even then, Stein would find a way to use those relaxing restaurant visits to remind his players of the standards he expected of them. His focus on detail extended to the point of checking the restaurant bill to see what had been consumed by his players and on one occasion his eyes alighted on a charge for a cigar. Stein duly called a meeting with the players about it to identify the culprit – Tommy Gemmell – and to make his displeasure known to the other players. His players might have won the European Cup but no one was to get above themselves by having a cigar! Any time Stein got a little opportunity to shake people up, he would take it and make the most of it. He made a big deal of small breaches of discipline to let players see that he wasn't going to stand for even the little things that he didn't like. That way, they would think twice or three times before carrying out a more serious breach of discipline.

'If you're winning and you're successful, how can you stop listening to somebody who's telling you how to be successful?' points out Macari. 'You would stop listening to somebody who was telling you what to do when you were not being successful – as a matter of fact, you're a bit daft if you don't because it's there in black and white: I'm listening to this fellow and we ain't winning anything so what's the point of listening to him? If you stopped listening to Jock, then you were a fool. At the time you might have stopped listening because you didn't want to hear some of the things he was saying but it becomes perfectly obvious to you when you get a lot older and a lot wiser that he was an expert in every single aspect of management.'

The Quality Street Gang, as Hay, Macari and their fellow promising youngsters were nicknamed, were of such a high calibre that the 1970s saw them pour through into the first-team. The new generation had been teenagers in the liberating years of the 1960s, when modern youth culture had been born, and unlike their predecessors they had never been threatened with national service.

Youngsters such as Kenny Dalglish, George Connelly, Vic Davidson, Lou Macari and David Hay also had the long hair and gaudy clothes of the early 1970s but Hay dismisses any suggestion that Jock Stein was fazed by a generation gap between him and his players. 'I think some of the Lions might have had long hair at the time – we were maybe just younger with long hair!' he says. There was a bigger problem than the generation gap, and it was a more traditional one: money. It was an issue that would drive a wedge between Stein and some of these new men. Stein had always used money extremely cleverly and cannily as a means of motivation. Celtic's pay structure was weighted towards bonus payments for results, which meant that if a player was not in the team he would lose out financially in a seriously damaging fashion. It kept players hungry for success and ensured no cobwebs of complacency were allowed to settle on Celtic Park. The players who had been at Celtic Park in the mid-1960s, when Stein arrived, had benefited drastically from this pay structure. They had been transformed swiftly from losers into winners, which meant they noticed an enormous difference in their financial rewards in comparison to the days of Jimmy McGrory's management.

The new generation were less easily satisfied, especially as they were hearing how footballers' pay was mushrooming in the higher echelons of the English League, even at clubs whose players could not compare in talent with those at Celtic. Lou Macari was the first of the Quality Street Gang to become so disillusioned by the wage structure at Celtic Park that it forced him to request a transfer. He left for Manchester United in January 1973 for a Scottish record fee of £200,000. With the benefit of experience, Macari can now look back on Stein's pay structure and see the sense in it. 'Even when I left I didn't have a run-in with Jock. I had been at Celtic Park for four or five years and a new contract came up and he offered me a fiver increase, which I was a bit stunned by, because I thought I had done OK. I just took the view that I wasn't going to accept it.

'Looking back, I can't criticise him for that. At the time it might have felt harsh but it is a way of keeping you hungry. I was on £50 a week and my increase was to £55 and I thought it was a disgrace but, looking back now, it was cunning on his part. He knew that, when the Rangers game came round, for instance, and they were going to give you £1000 if you won, that that was a driving force to get players to play. If you were on £55 a week and had the chance to earn £1000 you would kill, wouldn't you! The bonus system was the proper way. I can look back now, having been through all the other ways, and can say that all the other ways don't work. If you give them loads of money, players don't go away thinking you are wonderful and wanting to try harder for you. It doesn't work like that. The thing that actually happens is that years later your club will be bankrupt, which is the case now in England with a lot of clubs.

'So Jock was ahead of his time. He knew where the pitfalls could lie by giving players substantial amounts of money. I must say that after we had beaten Rangers and you were getting your pay on a Tuesday and it was now £1,055 instead of £55, it was a wonderful feeling. Figures of £500 and £1000 as bonuses were normal for big matches. There was a real carrot there for you and after you had achieved what you had wanted to achieve, which was to beat somebody, you had another benefit coming. You were on a high and you had another high coming when you picked up your wages because £55 to £1,055 was a massive increase.

'The only time I can really remember anyone having any legitimate gripe against Jock was when we played Inter Milan in the semi-final of the European Cup and we lost on penalties at Celtic Park. The place was packed – the attendance given was 75,000 but there were probably thousands more inside the ground that night – and because we lost we didn't get a penny. That was wrong because you had still played, the crowd had still come in. You didn't want money for losing but a little appreciation would have gone down well. I think Billy went and asked him and Billy came back and said, "No, there's nothing there for you."'

The mechanics of Lou Macari's transfer to England illustrate that Stein was determined to control the destinies of his players even when they were leaving the club. 'My move was strange,' adds Macari. 'Apart from playing football and getting on with the training you don't know about anything else as a youngish player. You don't know the ins and outs of football. You don't know how it operates; who is friendly with whom and how the strings are pulled. I had said to Jock that I wanted to go and for a couple of weeks I had no response and didn't really know if that was normal or abnormal. Then, one night, around midnight, I got a call from Sean Fallon saying he was going to come down first thing in the morning to pick me up and take me to England. That was it. I didn't even get a chance to ask questions. I didn't have an agent; nobody had agents. The car arrived with Sean in it and I headed south. I didn't know where I was going; I hadn't been told. We stopped for tea at Southport and two hours later I was going through the gates at Anfield.

'Sean took me into the office and Bill Shankly, who was Jock Stein Mark II, was there. It was the same patter, the same approach. So I was going to sign for Liverpool. He put a contract in front of me, which was for £200 a week; almost four times what I was getting at Celtic. At the time you got a percentage of the signing-on fee; five or ten per cent. So there was another £10,000 or £20,000 coming my way; it was Liverpool Football Club and it was really enough to make you sign. Kick-off time was coming round – they were playing Burnley in the League Cup – and Bill Shankly said, "Go and watch the game and I'll see you after it." So I went into the stand with Sean on one side of me and sitting on the other side of me was Pat Crerand, who was assistant manager at Man United at the time. Having come from Celtic himself he knew who I was and said, "What are you doing down here?" I said, "I'm supposed to be signing for Liverpool." "Oh," he said, "We didn't know you were available."

'Then I started to think to myself, "Well, it's never been in the paper that I was available." Really, it was just Jock pushing me to a pal of his who seemingly had asked that if I was ever available that they would get first shout on me. Pat Crerand said, "Well, we'd be interested in you at Man United so don't be doing anything until we speak to you." So as the game went on I was wondering to myself how I had ended up there without Man United being informed. I began to understand that I had been taken to Liverpool because it suited Jock and his pal Bill Shankly. I was a bit annoyed that I had been just shuttled down there. I had been under the impression that everyone in England knew that I was available for transfer but that wasn't the case. So after the game I told Bill Shankly I wanted time to think over their offer. The following day, I met Pat Crerand and Tommy Docherty in Glasgow and within an hour I had signed for

Man United. If I'd had had a choice of Man United or Liverpool I would have gone to Man United anyway. So that is how I departed from Jock and Celtic. Jock was annoyed and made one or two comments in the paper.' Macari's transfer created a record fee of £200,000 for a Scottish player's transfer to England. It is difficult to avoid the conclusion that if Stein had travelled south to Anfield with Macari he would have become, inevitably, a Liverpool player.

Goalkeeper Ally Hunter joined Celtic from Kilmarnock in a £40,000 transfer six days after Macari's departure in January 1973. An informal approach, through a work colleague, had been made to Hunter to ascertain whether he would be interested in joining Celtic and he had made it clear that that was a prospect that interested him greatly. 'It was all done pretty quickly,' he says, as he looks back on that time. 'Nowadays everything goes through various people and various circles but then you just said, "Yes, all right, I'll join." They just said, "We'll give you such-and-such a figure" and you would just say yes to it. It has changed now, where it goes to negotiations, but in that day the chance of playing for Celtic meant that you would just say you would play, no matter what the figure was. I think we're all a lot wiser now.

'I did not have any particular idea about how much money to expect. I personally hadn't had a great deal of experience of how much money was available. I got about £3,500 as a signing-on fee, which, at that time, was a lot of money but it wasn't the be-all and end-all. The money at Celtic itself wasn't all that good, to be honest. I think we were on £45 a week basic when the average wage was £20 a week. The only way you made any money was through playing in the first-team and winning every week. Then your money would go away up to a few hundred pounds. That's the difference between then and today. Today you don't need to play to make money. Then, you had to play and win to make any money.

'Jock Stein was a big man in all kinds of ways. There was that presence about him. He was a legend then, in '73, after winning the European Cup and because of the run the club had had since then. He was really the top man, the top wheeler and dealer in the country, and he was obviously a man to be reckoned with. Kilmarnock were a good side then – it was only a few years since they had won the

League – but when you went to Celtic it was a completely different set-up altogether. The atmosphere in the place was that generated by a successful side. I was lucky to catch the end of the European Cup-winning side; there were still a good number of them in the pool around about then.

'Training was good. For me, there was no goalkeeping coach as such but to be fair, a lot of the main work was work with goalkeepers. The players did a lot of work that involved playing the ball up, laying it off and shooting at the goalkeeper. So they were rattling the ball at you all the time and you were worked hard all the time. You weren't coached as such, you were just in goalkeeping situations at training. He was good at training; he kept your interest in it. You weren't slogging about doing boring things. You were always working with a ball. I've been at clubs where you just seemed to run round and run round and you would get really fed up with it. In general, with Jock Stein, you would just do a warm-up and a good few stretches and a couple of bits of hard stuff and then it would be ball, ball, ball all the time. There is a lot of interaction between the players when you are playing with a ball so it's good fun. So although you're working hard you don't realise you're working hard because you're working with a ball all the time. A lot of work was just playing balls, playing them back, shooting in, crossing, or creating situations with players crossing over and shooting in, so the goalkeepers were involved all the time.

'So when I joined Celtic they were a really good side, with really great players and Jock Stein stood out like a sore thumb. He was not a likeable person; I wouldn't expect anybody would actually like him as a person. You'll find that there are different categories of football managers and it's the same, I suppose, with any boss. There are some who rule and manage by being nice and helping you as you go along and there are some who rule by fear and I would say Jock Stein was one that managed by fear to a great extent. He was obviously successful in that way.

'These days the situation has changed in such a way that the balance of power has moved a good bit towards the players but then, a strong personality like him could manipulate players. Your livelihood depended on him because managers could make or break you then. They could put you out of the game and keep you out of the game. He could look after himself in that department. In saying that, as a manager he would send you out on to the park knowing you were going to win. Without being big-headed or anything, you went out on that park and you knew you were going to win that game, come hell or high water, and he could just catch you that right way. He knew the game, knew the other team, knew what they were going to do, and we had our plan to play to hit their weaknesses. I'm maybe not the most confident of people but when you went out on the park as part of one of Jock Stein's teams you were full of confidence without being complacent. You knew when you went out there that it was going to be all right and that if things were going wrong they would be sorted. Before a match, he would come to you and talk to you and put things over to you and inspire you.' Stein would always give his players clear, precise instructions and his confidence of manner imbued confidence in his men.

'You knew you had to do your job,' adds Ally Hunter, 'because you knew you would get sorted out if you didn't. He could be cruel to you although he could also help you. I had a crisis of confidence after the Scotland–Czechoslovakia match. I had a bit of a crisis after that. It was the biggest game Scotland had played for a long time and I let in a stupid goal although we still managed to win the game and qualify for the World Cup in 1974. I took quite a knock with that and my form shaded a bit. After it happened, he knew I was having problems and he was good about it. He suggested that if I wanted to go for a holiday for a few weeks it wouldn't be a problem.'

Hunter also witnessed another side to Stein that was kept well hidden from the public and that exemplified both the manager's single-mindedness and fearlessness. 'He would confront people. He would have a square go if it was on. I did see that on occasion, not with players as such, but I saw him in situations abroad when people stepped out of line in front of the players. I remember blows being exchanged on a couple of occasions. On one occasion he got involved in a fight with a press man and the other was with one of those types of flash guy you get who go on trips with the supporters. This guy came in and was making a nuisance of himself in the hotel in front of the players. Big Jock just picked him up, dealt with him and threw him out and there was nothing the guy could do about it. Jock could physically look after himself all right. He was a big strong guy. If need be, Jock Stein would be there to confront anybody. He would always make the right noises to show that he wasn't going to be messed about. I would say he was quite a fearsome character.'

David Hay had been an established first-team regular for five seasons when he carried out a challenge to Celtic's pay structure that was considerably more prolonged than Lou Macari's had been. 'Kenny Dalglish, myself, Louie Macari and Geordie Connelly all loved playing for Celtic as much as the Lions,' he says. 'I didn't want to leave but I felt I merited more money and there was no freedom of contract, no Bosman, at that time so I was out on a limb on my own. It was then that you realised that Jock was governed by the board in financial matters more than you would have imagined. He wasn't a Maley where he maybe controlled everything: those had been the days when bosses ruled employees. By the 1970s the era was arriving where, generally speaking, employees were standing up for themselves a bit more. It was difficult for me at the time to disagree with big Jock over a contract – when I was younger I would almost sign a blank paper – but I felt it was justified. I think, if I'm being honest, he could have gone the extra pound for some of his players but it was maybe a board decision that prevented it. Then again, he wasn't paid that much himself so you can almost understand his attitude.

'Jock wasn't changing but the individual player was changing. My only regret is that the team after the Lions never played long enough because we might have equalled what they had done in Europe. We were getting to semi-finals and we hadn't reached our peak. On the night Scotland beat Czechoslovakia to qualify for the 1974 World Cup five of the Scottish team were young Celtic players: Danny McGrain, Ally Hunter, myself, George and Kenny. So I regret that those players could not progress together at Celtic. It was definitely not the attraction of playing in England that took players away. Celtic had proved they were as good as anybody in England and were always playing in Europe. I would have stayed with Celtic for a lot less than I got from Chelsea but I was looking for more than Celtic were offering me. I felt we weren't getting paid the rate for what we were doing and there was an element where I had spent a year missing out on some bonuses because I was injured. So on that basis I felt I was justified in asking for a higher wage.' The basic weekly wage for Hay in 1974 was £65, which he wished to have increased to £100, a sum that he felt was not unreasonable given that the club was making frequent runs to the latter stages of the European Cup. Celtic, with such players as Hay, McGrain, Hunter, Macari, Dalglish and Connelly as regulars in the first-team, had contested the semi-finals of Europe's premier tournament in 1972 and in 1974.

Hay soon found himself dealing with chairman Desmond White more than with Stein as his dispute dragged on over several months during the 1973–74 season. White told him that if he gave Hay £100 per week he would have to do the same for every player; Hay audaciously told his chairman that he thought that would be only fair. Interestingly, Tottenham Hotspur and Manchester United were both after Hay's signature and Desmond White told the player that if he were to sign for Spurs he would receive a bonus payment from Celtic but that if he were to go to Manchester United, he would receive nothing.

The situation remained unresolved as Hay went off to play for Scotland in the 1974 World Cup in West Germany. The performances he gave for the national team proved of a similar high quality to those he had given for Celtic in previous months – despite spending much of the 1973–74 season in dispute over his contract with the club Hay had simultaneously come into some of the finest form of his career. That carried on into Scotland's games in West Germany, in which Hay had shown great determination and no little style, particularly in a 0–0 draw with Brazil. He returned to Celtic Park after the tournament, a proven world-class footballer, ready to resolve his dispute with the club. He had now decided to stay in Scotland and start a business as a means of supplementing his earnings from Celtic but the player found Stein in stubborn mood. 'He didn't force me to go but he knew my make-up and the way he approached it was almost as if to say, "You might be better going, Davie."

'He told me to come up to the park one Sunday. The park was shut and we sat in the car, his Mercedes, and he said, "It's better that you move on, Davie." I said, "What do you mean, boss?" He said, "Och, you had all your problems last season with your contract." I said, "I did, but it didn't affect my play." Then, and I always remember him saying this, "I had boys up there in the stand who weren't playing and you were playing." It was as if he was playing me when I had problems with him and these guys were not getting a game even though he had no problems with them. I said to him, "Boss, you played me because you thought I was better than them.'" Hay recalls vividly that Stein then began throwing his arms wildly up and down in the air in the car park at Celtic Park as if neither he nor the car could contain any longer his extreme frustration at the player's attitude. 'He started raising his voice and said, "There you go again,"' says Hay. Stein had manoeuvred the conversation round to a point where Hay would inevitably dispute what was being said. Having done so, Stein was able to suggest that the player was one who would always be looking for an argument with his manager. The intended effect was to ease Hay out of Celtic Park. 'I think,' says Hay, 'he had had this offer from Chelsea and he may have had a directive from above to take the dough.' The player's transfer for a £225,000 fee followed swiftly on from that dramatic car-park summit.

David Hay believes that none of the Quality Street Gang really wished to leave Celtic and Lou Macari agrees. 'I think that's spot on,' he says. 'I think little things cropped up where your pride was being hurt. After so long, when you are taking home £55 a week and you think you are going to be rewarded a little bit better, it does get to you a bit and I think in moments of madness, let's say, you do react. In saying that, how could I or Kenny or even David to an extent, say that it was wrong for us to leave Celtic at the time we did? I ended up 11 years at Old Trafford so it certainly wasn't the wrong move for me. Kenny ended up at Liverpool. David went to Chelsea. We've all been in management. So they were not the wrong moves for us. Even those moves happened because of the manager, so we were even fortunate in that. His style of management pushed us into a corner where we moved on. So, really, everything we've done we have got to credit him for it; even the moving, which really came about because he wanted to keep everybody on that wage structure, which, again looking back, you could not really fault him for because it has been the case at certain clubs, especially in England now, that there is more trouble because of the pay structure than anything else. He probably looked at the situation and said, "No, I can't afford Jimmy Johnstone on £80 and David Hay or Kenny Dalglish or Lou Macari on £100 or any figures different to what anybody else is getting." So he was sticking with his pay structure and we decided we weren't sticking with it.'

Stein was determined that no player would play havoc with his authority and his retribution could be careful and crafty. It could also be sudden and swift. Forward Jimmy Bone had joined Celtic from Sheffield United in early 1974 but had failed to impress Stein, scoring just once in 11 appearances. He was left out of the side for months and, although he was available for transfer, Stein continually told him that a suitable offer had not yet arrived for the player and that nobody was interested in him. One day at the training ground early in 1975, Bone, through extreme frustration at his situation, let loose with a sudden outburst at Stein, telling the manager exactly what he thought of him. It was the type of incident that could undermine a manager's authority irreversibly if the player was seen to have got away with it without suffering severe repercussions. Stein was well aware of that and Bone was transferred to Arbroath that very afternoon. Stein's authority had been usurped briefly by Bone but his speedy reaction to the player's dissent emphasised to the other players that he had the power to make or break them. His reaction to Bone's outburst had strengthened Stein's authority as manager.

A different type of Stein-related problem beset Ally Hunter. 'He hated goalkeepers,' explains Hunter. 'I think what it was was that he would send the players out on to the park knowing what all the outfield players could do and he had his system and people did their job but I think goalkeepers were the factor X. They were the thing that he could not really cater for. If you play a system on the park and one of the outfield players makes a mistake, someone else can fill in and cover for them but with the goalkeeper anything could happen. There was always that love–hate situation with goalkeepers. He didn't really want you there but he had to play a goalkeeper. He went through quite a lot of goalkeepers after Ronnie Simpson.

'He would actually say that he didn't like goalkeepers. He would curse goalkeepers. It was nothing vindictive: he didn't like them because he couldn't adopt a fail-safe system for them. You could play all your great football but when the ball comes through and the goalie flaps at it and misses it, there's nothing you can do about it. He liked to be in control of everything that happened and when it came to goalkeepers he couldn't be in control. It came down to that, basically.

'I remember playing at Easter Road once on this absolutely freezing cold day. The problem with playing in goal with Celtic was that half the time you weren't doing very much. I had three jerseys on and I let in a silly goal and he came in at half-time and started shouting at me. He actually physically manhandled me and pulled the jerseys off me, threw one back at me and told me to get out on the field and get on with it, which was probably fair comment, when you look at it. He probably thought I was namby-pamby or something like that. It was his way of impressing on me that I needed to be stronger. It was just a way of rattling your cage and getting you alive again. You accepted that sort of thing in those days.'

Football had, during the 1940s, provided Stein with a means of escape from his hard life as a miner in the Lanarkshire pits but he never forgot those early days. The adult Stein had been shaped by his time as a miner and he always retained affection for the tight-knit Lanarkshire community from which he had sprung. Ally Hunter, who had stayed on at school to sit his Higher exams and whose father was a businessman in Glasgow, feels that this created a bit of a barrier between Stein and some of his players. Hunter comments, 'He could be quite intimidating, just through his manner, and I felt that he was a wee bit so-so about people from different backgrounds to him. Jim Craig always said that Stein used to hate him because he was a dentist and I would agree that if you were that wee bit different from him he treated you slightly differently. That's the impression I got. He knew where he stood with people who were of a similar background. You had to be really strong to cope with it at times because he was intimidating and he could be intimidating to anybody through his bulk and his manner. Still, that's what made him successful so it's difficult to argue with that.'

Stein could even be intimidating in his more lighthearted moments. 'If he said something funny you had to laugh,' says Hunter.

'He would tell funny stories about situations, because in football there are always funny stories about players.' Such fun and laughter would only be on the agenda if and when Stein decided he wanted to have a laugh. Adds Hunter, 'If he told a story it would be fine but if somebody else did it he would not always laugh.' Instead, Stein might turn a withering glance in the direction of the budding comedian as if to question why they thought they were at all funny. 'He was the man who ruled the roost,' says Hunter, 'put it that way. If he was in a good mood, we were all in a good mood. That was his strength – he could control people.'

A decade on from his triumphant return to Celtic Park, Stein, now in his early 50s, looked quietly satisfied rather than elated as he left Hampden Park on 3 May 1975, following a straightforward 3–1 victory over Airdrieonians in the Scottish Cup final. His ten years as manager up to that point had yielded nine League championship titles, seven Scottish Cups, six League Cups and the prize of prizes, the European Cup. The intense detail that he applied to his preparations had paid off extensively. Stein thought deeply about the game and his extensive planning would even reach as far as discussing with his players what they ought to do when they were preparing for the restart of a game after Celtic had scored a goal. He would suggest ways in which his players lined up after the team had scored that would create a situation, just as the other team were kicking off, that would enable Celtic to hit the opposition once again. One of the most successful uses of this tactic had occurred in the 1971 Scottish Cup final, when Celtic hit Rangers with two goals in two minutes midway through the first half. That match ended in a 2–1 Celtic win.

'You would think that things that go on for that long would obviously get slack but they didn't really,' says Ally Hunter as he reflects on the latter part of that ten-year stretch. 'Although they lost the championship after the nine-in-a-row I still think they were a good, strong side. They still had that strength in the team. He wouldn't let standards slip. That's where his strong character and the fear factor came into it. Sometimes, if you've got a soft manager and you lose a game you don't bother about it. With Celtic, you had to win every game and he did maintain that. Football was his life and he put everything into it.

'He wasn't the kind of guy you would have for your best pal. I don't think he was the sort of person you would want to confide in and he wouldn't confide in you. There would always be a distance between you and him; even when you saw him with his own pals, the ones who used to come on trips, there would always be that distance between him and them. He ran the show and if he wanted to do something that's what they did. Your pals are the people you tell your innermost secrets and worries and I couldn't imagine anybody going to him like that. He was so focused on everything he was doing in his job that everything else paled into insignificance. That's not to say anything bad against him; it was just the way he was. I suppose football managers are always watching themselves with the press to a certain extent. I think they're always watching their back in that direction so they maybe don't want to give too much away.'

That summer of 1975 Stein jetted off to Minorca for a well-deserved holiday but on his return, as he drove back to Glasgow from Manchester Airport, Stein, his wife Jean and accompanying friends, bookmaker Tony Queen and his wife, were involved in a dreadful car crash on the A74 close to Lockerbie. As doctors at Dumfries Infirmary battled to save Stein's life, they performed a tracheotomy on him to allow him to breathe while they attended to chest and head injuries that he had sustained in the crash. He survived but the after-effects were so severe that Stein would be absent from Celtic Park for a year while he underwent a full recovery.

Billy McNeill casts his mind back to that traumatic time and says, 'The thing that always nagged me was that I stopped playing earlier than I might have done. I stopped after the cup final with Airdrie, which seemed a great idea at the time. Liz and I went on holiday, on a cruise, and we had literally stepped back on these shores at Southampton when, strangely enough, just as we were waiting to come off the ship, one of the young officers came and told us, "Jock Stein was in an accident last night." On our way up the road, we jumped in to see him in hospital in Dumfries. That summer, I fully expected somebody at Celtic Park to phone me and say, "Look, would you reconsider?" which I would have done. It would probably have altered my thoughts but nobody ever did. It was a strange one.' Assistant manager Sean Fallon, who took over the running of the team in Stein's absence, later told McNeill he had been hoping McNeill would have phoned him. McNeill told him he felt it would have been a bit vain of him to offer and that he felt it would have been much more sensible for the offer to have come from someone at Celtic Park. The type of leadership that McNeill might have been able to provide would not have been amiss at Celtic Park in the 1975–76 season. Fallon, as Stein's assistant, took over and Celtic failed to win a trophy for the first season since Jimmy McGrory's time as manager. At the conclusion of the 1975–76 season, Fallon was replaced as assistant manager by Davie McParland, who had been previously the manager of Partick Thistle.

'That was a strange period,' says Ally Hunter. 'You were so used to big Jock being there and that sort of atmosphere about the place that when he was not there, things were different. When you heard Jock Stein coming, you would sharpen up your attitude; things were no longer like that when he wasn't there. There just wasn't that edge. In football the difference between winning and losing is so small and possibly the lack of that wee edge that you always had under Jock Stein wasn't there that season. That fear factor, that fear of losing, just wasn't there. If you could measure that difference between winning and losing it would probably measure about a millimetre. That's all it is, that wee edge, but it makes all the difference.'

The long-term effect of the car crash on Stein was deep and pronounced. He lost a degree of vigour and seemed drained at times. It was his second close encounter with mortality; he had been hospitalised for a fortnight with heart problems in early 1973. So it was a more subdued Stein who returned to the manager's office in 1976. 'The car crash seemed to take his enthusiasm away,' muses Billy McNeill. 'It seemed to take his personality away to a degree. He never quite seemed the same big, enthusiastic, outgoing personality that he had been. It probably encouraged him to think of himself and to look after himself more than anything else.'

Stein still proved able to assemble a useful team for the 1976–77 season, a team that won the Scottish League and Cup Double, but the departure of Kenny Dalglish in a £440,000 British record transfer to Liverpool in the summer of 1977 was a serious blow to Stein, who tried every ruse possible to keep Dalglish at Celtic Park. Early in the 1977–78 season, the other world-class player available to Celtic, right-back Danny McGrain, suffered an ankle injury that finished his season. Pat Stanton, a superb passer of the ball who had done much to glue the team together in the 1976–77 season, also received a severe early-season injury, in the opening League fixture against Dundee United, that would, ultimately, end his career. The loss of those three players ripped the heart out of Stein's team and Celtic stumbled blindly through the remainder of the 1977–78 season. At one point they hovered close to the relegation positions and they ended the season in fifth position in the Premier League, a disastrous fall from grace when set against the high standards of the earlier Stein years. It was their lowest League position for 13 years. Jock Stein's final match in charge of Celtic was a 3–1 defeat by St Mirren at Love Street in April 1978 that killed off Celtic's final hopes of being involved in the following season's European tournaments. It was the first time they had missed out on European competition since the 1964–65 season. The St Mirren manager was Alex Ferguson, then an up-and-coming 36 year old.

A degree of mythology has grown up around Stein's departure from Celtic in the summer of 1978, which portrays him as a victim of a manipulative board, one that was ungrateful for his long and distinguished service. The story goes that the Celtic board offered him a demeaning post on the board, one with responsibility for commercial duties and that, insulted by their removal of him from footballing matters, Stein walked away from the club. Yet Stein was never a victim. He was never a man to stand back and allow himself to be stung by the slings and arrows of outrageous fortune.

When Stein decided, in tandem with the board, that it was time to step down as manager in the spring of 1978, he had very much in mind his testimonial match against European champions Liverpool, which was scheduled for August 1978. Stein didn't smoke or drink but he had a passion for betting on horse races and it was widely believed that Stein's gambling debts were such that he required the income from the Liverpool match to help meet them. Accordingly, Stein played along with the board's offer of an 'executive directorship' throughout the summer until the Liverpool match had been played, a game that attracted a 60,000 Celtic Park crowd and that brought £80,000 through the turnstiles. Within hours of the final whistle, Stein was talking openly to Leeds United chairman Manny Cussins and one week later Stein had quit Celtic altogether and was being announced as the new manager of the Elland Road side after having neatly obtained the takings from his testimonial. Rather than retiring as a manager, he had moved to Elland Road, where a handsome annual salary of £30,000 was on offer, considerably more than he had been earning at Celtic Park. Even then, Stein delayed signing a contract with Leeds just long enough for an alternative offer to arrive from the Scottish Football Association for him to succeed Ally MacLeod as manager of the Scottish national team, a post for which he then left Leeds in October 1978.

Stein had approached Billy McNeill on Celtic's behalf that spring of 1978 with the proposal that McNeill take over as Celtic manager and McNeill firmly believes that Stein was always several moves ahead of everyone else. 'I always felt Jock had a hidden agenda,' says McNeill as he thinks back to that time. 'You know, he said he wanted to retire but I never, ever believed that. I think he had his career mapped out. He never did anything ad hoc; he never left anything to chance. I think the club handled it badly but I am sure he knew he was going to Leeds. I don't think the board would have known that. I thought he had everything mapped out because he wasn't a person who ever did things without having planned them and without having looked at the whole thing carefully.'

Stein had transformed the job of Celtic manager during his 13 years at the club. He had hauled Celtic's managerial procedures out of the Victorian age and quickly brought them up to date. His futuristic managerial methods left his rivals bamboozled by his brilliance. He had been in a position of strength on his arrival at Celtic Park – the club's lengthy, undistinguished progress under the influence of chairman Kelly and the non-intervention of manager Jimmy McGrory in the period prior to Stein's arrival had given him a blank canvas. It had been the perfect situation for Stein, who desperately needed to be in full control of all aspects of management. He had also had the vision to understand that there could be more to football than simply getting players physically fit and putting 11 men on the field of play every matchday.

Stein believed that a football club and its players could be infused with an ethos, a spirit, to create a positive, all-round atmosphere that would generate a winning mentality and that hundreds of small, seemingly unrelated, positive actions on the part of the manager could combine to create this effect. Jock Stein was so involved in all aspects of the club that he would often answer the telephone inside Celtic Park. Imagine that . . . the greatest manager in the history of Scottish football being prepared to muck in and answer a random telephone inquiry, a task that many lesser managers would consider beneath their dignity. Jock Stein's 13 years as Celtic manager had been undeniably unique.

FIVE

Billy McNeill – The Lion's Art

Billy McNeill was looking forward to a relaxing fortnight's break in a rented holiday home in Troon as the summer of 1977 drew near, so he was surprised when Jock Stein came on the phone seemingly to advise him that the McNeill family should consider taking their annual holiday elsewhere. McNeill had been used to Stein's desire to control every detail of McNeill's life as a player, but two years into McNeill's retirement from Celtic this seemed ridiculous. He remembers that telephone call clearly. 'Jock phoned me and said to me, "Have you got anything fixed up for the holidays?" So I told him that Liz and I had rented a house in Troon. He said, "Would you fancy going to Aberdeen?" I said, "On holiday?" He said, "No, Dick Donald was asking me if you would fancy going up." I said, "Oh, that would be great." ' McNeill, who had been in his first managerial job, at Clyde, for only a matter of weeks, met the Aberdeen chairman Donald in Perth and felt such confidence in him that he agreed to take the manager's job at Pittodrie there and then, without even discussing what his salary would be. His belief in Donald would not be misplaced.

One year later, after McNeill had completed an impressive debut season at Pittodrie, taking Aberdeen agonisingly close to winning both the League and the Scottish Cup, Jock Stein engineered his former captain's next move in management. This time the job on offer was the Celtic one. As the captain of Jock Stein's European Cup-winning side, Billy McNeill had always had a close relationship with the manager and that paved the way for him succeeding his mentor. 'The only person I had any contact with was Jock Stein,' says

McNeill as he recalls how he was approached to return to his spiritual footballing home. 'I wouldn't have gone to Celtic Park, I don't think, if he hadn't asked me. To be quite frank with you, I wish he hadn't asked me because it wasn't the right time for me to move. I had a great job at Aberdeen. I had a great board of directors; in fact, I had the best board of directors I have ever worked with. I doubt very much if anybody had a better group of directors than Aberdeen had. It was a great learning process for me. When I came back to Celtic Park I couldn't believe what I had joined. I remember Dick Donald only said one thing to me, "You'll not enjoy working with that board as much as you've enjoyed working with us." I didn't really appreciate what he was saying at the time but I came to appreciate it soon after.

'I should have stayed longer up there at Pittodrie. From my own personal point of view it would have been much, much more beneficial. It really would have been. They were much more attuned to assisting and helping. There were only three directors, all of whom had played for Aberdeen: Dick Donald, Chris Anderson and Charlie Forbes. Chris was absolutely great; Chris used to mark my card and tell me to do this and do this and any time I had a wee problem I used to be able to go and talk to him. That way, I was able to get it straightened out so that when I went to a board meeting I knew how to approach Dick. They were good when you were under a bit of pressure. I remember we got hammered by Rangers 6–1 and I was totally distraught. Then the chairman came in and said, "We've never, ever talked about a contract, you and I. If you want a contract, just tell me. You can have three or five years, just tell me what you want and you've got it." He was that kind of person. He seemed to know when to come and talk to you; when to offer his assistance. I left it all but I couldn't have resisted the challenge of Celtic.'

Billy McNeill returned to Celtic Park that late spring of 1978 determined to make the club he loved great again. His energy and vitality were needed to return to life a Celtic side that had become drained of spirit. The new manager, still only 38 years of age, would bring to the job tremendous desire. His enthusiasm and dynamic approach to life would quickly spark the Celtic players into action and under the guidance of the captain of the Lisbon Lions, Celtic would soon be ready to roar back to life. McNeill appointed John Clark, his central defensive partner in the Lions, as his assistant manager. At 6 ft 1 in., McNeill possessed a military bearing that commanded people's immediate attention. He was a restless bundle of energy and his infectiously positive approach transmitted itself to those around him. As he patrolled the corridors of Celtic Park, he would be taking in every last detail of what was happening and although he could be lenient, if he felt that was the best approach to a particular situation, everyone at the club knew that no liberties could be taken with him.

McNeill was to achieve success as Celtic manager but despite all that he still looks back on his move to Celtic as being too much, too soon. He was placed in the dilemma that May of 1978 of knowing that if he turned the job down it might never be offered to him again. It does seem certain that if he had continued to make progress in his managerial career elsewhere that, given McNeill's standing with the Celtic support, the offer of the Celtic manager's job would have come his way once again. McNeill, as the man caught on the horns of that particular dilemma, could not afford to be so objective. 'I don't know whether it would have or not,' he says. 'I just couldn't take the chance that it wouldn't.'

To those who could look behind the facade at Celtic, it was clear that the chairman, Desmond White, who had succeeded Robert Kelly in 1971, was simply using the club as a licence to print money. The dedicated, captive support would fill the terraces dutifully and White would cream off the profits. Celtic have always had marvellous supporters, real lovers of football, people who live for the game. It means that if the club's board is of a cynical bent, the good faith of these people can be exploited mercilessly. With White as chairman, the club was living off its name and its magnetic attraction to those supporters. 'Desmond White wasn't interested in investing,' adds Billy McNeill. 'Everything was done on the cheap – it was murder. The Aberdeen that I left were far better than the Celtic that I joined. They finished second in the League and lost to Rangers in the cup final and it was a well-organised and positive set-up. You had to prove your case with the Aberdeen chairman in everything; you had to prove your case with the board but they were helpful and they were anxious to get Aberdeen moving up. I felt when I went to Celtic that it was the opposite; that what had happened in the past was good enough for them. It frustrated me.

'I wasn't ready. I shouldn't have gone. The problem was that my heart couldn't let me say no to it. My head was telling me not to go, my head was telling me to stay where I was, but I didn't listen to my head in that situation. My wife didn't want to come back down. She wanted us to stay in Aberdeen and she was right. We should have stayed in Aberdeen; we were happy in Aberdeen. We had a wonderful year up there. I was too young. I could still have been playing at 38, as it so happened. It was the wrong thing to do at that particular time, however exciting it was and everything else. I've got to be honest, I found great difficulty in establishing any kind of relationship with the then chairman, Desmond White, I really did.'

McNeill recalls his days as a player in the 1960s to illustrate the uninterested approach of the club's directors with regard to the employees of Celtic. 'The directors never gave you any advice. I remember Liz and I buying our first house and, coming from my background, I didn't know a single person in Bellshill that owned their own house. Liz's father worked in the shipyards and they were of a similar nature. We had a stockbroker, a lawyer and an accountant on the board and not one of them gave you one iota of advice as to what to do or what not to do. You just stumbled along in the dark. So, really, I should have appreciated that there wasn't going to be a lot of assistance for a young manager – and there wasn't. They were hard to deal with.

'I had just left the best board that I ever worked with and it was chalk and cheese, night and day. I never, ever established a relationship. I remember saying to Desmond White one day, "You and I are supposed to be heading in the same direction but every time we have a talk it's you against me. The directors were just impossible to work with: having employed a young manager they should have ensured that he got every bit of advice but I didn't. You had to go and do things on your own. Money was always a problem. There was no real ambition about developing the club. At that time everybody else was starting to develop their grounds. Rangers had massive plans and Aberdeen were changing to an all-seated stadium and putting in covered areas. English clubs were way ahead of us, as usual. Celtic were lagging way, way behind and the stadium was almost archaic.

'When I moved to Celtic, Liz was still up in Aberdeen and a few weeks after I had joined Celtic as manager I remember going back up the road and thinking to myself, "Oh, dear God, what have I taken on here?" It was something else. You had to argue and argue and argue all the time to get things.' McNeill had noted that Norwich City had built a new stand at the River End of their Carrow Road ground, bringing spectators right to the action, and that the work had been completed at speed. He wanted similar action carried out at Celtic Park, where both the east and west terracings, behind the two goals, were set back a considerable distance from the playing surface, making for a hollow atmosphere at times. Nothing was done about this; nor was the club interested in the then progressive idea of installing undersoil heating.

Despite the unhelpful approach of the board, McNeill still managed to regenerate the playing side of the club through his huge enthusiasm for the task of managing Celtic. He loved being a manager and considered his major strength to be his ability to tune in quickly to the players' various wavelengths. 'I thought I was able to talk coherently to players,' he says, 'to talk straightforwardly to them. I think I was able to lift them; I was able to make them more ambitious and to lift their confidence. I loved the involvement. It was nothing like playing; playing is the essence of the game. The other thing is that management is much, much more difficult. You find very quickly that half your job is protecting players and ensuring that players don't get themselves into bother; that they sneak away from it and stay away from it. That is often difficult.' McNeill's leadership of the Celtic team as a player had imbued him with the ability to think on his feet and he believes that flexibility is essential to effective management. 'There is never a time when you can say, "I'm going to do this" and then you do it exactly as you intended. You've got to look at the situation and try to understand that players are different. They each need a different approach; not every player will be motivated by the same approach. I think you've just got to vary it depending on what the situation is.'

McNeill's opening season as Celtic manager proved a memorable one. He quickly freshened up the side with two players whose drive would help steer the club in the right direction. Outside-right Davie Provan was signed from Kilmarnock for a Scottish record fee of £120,000 and the sturdy, energetic midfielder Murdo MacLeod moved to Celtic Park from Dumbarton for £100,000. 'Davie Provan would have been going to Aberdeen; I would have taken him to Aberdeen because I couldn't believe that nobody had bothered taking him,' remembers McNeill. 'What a good buy he was for Celtic! Murdo MacLeod was great too – I watched Dumbarton and they had two good players and I said to myself, "That can't be true. Dumbarton can't have two good players; you're pushing your luck there." So I just went for Murdo MacLeod; the other fellow was Graeme Sharp, who was an excellent player. I just couldn't believe that a team like Dumbarton could produce two players who could play at the top level but they did. So that was an error of a young manager.' Sharp went on to Everton, where his goalscoring in the 1980s helped them take league titles, the FA Cup and the European Cup-Winners' Cup.

'Billy's confidence was his biggest strength,' says Murdo MacLeod. 'He just had something about him because of his big association with the club. Some managers you have got to go in and listen to them and see how good they are tactically or what they are like as motivators but Billy had a presence when he walked into the dressing-room. He had immediate respect because of what he had achieved. He gave the players great confidence and he was always ready to kick you up the backside as well. He kept everybody on their toes; he never let anybody think they had made it.'

Celtic sides under McNeill's guidance were geared to go forward and players such as Provan, MacLeod, Danny McGrain, Roy Aitken and Tommy Burns combined a high workrate with the ability to create something unexpected. McNeill ensured that he maintained a stable framework in which they could operate. Changes would only be made as and when necessary. 'He knew the game,' says Murdo MacLeod of the then Celtic manager, 'but I think tactically he didn't change it often because he didn't need to. He knew the strengths of the team. We had four at the back, with four in the middle, including Provan wide on the right, who would be going forward at times. So you were playing something like a four, three-and-a-half, two-and-a-half and we knew how to play it. So he didn't need to change it. Nowadays you see managers changing tactics three and four times throughout the 90 minutes but sometimes they are just changing it for the sake of change if their team is not playing well. I think the system we were playing then was perfect for us. We were very hard to beat.

'We had good full-backs, good wide players, especially Provan, who would get forward and cause all sorts of problems. So he was an extra forward and a lot of times in midfield you were playing three across the middle so there was a good balance to it. I don't think Billy had to change it very much and very rarely would he change it going into different games because I think we were the strongest side at the time. So it was just a matter of going out and beating the opposition and making sure we played well. I think with him not changing the side or changing systems it helped the players.'

The manager also ensured that the players were shielded as far as possible from the difficulties he was experiencing with the board. 'In those days the boardroom problems were kept very quiet,' adds MacLeod. 'Nowadays every club has got their boardroom problems and they are in the newspapers but in those days it wasn't an avenue newspapers went down. Billy would never come out and moan about it. Billy was the type of person who would keep all his problems to himself to protect the club. He would keep everything quiet and made sure the players didn't get involved if there was a problem at the club. We knew, time and again, when we were looking for bonuses for games that the money was never forthcoming. Billy would fight for you on that and would get it now and then but it was always a struggle for the manager to try and get more money. We knew that, because players that actually spoke to the board at the time – for bonus money for winning cups or whatever else – knew that the board were quite mean with their bonus money. We just accepted their decisions and got on with it.'

The new manager had initially aimed only for European qualification in his first season as manager but, refreshed by his new signings and the return of the inspirational full-back Danny McGrain after a lengthy injury, the team powered on to take the title. It seemed typical of a McNeill team that the victory would take place in the most dramatic possible fashion. Celtic's final match of the season had pitted them against Rangers, who needed a win or a draw at Celtic Park to almost guarantee them the 1978–79 Scottish League title. Celtic needed to win to clinch the title. The Celts survived the sending-off of winger Johnny Doyle to force a 4–2 victory that was clinched by a long-range shot from MacLeod in the dying seconds of the match. At the final whistle, McNeill rushed from the dugout to punch the air in celebration of the achievement.

The title win provided entry to the European Cup and an exciting, energetic performance in the home leg of their 1980 quarter-final with Real Madrid gave Celtic a 2–0 victory. Nothing went Celtic's way in the return in the Bernabeu, though, and a 3–0 defeat ended their European challenge. It precipitated a collapse in the League that saw Aberdeen come from ten points behind Celtic to take the 1979–80 title to Pittodrie. Compensation for McNeill came in the form of a 1–0 Scottish Cup final victory over Rangers in May 1980.

Celtic's record in European competition under McNeill was a fair one and he was the only Celtic manager of the 1980s and '90s to keep the club in European competition after Christmas with that quarter-final against Real Madrid. Celtic's two other European Cup entries under McNeill ended with defeats to Juventus in 1981 and Real Sociedad, the latter after a buccaneering Celtic victory over Ajax in Amsterdam in the autumn of 1982. It was a useful record – unlike Stein in 1965, McNeill had inherited a number of players who'd had to be replaced. He had also brought several young players in their early 20s into his side. They had just begun to experience top-level Scottish football when Celtic had been pitched into the even more testing sphere of top-level European competition. Another factor that mitigated against success in Europe was that counter-attacking football was proving successful in the European Cup during the late 1970s and early 1980s. It was a style that was alien to McNeill's Celtic and one with which Celtic teams often found it difficult to cope.

'I think it was difficult for us in Europe because we did not change the system throughout the year in Scotland,' comments MacLeod, 'although in European matches the likes of Davie Provan would play more across the middle and you still had the two up front. I think when you look at the Real Madrid game we were holding our own for 45 minutes. We then lost a goal right on half-time, then lost another goal just after half-time and then a late goal knocked us out. I don't know whether that was for tactical reasons or just the players giving away soft goals. The first one was from a corner-kick right on half-time and even with the best tactics in the world that can happen. I think in European football the players themselves were a bit naïve about going forward all the time. I think when you watch European sides they can sit back so long in the game and hit on the counter-attack. We never played that throughout the year so I think if you change it for one game you would all be sitting thinking, "What do we do here?" I think Billy, as much as possible, always kept us playing to our strengths and I think that worked.'

The early 1980s was a challenging period for Celtic. Aberdeen, managed by Alex Ferguson, and Dundee United, managed by Jim McLean, were each proving to be superb and consistent competitors whilst Rangers were always a threat. In the face of that competition, McNeill's record in his initial five years as manager at Celtic Park is impressive. Between 1978 and 1983, Aberdeen won three domestic trophies; Dundee United won three; Rangers won four cups but never the League title. McNeill led Celtic to three League titles, a Scottish Cup and a League Cup, making him the most successful manager in Scottish domestic football, although an honourable mention must go to Alex Ferguson for leading Aberdeen to victory in the 1983 European Cup-Winners' Cup final.

'It's strange when you look at it that he did manage to keep it going year in and year out,' says Murdo MacLeod as he thinks back to McNeill's time. 'Again, when you worked with the players that we had at that time it would have been fairly easy because all the players had the right attitude. They were all winners. Big Billy is a winner and you had Danny McGrain and big Roy Aitken, Davie Provan, Tam Burns, big Peter Latchford in goal. He was so laid-back but he wanted to do well; he didn't like losing goals but he didn't show it like other goalkeepers. Then when Packie Bonner came in he was the same. He was a workaholic as well and wanted to do well . . . when you have got players like that and the boys up front – George McCluskey, wee Johnny Doyle and Bobby Lennox – you had players who were desperate to play for Celtic. So they kept it going. It was easy for them every week because they wanted to play for Celtic so badly. I think the attitude of the players was that they didn't want to let anybody down. Big Billy had been a major player in the club's history so when you were playing for him you made sure you didn't let big Billy down. I think he picked his best 11 and that 11 always had the right attitude. Throughout the club at the time there was a wonderful spirit. His leadership meant that everybody, in training and in games, wanted to do well for him. There was no way we were going to let our standards drop.'

McNeill relished the rich variety of challenge that his team faced in the early 1980s. 'Going head to head with Aberdeen and Dundee United was fine; they were the emerging challengers. My record against both of them in those five years was fine. We lost out once in the league to Aberdeen and we lost out once in the league to Dundee United but both of those sides were full of top-quality international players. If you looked at it from an international point of view they were better staffed than we were.'

Two successive league titles arrived at Celtic Park in the 1980–81 and 1981–82 seasons and those years also saw McNeill carefully and gradually introduce good young players to the team, most notably Paul McStay and Charlie Nicholas, both of whom benefited greatly from McNeill's emphasis on attacking football. Nicholas was unfortunate in suffering a broken leg midway through the 1981–82 season but he made a problem-free comeback and was still only 21 years old when he ended the 1982–83 season having scored 46 goals, many in exquisite style. Nicholas had made a stunning impact on Scottish football and his goalscoring, in tandem with his 'gallus' Glaswegian public image, had captured the imagination of the Celtic support.

Nicholas had barely established himself in the Celtic side, however, before rumours began to surface of his imminent departure. The arrival of spring 1983 saw Nicholas become the most feverishly pursued talent in British football, with Arsenal, Liverpool and Manchester United from England's First Division slavering after his signature. Nicholas was courted very publicly and assiduously by each club before plumping for Highbury. Arsenal, under their talkative manager, Terry Neill, were a mid-table side in contrast to FA Cup-holders Manchester United and League champions Liverpool and it seemed, at the time, a strange choice of destination for Nicholas. He became a big favourite of the North Bank because of his confident style but the move stunted his career. It would have an equally damaging effect on Celtic, whose manager, McNeill, had tried everything he could to advise Nicholas to remain in Glasgow. McNeill, who had a good working relationship with Nicholas and knew how to handle his many youthful indiscretions, believed that the player was too young, too callow, for the top level in England. His words of wisdom had not been able to compete with the desire of chairman Desmond White to sell the player.

That spring of 1983 had seen Nicholas summoned to the business office of Desmond White in West Nile Street, Glasgow, because the player had told McNeill that he was dissatisfied with Celtic's modest offer of an increase in pay. Nicholas found it strange that he had been asked to meet White since it was McNeill who habitually dealt with all transfer business. When he came face to face with the Celtic chairman, White told Nicholas that he would understand fully if the player wanted to move on from Celtic to take up other challenges. It was hardly an exhortation to the player to remain at Celtic – quite the opposite. White had been swayed by a challenge that he himself had found to be irresistible: the offer of a fee of approximately £625,000 for Nicholas, then a massive amount.

'To this day, Charlie Nicholas was sold behind my back,' says Billy McNeill. 'I would not have sold him to Arsenal. There were several clubs interested in him. It was the wrong time for Charlie to go, never mind anything else, and it was certainly the wrong time for Celtic to sell him. I still to this day don't know what money they got for Charlie Nicholas. The chairman refused to tell me. Much was said about me leaving because it was an argument over money. It was never an argument over money; it was over principles such as them selling Nicholas over my head, such as not even involving me in the deal, such as not even telling me what the fee was. I remember, funnily enough, just before Charlie Nicholas went, playing in a pro-am at Haggs Castle. Our Martyn was only a youngster and I remember getting a photograph taken with Martyn on my shoulders so he could see over the crowd. I remember being as happy as Larry and then just a few weeks later I was heading for Manchester.

'I was never treated as the main person at the club. I was so low down the scale of wages in comparison to other managers, considering I was Celtic manager, that it was frightening.' Four other Premier League managers, including Ricky McFarlane of St Mirren, were paid more than McNeill, who was earning £20,000 per year in 1983. 'Managers are like any other human beings,' continues McNeill. 'You can fight against the tide for so long. I'm not saying I was the easiest fellow to get on with. The first time I was there I narked and narked and narked at the board and I suppose I was cheeky and aggressive but it was because I wanted Celtic to be successful. When the response doesn't come back, it just becomes impossible, it really does.'

The feisty McNeill had one final argument with Desmond White that spring of 1983. McNeill angrily slammed the door behind him as he walked out of that last meeting before deciding to accept the offer of the job of Manchester City manager. It was an almost inevitable denouement to a relationship between chairman and manager that had, all along, been an uneasy one. It still seemed an unnecessary conclusion to a five-year spell under McNeill's management that had reinvigorated Celtic. White and his board had, after all, known what they were getting when they recruited McNeill in 1978: a passionate, impatient young man, raw in management but restless and determined to do the best he could for Celtic. A wiser, more tolerant board would have understood McNeill's moods and would have been pleased to work with such a passionate, charged individual. If they had been more mature, better able to see the bigger picture, they would have been able to help him channel his energies even more productively. Billy McNeill had proved to be a dynamic manager for Celtic, but as he journeyed south that summer he could only reflect bitterly on how much unfinished business and unfulfilled potential he had left behind at Celtic Park.

SIX

David Hay – Solid Service

A cosmopolitan collection of players stroll in and out of Livingston Football Club's reception area on just another day in early twenty-first century Scottish football. A Trinidadian, an Englishman, a Canadian and a Spaniard amble past as the receptionist tries with difficulty to establish telephone contact with a player in Argentina. David Hay appears in full training gear and communicates with a potential signing from southern Europe with the help of translation by the player's female partner. The cohesion of such diverse individuals into a team capable of landing Livingston qualification for the UEFA Cup in 2002 after their first season in the Premier League owed much to Hay's input as head coach. Livingston manager Jim Leishman is the figurehead who motivates the players on a Friday and Saturday; Hay and first-team coach John Robertson work closely with them throughout the week. Hay, now in his mid-50s, can deal with his multinational charges by drawing on wide and varied experience from numerous managerial and coaching posts in England, Scotland, continental Europe and the USA. He is thoroughly enjoying life at a new football club in a new town. 'Football is the best place in the world to be,' he enthuses. 'It's got a special magic and I think even people who are not involved in it realise it has got a special magic.'

David Hay's experience was considerably more limited when he was approached to become Celtic manager in the early summer of 1983 after Billy McNeill had swept out of the club. At that time, Hay was 35 years old and although he had played at the top level with Celtic and Chelsea throughout the 1970s, he was a fledgling manager. There were no problems for Celtic in prising him away from another club for the curious reason that he was not, at the time of his appointment, involved in football and was instead the owner and operator of a public house in Paisley. If Celtic had not come calling, it is quite possible he would have remained out of the game.

Hay's brief managerial CV was, admittedly, impressive: he had been assistant manager to Ally MacLeod at Motherwell for two years before taking over as manager himself in the autumn of 1981. He immediately won the 1981–82 First Division title with Motherwell in emphatic fashion. That summer, he went on holiday to the USA, where he became intrigued by the possibility of becoming involved in opening up an indoor soccer complex. It appealed to Hay, together with the American lifestyle, and his children were young enough to move to the USA without too much disruption to family life. Enthused by these plans, Hay decided to leave Motherwell rather than keeping the club hanging on whilst he awaited clearance from the American immigration authorities. He then came up against a visa problem that prevented him from emigrating to the USA and when, in early 1983, he opened his pub in his home town of Paisley, he had not been involved in football since his departure from Motherwell in the middle of the previous year.

As an intelligent individual, Hay has always been able to see more than one side to any situation and has never been blinded by the superficial glamour of football. His initial hesitation over whether to accept the Celtic manager's job was characteristic of him. It mirrored his approach when he had been asked to join Celtic as a player in the mid-'60s. He joined the club on a full-time basis but after three months decided to go part-time to study to become a chartered accountant before, two years later, deciding to go full-time again to accelerate his progression through to Jock Stein's first-team. Hay's rounded personality and ability to take a mature view of things helps make him an approachable coach in the modern era.

'I was asked to take the Celtic job,' he says, casting his mind back to the summer of 1983. 'I remember at the time I hesitated a wee bit on the basis that I had just taken over this pub because I knew that the Celtic job would prove a liability in running the pub. So it proved. Eventually I sold the pub when maybe I should have kept that as my insurance policy for what happens in football management. That was the delay in making the decision but I always knew I would take it. I had had a wee bit of experience because I had taken the Chelsea youth team, had been assistant to Ally MacLeod and had managed at Motherwell so I wasn't a total novice – but I was a Celtic novice. I was 35 and that is too young for someone to become Celtic manager. I think because I was an ex-Celt and had done so well at Motherwell I fitted the bill. I think my Celtic background swayed it. I admit I didn't have enough experience but, at the time, through youthful exuberance, I probably thought experience meant absolutely nothing.

'On reflection, and I am not taking anything away from John Clark, Billy McNeill and I would have been an ideal combination on the basis that we've both got similarities. Billy was maybe more outgoing in dealing with the press although I had my strengths there as well. I think if Billy had been manager and I had been his assistant it would have worked to a tee. It would have been an ideal combination on the basis that Billy did have the experience. If the progression had gone on, he would have moved up and I could have done so too. I have often thought about that and it is ironic that I took over from him and he took over from me.'

David Hay's playing career with Celtic had stretched from the mid-'60s to the mid-'70s, when he left the club after a dispute over his earnings. On his return to Celtic as manager he picked up where he had left off, by trying to negotiate a better financial package. 'I always remember at the time I tried to dig out for a couple of bob more even then – so things hadn't changed that much!' he says. 'I feel honoured that I was asked to be Celtic manager . . . It's something you can't really refuse. There were wee pitfalls but there were more happy times than sad times.'

Frank Connor had been appointed as Celtic assistant manager prior to Hay being given the job and Connor himself asked Hay if he had any objections to working with Connor. It was a strange situation – Hay had not requested Connor as his assistant but because Hay was such a young manager he felt that he had no contemporaries to take on in that role. The Celtic directors had actually asked McNeill to replace John Clark with Connor – McNeill's refusal to do so had added to the friction between the manager and the board. Now, with

Hay, they had had their way. Hay's multifarious duties as Celtic manager meant he played a vital role in the smooth running of the club. 'I did contracts, I organised trips, I did all the training. I would physically sit down with the boys and say to them, "Right this is what you're getting." I would sometimes write the contract in myself.'

Hay made few alterations to the style of football that Celtic had played under McNeill, which had, after all, been a largely successful one. The same playing staff remained largely in place, with the notable exception of Charlie Nicholas. His departure was more than adequately compensated for by the introduction of Brian McClair, whom McNeill had signed from Motherwell after the end of the 1982–83 season for a £70,000 fee. McClair would finish each of the next four seasons as Celtic's top scorer.

The summoning of Hay from behind his saloon bar to the job of Celtic manager was reminiscent of a retired gunslinger being brought out of action in a Western. Hay was the archetypal hired hand; relaxed in the face of danger, laid-back, laconic and undemonstrative, doling out a succession of one-liners with his slow drawl, all the time keeping an alert eye on events unfolding around him. He even, Clint Eastwood-like, had a penchant for chewing on the occasional cigar. At the point when he was provoked, though, it was advisable to stand well clear before the bullets started flying.

'Davie was more aggressive than Billy,' says Murdo MacLeod, whose driving play in midfield was essential to both McNeill and Hay. 'He would be quietly spoken and would organise things but if things weren't happening the way he wanted, then you would know about it. The players respected Davie as a manager and as a player and got on well with him and knew he had been a hard man on the park. I think when he snarled once or twice in the dressing-room the players knew they could not push this man too far. Every manager is different; no two are the same. When you are a player you adapt and adjust to the manager's way of thinking and how they want things done. Davie was a strong, hard guy and when he would ask you to do something you would go and do it. If you didn't do it, you would get a mouthful from him. He kept the same system as Billy, which, it had been proved, was a winning formula.

'He would get annoyed if players were not performing as well as he had hoped and not doing the right things on the park. He would have a go at them and if somebody said anything back, maybe to try and defend themselves, and Davie felt he was right and the player was in the wrong, Davie would get angry and the player wouldn't argue back again. He would allow players to have their say, which was really good, but in the heat of an argument you would just keep your mouth shut. You knew that when Davie was getting angry then he had a strong point. Most of the time he would get on well with the players, organise the players, talk to the players, encourage the players. He had been the type of player who would kick his granny to get a result and when he became a manager he kept that attitude.

'The age difference between Davie and ourselves wasn't too vast – he was only about ten years older than a lot of us. So when you went on a pre-season tour you would have a beer together. He would join in with the guys but you wouldn't overstep the mark. I think the players would give an awful lot for Davie, the way he looked after them. He was a players' manager so the players used to give him that wee bit extra.'

Hay's aggressive streak ensured that the Celtic players got tight on to opponents. Every team they faced knew they had been in a game – Hay never allowed his players to forget the need to battle for the ball. McClair's goals helped push on this settled Celtic side to the final of the 1983–84 League Cup, where a debatable extra-time penalty awarded to Rangers by referee Bob Valentine led to their 3–2 victory. Celtic also reached the final of the 1984 Scottish Cup and were once more unfortunate when Roy Aitken was sent off early in the match, again by Valentine. Celtic fought hard after that and took the match to extra-time, but with only 10 men ended up losing 2–1.

Aberdeen, managed by Alex Ferguson, were engineering an extraordinary period in Scottish football, in which the Pittodrie side were the dominant force in the Scottish game. Ferguson's side, rather than Celtic or Rangers, were the team to beat. Dundee United were also a top-class force, and, as with Aberdeen, not only in Scotland but also in European competition; in the spring of 1984 United reached the semi-finals of the European Cup. Rangers, as Celtic's main rivals, were always formidable opponents in the heat of an Old Firm match. It meant that Hay's team was faced by extremely competitive and technically adept opposition and throughout his time as manager they kept abreast of that opposition. Aberdeen duly became the 1983–84 champions with Celtic runners-up, seven points behind. The UEFA Cup had featured a memorable 5–0 victory over Sporting Lisbon at Celtic Park, then an impressive 0–0 draw with Nottingham Forest at the City Ground.

The first-leg draw with Forest in England primed the fans for the return at Celtic Park, which was crammed to its then 67,000 capacity, only for Forest to expertly hit Celtic twice on the break and take the tie. Brian Clough, the Forest manager, had taken his players for a drink in Davie Hay's Paisley pub on their way in to Glasgow from the airport. Before leaving, Clough had cheekily told the staff that Hay would pick up the tab for the drinks.

That 1983–84 season had been a good one for the fans, with plenty of excitement and big occasions. There had been a lack of luck but the failure to win trophies made Hay a hostage to fortune thanks to a pronouncement he had made on becoming manager. 'The first season I was there I said that if we didn't win something I would resign,' he explains. 'It was almost to protect the players because you're taking away the pressure from them and putting it on yourself – even though I was that young. I also meant it quite genuinely. I remember we played Aberdeen in the Cup final and we lost in extra-time and the first question in the press conference afterwards was, "Are you going to resign?" I probably shouldn't have said what I said but there is an element of truth in it, and I'm big enough to say that if you don't win something as a Celtic manager, maybe you should say, "Well, wait a minute, at this club you should maybe stand back." Where I got out of jail was that we won the BP Youth Cup!'

There was less to laugh about in Hay's second season. Europe once again offered an entertaining diversion as Celtic defeated Ghent before facing Rapid Vienna. Having lost 3–1 in Austria, Celtic powered to a tough-tackling 3–0 home win and a place in the final. The evening had, however, been spattered by Austrian gamesmanship and resulted in a protracted, cynical appeal by Rapid, which centred on a bottle having struck one of their players. Television evidence showed the bottle, stupidly launched on to the park from the Jungle terracing, had not made contact with any player. Rapid's Weinhofer, who had only just been sent on as a substitute with a few choice instructions in his ear from his manager Otto Baric, had still left the field with his head swathed in bandages. Baric, at one point, had himself even thrown a bottle on to the pitch from the touchline.

'It was almost as if they planned for it,' says David Hay. 'The thing that was lost in all the controversy was how well we played on the night.' UEFA initially threw out Rapid's case. They then, inexplicably, allowed the Austrians to change their story to the player having been hit by a coin and, even more inexplicably, ordered the match to be replayed at a neutral venue. That game, at Old Trafford, brought a freakish 1–0 defeat for Celtic and an exit from a European competition that Hay's team might even have had a chance of winning; Rapid, who had been defeated fairly by Celtic over the initial two legs, went on to contest the final with Everton. 'I maintain that if we had got through that tie, which we should have done, we would have gone all the way,' says Hay.

Celtic's league form stuttered in the wake of that episode and although they were again the principal challengers to Aberdeen in the 1984–85 Premier League competition, Celtic again finished seven points adrift. It meant that as Hay's team approached the 100th Scottish Cup final in May 1985 against a fine Dundee United side they needed a victory to land a first trophy for their manager. After going behind to a Stuart Beedie goal, Hay pushed on two substitutes, Pierce O'Leary and Brian McClair, to provide greater spring for attacks from midfield. Roy Aitken was told to move from centre-back into midfield. It worked – two spectacular late goals from Frank McGarvey and Davie Provan saved the day.

Unlike Billy McNeill, David Hay enjoyed his one-to-one relationship with the Celtic chairman, Desmond White. The relationship had its roots in the mid-'70s, when Hay had been involved in an ongoing debate over his contract with the club. His dealings at that time had been more with White than with Jock Stein. 'I found Dessie straight,' says Hay, 'a man who would give a straight answer to a straight question.' He appreciates having been given the authorisation from White to buy the striker Mo Johnston from Watford for a Scottish record fee of £400,000 in 1984, shortly after

Celtic had agreed a lucrative deal to allow shirt sponsors on the club's jersey for the first time. Tragically, Desmond White died suddenly on holiday in the summer of 1985. 'After that,' says Hay, 'there was a power struggle for the chairmanship and I probably got caught up in that a wee bit. When Dessie died, they made Mr Devlin chairman, where I thought it should maybe have been Mr Farrell, and I think Jack McGinn and Tom Grant were able to manipulate Mr Devlin more than they could Mr Farrell.' Alliances and allegiances were formed and it is Hay's opinion that Tom Grant's attitude towards him was less than favourable. 'At that particular time I think he was probably more of a pro-Billy man than a pro-Davie man,' adds Hay. 'I think there was an aspect of that crept in. Eventually, Jack became chairman. The thing is, if you win, all of these things don't matter. If you lose, then maybe if somebody is more of an ally to you it extends your period – or your losing run – longer.'

Early exits from cup competitions in the 1985–86 season left Celtic focusing solely on the League title. This time Hearts led the race for the title for most of the season although a 15-match unbeaten run drew Celtic closer and closer to the Edinburgh side as the season progressed towards its conclusion. 'That was Davie's type of fight,' says Murdo MacLeod. 'When Hearts went top of the league we knew we had to keep on winning and scrap for every point just to keep up with them. Even in games when it was 0–0 late on we would keep on pushing because we had nothing to lose. Davie just kept pushing you all the time.'

A dramatic final day found Hearts needing just one point to take the title. Instead, they lost 2–0 at Dundee. Even then, Hearts might have expected to finish in front of Celtic as their goal difference had been four better than that of Hay's team before that afternoon's matches. A superb 5–0 victory over St Mirren at Love Street, Paisley, had taken care of that small problem for Celtic and Hay had won his first Premier League title as Celtic manager. The manager allowed himself one or two of his customary small cigars that May evening as he celebrated a victory that had been achieved in classic Celtic fashion. 'That team had the capability of doing well,' says a wistful Hay, 'but we needed to strengthen the defence in one or two areas and the money wasn't made available.' The money that had been released for the Johnston signing had proved to be a rare exception for Hay; for the rest of the time he had had to patch up the squad here and there with players attained for unspectacular fees.

'We won that championship from Hearts just by hanging on for any slip from them,' says Murdo MacLeod as he thinks back to that spring of 1986. 'We managed to do it on the last day and the board seemed to think, "The team has won the championship; we will just keep that team going." I think we needed a freshness, a couple of extra players, just to give the players a lift. That didn't come about. We never won anything the following year so Davie would be under a wee bit of pressure but I think when you look at his track record before that they should have said, "Let's build on that now. Let's start again." '

Hay had also had to contend with another spectre as he approached the 1986–87 season. The arrival of Graeme Souness as player-manager at Rangers in April 1986 had increased the stakes for all involved in Scottish football. Rangers had quickly invested heavily in purchasing English internationals such as Terry Butcher, Chris Woods and Graham Roberts and had paid them wages similar to those that were expected at the top level in England. It swiftly and suddenly brought to an end a long-lived tradition through which both Celtic and Rangers had paid poorly in comparison to top-level clubs in England. Both clubs' directors had previously played on the magnetic pull of each Old Firm club: players were expected to play for the jersey and for the love of the club and that was to compensate for their reduced earning power at Celtic Park and Ibrox. It was an approach that was no longer working for Rangers by the mid-'80s. They had spent the early part of that decade constructing an ultra-modern stadium but now that it had been completed they discovered that they had a team mired in mediocrity, whose paucity of ability saw them play home matches in front of banks of empty seats. Those problems resulted in the Ibrox club consigning old-style manager Jock Wallace to history in the spring of 1986. They then introduced the unsentimental Souness, who had had no previous connection with Rangers or with Scottish domestic football, to modernise the club's approach.

Rangers' new policy had no immediate effect on Celtic: while

Souness experienced teething troubles in the opening months of his managerial career at Ibrox, Hay's team built up a nine-point lead in the League during the autumn of 1986. That was gradually eroded as Rangers' new players bedded in and Souness's team found the consistency to keep winning whilst Celtic scattered points to the wind during the second half of the season. Hay, in an effort to refresh and revive his team, sacked his assistant Frank Connor in February 1987 and replaced him with Tommy Craig.

The new Rangers players, as experienced internationals, had, though their professionalism, vastly reduced the number of errors made by their team. Hay requested funds from the Celtic board to improve his own side in a similar fashion to Rangers and maintain a challenge on Rangers but found that such funds were not forthcoming. Jack McGinn, at one point, suggested that if Hay wished to sign a player the manager would have to dig into his own pockets for the cash. 'The irony is,' says Hay, 'that halfway through that season they gave me a rise for no apparent reason; I don't know whether it was to win me on to their side a wee bit and take the party line a wee bit. I always tried to take decisions for the good of the club whilst being realistic. If we had signed three players at the time we would have gone on and won the League that year. Before Souness came there was almost a parity between Celtic and Rangers with regard to wages. There wasn't a cartel but it was as near as you would get to one. Strangely enough, Celtic were probably paying slightly more but the press always seemed to write more about Celtic's wages problems rather than Rangers'. If you look back to Baxter, why did he leave? Then, when Souness came, that changed – the English players came up to Scotland because Rangers were paying so much money. I probably didn't get enough backing from the board because if we had signed two or three players we would maybe have won the league that year. It wasn't to be and I can't cry over spilt milk now.'

Funds were finally released to Hay at the very end of the 1986–87 season, after Rangers had wrapped up the Scottish Premier League title by finishing six points clear of Celtic. Ten days after the League season had ended, Hay was given the money to sign the rugged centre-half Mick McCarthy from Manchester City for a fee of £425,000. 'I did the negotiations for the contract,' says Hay, 'and I almost broke the wage structure off my own back.' Hay believed it was necessary to do so if Celtic were to compete with Rangers. 'I always remember the wage structure was such that the top player at Celtic was on about £35,000 to £40,000 a year. So when Mick came I offered him £1,000 a week and a signing-on fee. He never hesitated in signing because I knew the figure to hit to get him up here. I had other targets for the next season. I offered Brian McClair identical terms to those I had offered Mo. Mo was always going to go but Brian, I think, was almost going to sign. So I had the structure of a team. That was in the week before I got the sack.'

Days after McCarthy signed for Celtic, the Lisbon Lions got together to celebrate the 20th anniversary of their victory in the European Cup final at a sizeable function in the Normandy Hotel. Hay had been invited to attend but had made an arrangement to visit England that weekend. On the evening of 25 May 1987 Billy McNeill made a speech that received a standing ovation. 'Billy was lauded that night, rightly so,' says Hay, 'and the directors were there and I think they saw a main chance that night.' Hay believes that, in his absence, and seeing McNeill's obvious popularity with the support, the directors envisaged the opportunity to bring in a new manager, especially as McNeill had been dismissed earlier that May by Aston Villa. 'You find that when you are invited to these types of functions it's a Palm Sunday kind of thing,' comments Hay dryly. 'So Billy had a Palm Sunday that week and I was the crucifixion the following week.'

McNeill's departure in 1983 had resulted from a personality clash with Desmond White at a time when McNeill had been a successful and popular Celtic manager. Now, with White having passed away, Celtic having failed to win anything in the 1986–87 season and McNeill looking for work, it struck the directors that the time was right to bring McNeill back to Paradise. Two days after the function at the Normandy, Billy McNeill attended the studios of Radio Clyde in Clydebank to contribute to a programme on the Lisbon Lions. Prior to that radio slot, on 27 May 1987, he received a telephone call from Celtic chairman Jack McGinn, suggesting that McNeill meet him in the car park outside the studios. McNeill agreed to do so and McGinn offered him the position of Celtic manager.

It seems strange that the Celtic board gave their blessing to Hay breaking the club's wages policy and paying a Celtic record fee for a player only to replace him a week later. Hay thus believes that the decision to terminate his managerial career at Celtic was made on a whim by the directors.

The end for Hay, on 28 May 1987, was short but not sweet. 'I went in that morning then went home and got a phone call from Jack McGinn's secretary and something in my bones told me that it was a strange one. So I went in to see Jack and he said to me, "Davie, I'm sorry to say it, but we are going to ask you to resign." So I said to him that I would resign once we had sorted out the basis of the deal; although I didn't have a contract I had been there long enough to be due some sort of compensation for losing my job. He said he would get back to me on it. I actually felt I took the news reasonably well, considering the shock. As God is my judge, this is the truth, and I don't know what made me say it, but I asked him, "Who is getting the job?" Right hand to God, he said, "Billy is one of the candidates . . ."' Hay left that meeting under the impression that the board were still considering whom they wished to appoint as manager.

'So I went away home and late that afternoon Billy was announced as Celtic manager – about four hours after Jack McGinn had spoken to me. I can live with that now – you realise that maybe these things happen in football. At the time it hurt. If they had said, "Davie, we feel it hasn't worked out. We're very sorry but we're going to bring Billy in," I would have said that I was sad it had happened and would have wished them luck, which, eventually, was a point of view at which I arrived, because life goes on. At the time, though, I felt they had gone behind my back and that became a bigger wound than the actual sacking; the manner in which they did it.'

Popular accounts of that era have it that Hay refused to resign and insisted that if the board wanted rid of him they would have to sack him. As such, it would have made him the first Celtic manager to be sacked, as opposed to having handed in an offer of resignation to the board. The truth is more prosaic. At the meeting with Jack McGinn, where Hay was informed that the board no longer required his services, Hay had told the chairman that he wished to discuss the conditions under which he would offer his resignation. Hay then left

Celtic Park with the impression that a settlement was to be thrashed out with Jack McGinn prior to Hay then resigning. Events quickly overtook the possibility of this. As Hay puts it succinctly, 'The fact that they appointed Billy three or four hours later obviously meant that I had been sacked.

'I always remember I got a letter from Cardinal Winning telling me that time would be a healer,' recalls Hay, 'and he was right. Celtic should be noted for doing things in the correct manner but the manner in which they sacked me was wrong. As I said at the time when I was sacked, I was more equipped then to do the job than when they offered me it.'

Jack McGinn was of the opinion that Hay had been too nice a man to be an effective football manager. 'He did say that at the time,' says Hay. 'Maybe that was genuine but, you see, if you win and you're nice there's nothing wrong with it. If you're nice and you lose, then there's something wrong with it. If you're a ratbag and you win, there's nothing wrong with it. If you're a ratbag and you lose, you should be nicer. So that season, basically, what happened was we finished second to Rangers and I was sacked, albeit I had won the League the previous season.'

Subsequent to his sacking, David Hay continued to follow Celtic's fortunes, although he made a point of paying his own way in to Celtic Park. He would also travel to away games on a supporters' bus with the David Hay Celtic Supporters' Club and enjoy his pie and pint with the fans before matches. On one occasion, sitting in a social club before a match in Dundee, his fellow supporters contrived for an announcement to be made over the speaker system: 'Is there a Davie Hay here? There's a Jack McGinn wanting to meet you out in the car park.' The warmth and camaraderie he felt through being amongst Celtic supporters helped to dispel any lingering bad feeling from his dismissal. Hay is also magnanimous enough to suggest that it may even have been better that he was sacked and for Celtic to subsequently enjoy winning the League and Cup Double in their 1987–88 centenary year than for him to have remained in position and the club possibly not to have won those trophies that year. He would certainly have liked to have been given another season to try to claw back some ground on Rangers but is big enough to acknowledge Billy McNeill's subsequent achievements.

'I have no malice towards Jack McGinn in the slightest now,' says Hay. 'I meet him – he has had hardship in his life – and we get on fine although there was a period for about a year afterwards when I could have smashed his gob in; his or those of any of those Celtic directors at the time.' Hay's analysis of his time as Celtic manager is typically rational. 'Celtic appointed me when I was, probably, inexperienced and sacked me when I was more capable of doing the job. Things were done behind my back and the hurt was deep. I felt let down because I had always been an up-front kind of person.

'As manager I felt I did relatively well. People used to say I was laid-back but my approach was to keep things on an even keel. I was never too demonstrative because I always felt that the traditions of Celtic made that the way to act. It was maybe my undoing because people looked at me and might say I didn't care enough. Nothing could have been further from the truth. We won a Cup, we won a League, we did all right in Europe; but for a break in certain games it might have been different but I wouldn't change it for the world because you go down in history as being a Celtic manager.'

SEVEN

Billy McNeill – Caesar Reigns Again

Four challenging years in England at Manchester City and Aston Villa had helped Billy McNeill to mature as a manager. He had done well at Maine Road, where he had a skimpy budget to buy players, and had won City promotion to the First Division two years after his arrival at the club. After a disagreement over what he saw as meddling at directorial level in his running of the team, McNeill quit City for Aston Villa early in the 1986–87 season. Villa were struggling and despite a brief resurgence under McNeill they finished the season being relegated. McNeill paid for that with his job.

Billy McNeill's frustrating final season as a manager in England meant that he had a lot of pent-up energy ready to be unleashed on his return to Celtic Park in 1987. He was delighted to be back where he belonged and from the first moment to the last of the 1987–88 season, McNeill could be seen driving on his players from the touchline, pressing them to give every last drop of energy to ensure that Celtic's centenary would be celebrated in style. The initial impetus of McNeill's return was so great that he pushed his team to play with passion and precision and capture the Scottish Cup and League Double. McNeill's special bond with the club and its support ensured that he was entirely aware of the importance of celebrating the sentimental milestone of the centenary in style at a club whose supporters have always been enormously conscious of its colourful history.

'Billy was able to get that spirit going,' says Billy Stark, who had been one of the manager's key signings in the summer of 1987. 'That was absolutely crucial and was the main reason we had such a good season. I think managers have got lots of different qualities. I don't think there are any of them that are brilliant at everything because there are so many facets to it. The one thing he has right away is presence and the legendary status that he had at the club. He was absolutely tailor-made to be Celtic manager, particularly for the centenary season.'

McNeill admits that there was a lot of luck involved in the club's success that season. 'I had been lucky in that I had still kept my contacts with scouts and with different people up here,' he says, 'so I knew the sort of players that were available. I knew Andy Walker had a right chance. We had a great shower of blokes; good personalities. Apart from their abilities on the pitch, they were good to work with and determined to progress.' A series of signings were swiftly made by McNeill as he rolled up his sleeves and got down to work: wing-back Chris Morris from Sheffield Wednesday, stylish midfielder Stark from Aberdeen and striker Andy Walker from Motherwell all arrived in the close season. Frank McAvennie from West Ham United and winger Joe Miller from Aberdeen joined Celtic in the autumn. Graeme Souness at Rangers had set the trend of importing players from England and beyond. Celtic were forced to follow that trend to try to keep abreast of Rangers – it contrasted severely with McNeill's first period as manager, when his teams had consisted of players reared by Celtic or purchased from other Scottish clubs. McNeill adopted a 4–4–2 system that season, with Chris Morris and Anton Rogan working as two overlapping full-backs by whipping up and down the touchline, and a dynamic, incisive approach saw his players pull opposition defences apart on a regular basis. Celtic worked extensively in training on pressing the ball to force opponents into mistakes.

'I remember during the pre-season,' recalls Billy Stark, 'that you could sense that the management were working very hard to get the players to gel quickly and I think the chemistry of the players was important in that as well. It wasn't easy to do it all so quickly but we did become a good squad of players. Jimmy Steele, God rest him, was still there and he was brilliant in terms of that. Tommy Craig obviously added another part to it as well.

'Tommy is very much a coach and played a big part in the shaping of the side. I don't remember Billy McNeill making very many poor signings as a manager and that was a big strength of his. Billy would work on the team spirit but Tommy was a more introverted character and they worked well together from that point of view. You could just see that big Billy loved every minute of being manager of that club and I think that gets through to players right away, without him actually having to say anything. Immediately, you can see that he is a good guy. You could just see he was ecstatic about being back and being manager of the club that he loved and he quickly instilled that in all of us, from young boys to experienced professionals like myself.

'Billy was always on the training ground and while Tommy Craig did the training Billy would watch players. He would take part in five-a-sides once or twice a week. You knew that you almost had to match his desire for success for that club and that's how he got the best out of you. Big Billy is not a complicated guy. He wears his heart on his sleeve; he wanted players to go out and give everything for the club and you did that because he told you to do it. That might sound simplistic but there are not many managers who are able to do that.'

That concerted effort helped to provide McNeill's team with a vital 1–0 victory over Rangers in the first Old Firm match of the 1987–88 season. Billy Stark scored an exquisite goal, curving the ball round Rangers goalkeeper Chris Woods' outstretched hand after the Rangers defence had been pressurised into giving the ball away. 'I remember him talking to me on the Friday before that game,' says Stark, 'after a light session at Barrowfield, but he did not talk to me in a serious way. He was good at that: he could be getting home a point but in a kind of jocular fashion and because of his presence and the respect that you had for him you knew what he was trying to do. I remember him saying to me about it being an Old Firm game and how big a game it was.' Stark had been brought up as a Protestant in a 'mixed' family and had not been a Celtic supporter at any stage. McNeill told him all about how Tommy Gemmell and other non-Catholics had still always relished defeating Rangers as much as those who had been brought up as supportrs of Celtic, the club that has traditionally had a large Catholic following.

'It was a help,' says Stark. 'It just took a bit of pressure off me. He must have had a million conversations and wee words in my ear but I remember that one maybe because it was my first Old Firm game. It certainly did help although not as much as getting the goal early on. He was basically saying to me to feel just as passionate as everyone involved; he was talking about big Tam and how he loved beating the Rangers and all the rest of it. That was just his way of getting that passion instilled in you in case it wasn't already there.'

A six-month unbeaten run between October and April captured the 1987–88 League title for Celtic and two hugely dramatic Scottish Cup comebacks, against Hearts in the semi-final and Dundee United in the final, made it a Double. Celtic, driven on by the great motivator McNeill, were simply irresistible that season.

'It was satisfying that you did that,' admits McNeill as he looks back on that time, 'but it was hard going. It was hard, hard work. It was a demanding job. I remember us battering up and down that road to England and getting back in at three o'clock in the morning and being in at training at nine o'clock in the morning just because we wanted to see games and we wanted to look at players. I remember getting a *Rothmans* book out and underlining every Scotsman in it who was playing in England and we tried to see them because half of them you don't know – and it just wasn't possible. We didn't have enough finance to have a proper scouting system. When I look at the staff at Celtic Park now, and I think of the staff that I had, I really just can't believe it. I think there's more connected with the first-team squad at Celtic Park than we had in total, including our scouts. I didn't have any scouts in England because we couldn't afford it. Our chief scout had to do that as well. We had six scouts. There was never anything like the financial resources necessary for a big-time club.'

The raw passion that had driven Celtic on in the 1987–88 centenary season could not be sustained indefinitely, not even by Billy McNeill. As things settled down and life returned to a more even pace, Celtic needed to invest if they were going to build on their success. It was not to be; only one major signing was made in the summer of 1988, when goalkeeper Ian Andrews joined from Leicester City for £300,000. Celtic needed one or two outfield signings in their mid-20s to augment the experienced players and keep the club moving forward but funds were not forthcoming for the manager to secure such signings. 'The frustrating thing for me,' says McNeill, 'was that here were you as the manager of a massive club that didn't behave like a big club, didn't finance things in the way a big club should. Souness and Rangers were looking massively to the future. Their stadium had been improved, they were financing players. In fairness to the Celtic directors, the money wasn't there . . . who knows where it went? Rangers recognised that the one important aspect of any football club is investment in players.'

Frank McAvennie had been outstanding at centre-forward during the centenary season, scoring 18 goals after signing from West Ham United in October 1987. Even before the 1987–88 season ended, though, the news escaped that the goalscorer wished to pursue his aims away from Celtic. The story went that he wished to rejoin his girlfriend in London but Billy McNeill suggests an even more basic reason for McAvennie's wish to go. 'He was superb but the frustrating thing was that money proved the downfall. As soon as he started making inroads about wanting away, that was us on the slide. You can keep people if you offer them enough money and we couldn't do that. It was frustrating that West Ham were in a position to satisfy a player more than we were.' McNeill sees the financial shortfall as the problem rather than the geographical estrangement of McAvennie from his blonde, pneumatic partner. 'You can get to London easily enough,' says McNeill, 'you jump on a plane and you're in London in an hour.

'The second time was just absolutely desperate. It was much worse than the first time I was there, because Rangers were oodles in front of us. Graeme Souness bought good players. He got England's captain and England's goalkeeper up here and he produced really good sides. I think the best Rangers teams I saw were under Souness because they had quality, steel and class. They had the quality up front, the power up front. They had the skill from midfield. They had really, really good players. I thought his teams were great and that was really frustrating. Souness was a hard adversary and Murray at that time was really determined to make them into something else. I was envious of what they had.

'David Murray was prepared to support his ideals and his ambitions and he supported his manager. So it was always frustrating;

it was hard. The second time was the hardest time because with what we achieved in the centenary year there was no way we were going to be able to sustain that, no way whatsoever, and then the whole thing started to break up. Macca wanted away and other players wanted away. We just didn't have the players. Those players that did the League and Cup Double couldn't do it again without improving the structure. There just were not the resources to do it. The thing that Souness did was he went out and strengthened Rangers. There wasn't any player whose signing it was beyond their capability of obtaining. To go down to England and take their best players, as he did . . . You know, the English are very, very proud of their international team and their captain was suddenly whisked up to Scotland and their international goalkeeper was suddenly whisked up to Scotland and big Hateley was whisked up to Scotland, as well as Mark Walters, Ray Wilkins and Trevor Steven; these were all good, quality players.'

The club's infrastructure was being equally badly neglected, as McNeill points out. 'I remember the Belgian club Mechelen came over here to play St Mirren and their manager phoned me up and said, "We're over to play St Mirren and they don't have a training ground. I was wondering if we could use Celtic's training ground." I told him it was no problem and that they should come to Celtic Park and get changed at Celtic Park since the training ground was only half a mile away. So they duly came down. I was interested to see what their training was like and when I went along to see their manager at training he said, "Ah, Billy, this is not your training ground." I said, "I can assure you it is." He said, "No, no, this is for the younger kids. You've put me on the children's pitch." I said, "The children use this pitch, the youths use this pitch, the reserves use this pitch and the first-team use it." He said, "No, I can't believe that – a club like Celtic!" I always wanted something done about it. I argued with the board the first time I was there and I argued with the board the second time I was there and nothing was done about Barrowfield.

'They were never willing to invest in youngsters. I wanted to alter the whole aspect of the Celtic Boys' Club because I think the Celtic Boys' Club was a wonderful vehicle for Celtic to use but they had to structure it to suit Celtic. It did produce a lot of youngsters but a lot

Willie Maley, Celtic's first manager, was never without a soft hat and a hard stare. Here he basks in yet another triumph as Celtic manager, the capturing of the 1933 Scottish Cup. Maley won more major trophies than any other Celtic manager: 14 Scottish Cups and 16 League titles.

Team captain Jimmy McStay leads Celtic out in the 1930s. McStay, who became Celtic manager in 1940, is part of a dynasty that includes his brother Willie, who was also a Celtic captain. They were great-uncles to brothers Paul, Raymond and Willie McStay, all of whom joined Celtic as players in the late twentieth century. Willie is currently head youth coach at the club.

Jimmy McGrory was loved for his good humour and kindness but as a manager he lived under the shadow of autocratic Celtic chairman Robert Kelly. One of Celtic's greatest players, Jimmy later became the club's first public relations officer to round off more than four decades of service to Celtic.

A seriously sharp operator, Jock Stein never overlooked the slightest detail in his preparation and planning for each and every match. His fearsome temper could be ignited with any indiscretion on the part of the players, but there was also a big, soft side to him that he did his best to disguise.

The measured, canny approach of David Hay to the job of Celtic
manager produced some memorable highlights in the club's history.
His deceptively laid-back demeanour masked a quiet, sincere
determination and his players were left in no doubt as to Hay's desire
to achieve results for Celtic.

The delight on Billy McNeill's face shows how much winning with Celtic means to him as he watches his players lift the 1989 Scottish Cup. McNeill's coach and right-hand man Tommy Craig is by his side. The dynamic, driven McNeill is the only man to have had two separate periods as manager of Celtic.

Liam Brady exhorts effort from his team during his first Old Firm game, an ominous 2–0 home defeat by Rangers in August 1991. Backroom staff Brian Scott, Neil Mochan and Jimmy Steele appear to share the crowd's muted apprehension. Anton Rogan and Paul McStay avert their eyes.

Lou Macari hails the opportunity to become manager of Celtic in October 1993. The strong-willed, determined Macari had walked into a maelstrom of difficulties that would soon suck him under. His eight-month stay made his time as Celtic manager the shortest up to that point.

Tommy Burns looks thoughtful after a 1–0 League defeat away to Dundee United in February 1997 during his final season as Celtic manager. The efforts of Burns, in testing circumstances, did much to build a base that allowed for the successes of Celtic in the modern era.

A pensive Wim Jansen looks on as Celtic play Parma in a pre-season match during the summer of 1997. Jansen was a shy, inscrutable individual whose thorough preparations, tactical sophistication and economical use of resources brought the club success in his sole season in charge of team affairs.

Dr Jozef Venglos was a perfect gentleman with a professorial demeanour and a keen intellect. It made him a perfect manager for the modern age and he brought many useful ideas to Celtic. He harnessed the resources available to him to create a Celtic team with a fast, fluid, attractive style.

Kenny Dalglish (left) and John Barnes (right) were hailed as the dream team when they took charge at Celtic in the summer of 1999. Their joint venture soon turned into a nightmare as Barnes' inexperience in football management led to his demise at Celtic after seven months as head coach.

John Robertson (right) confidently points to the heights as new Celtic manager Martin O'Neill (left) supervises his team during the 3–0 victory over Hibs in September 2000. That win took Celtic to the top of the Scottish Premier League, a place that they would be able to call their own under O'Neill's inspirational management.

of them were brought to the club, so artificially Celtic got the credit that they didn't really deserve for bringing in an awful lot of players. The club should have structured it and financed it and employed the people to run it and done what we wanted with it. They would never listen and I think that's what went wrong. There was a period when they weren't prepared to invest in youngsters. When the Lennoxes and the Johnstones and the Gemmells came along there was no cost at that time and even to a degree when the Dalglishs and Hays and McGrains and Macaris came along there was still no cost but then the world started changing because everybody started seeing the importance of producing your own and Celtic never did it.'

The departure of McAvennie early in 1989 saw Celtic fielding Joe Miller, more usually seen on the wing, at centre-forward and the player scored the only goal of the 1989 Scottish Cup final with Rangers to take the trophy to Celtic Park. During the week prior to the final, McNeill had taken his players to Portugal for a golfing break and some light training. If the result had gone against Celtic McNeill might have found himself pilloried by the press, but he was sure in his mind that it was the right thing to do at that stage of the season. He recognised that in that week he wouldn't be able to do a great deal tactically. It was important to forge a spirit in the team to win the game. On their nights out, Billy would be right in the middle of things, encouraging the players to have a few drinks and a sing-song. At the end of one night – a night that full-back Anton Rogan ended by sitting on top of some traffic lights – Billy McNeill stood in front of a revolving door and his players, one by one, spontaneously emerged from the contraption to take their turn at pouring a pint over their manager's head. The players could see that he was prepared to muck in with them when the time was right but he was clever enough to then be able to get back on to a managerial level and command the full respect of the players the following day.

That 1989 Cup final victory salvaged a season that had been almost as disappointing as the previous one had been uplifting. A poor start to the 1988–89 League season had seen Celtic go down 5–1 at Ibrox and a series of subsequent League defeats were augmented by an early European Cup exit to Werder Bremen. McNeill knew he required a genuine striker to replace McAvennie and attempted to bring Maurice Johnston back to the club. The player had been with FC Nantes in France and he was paraded by Celtic in May 1989. There then followed two months of confusion over whether or not Johnston had actually signed a contract with Celtic. Eventually, in July 1989, he turned up again in Glasgow, having joined Rangers. Rumours swept the streets that Rangers' financial offer to Johnston had been, in whatever shape it was offered, simply irresistible. He became the first Catholic player at Ibrox in modern times and for McNeill it was further hard evidence that Celtic were slipping further and further behind Rangers on a daily and weekly basis.

Finding himself priced out of the top-quality British market, McNeill employed some imagination to find a goalscorer both affordable and of high quality. He purchased Polish international Dariusz Dziekanowski from Legia Warsaw for £600,000. A burst of brilliance initially endeared the Pole to the supporters – he scored four of Celtic's five goals in a 5–4 Cup-Winners' Cup victory over Partizan Belgrade in September 1989 – but he found it too difficult to cope with the freedoms of the West, after the privations of communist Poland, and soon his off-field activities were sapping his athletic strength.

'Dziekanowski was much maligned,' says McNeill. 'I think it was a difficult process for him as well because those nations at that time had an iron grip on everything and for him suddenly to be exposed to the much more relaxed, free attitude in this part of the globe must have been difficult for him but the whole reason behind it was because we couldn't afford to barter for top-quality players in this country. So I had to look here, there and everywhere to think of ways of getting in players. Paul Elliott was a classic example of that,' adds McNeill in reference to the English centre-half he purchased from Pisa for £500,000 in the summer of 1989. 'I always felt that Paul would use the club to get his career back in vogue but money would have solved the problem. He would have been happy enough staying up here if the money was equitable. That was always the difficulty; not having the resources behind me.

'Dziekanowski was no problem in the dressing-room. People say that he didn't train – he was a magnificent trainer. He was fit as hell;

he had great fitness and they had been brought up properly. He used to go and clean his own boots and things like that. It was off the field that you had the problem with Jacki. There are things that you have just got to put up with at times; things that you have just got to control and with which you have just got to assist. Unfortunately, it wasn't to be.' Dziekanowski's bubbly early form fizzled out and Celtic's fortunes dipped low in the 1989–90 and 1990–91 seasons. McNeill's side failed to win any trophies; the first time since the pre-Jock Stein era that such a two-year sequence had occurred.

It was a difficult time for the manager and his problems were exacerbated when, in January 1991, the Celtic board took the decision to appoint the club's first chief executive, Terry Cassidy, whose brusque approach made McNeill suspicious. 'I felt that if the board felt I wasn't doing it they could have sat down and talked reasonably about it,' says McNeill, looking back on those troubled times. 'That's down to the board. At the end of the day, I think there is a way that you can treat people who served you well and I think I served Celtic very well. You can treat people properly; you don't treat them like a bit of dirt that's attached to your shoe.' Late in May 1991, the long-running rumours that Billy McNeill had heard that the board had been manoeuvring to dispense with his services finally became reality. He parted company with the club, making his final departure from Celtic Park as an employee after a playing and managerial career that had stretched over five different decades.

'I felt very bitter,' he states, 'and it took a long time to lose the bitterness; not to the club – to the board of directors. I felt I was entitled to an awful lot better treatment. I could have screwed them into a contract after the first year but I didn't do it. I could have done that but I didn't do it because I thought, "They know who I am now." I hadn't been treated well the first time – and people could easily say that I maybe contributed a lot to that myself and that might well be the case, I'm not going to argue that point – but my aggressiveness was to try and get Celtic on the road because I thought that was what they had employed me for. It was like being in a boat and one person is rowing one way and the other is rowing another way. That's the feeling that you got. It was a nightmare. For me, there was always the frustration that Celtic should have been doing a helluva lot more and should have had a far bigger face than they had. Big clubs everywhere were looking to get better and better but Celtic kept rolling against the tide.'

A disillusioned McNeill turned down the offer of the job of Dundee manager shortly after his exit from Celtic – he was now 51 and the demands of the Celtic job had drained him of much of his youthful resilience. 'I was tired and I was hurt and I was bitter and it was not the right combination to take a job on. I would've taken a job for the wrong reasons. Dundee had offered me the manager's job just after I packed it in at Celtic. Ian Gellatly, the chairman, had agreed with me that I would take the job and I said I would but I didn't sleep well the night before I had to go through and finalise everything. I thought about it and thought about it and picked up the phone and said, "Look, Ian, I'm sorry, I'm not coming through. I was going to take the job for the wrong reasons. I was going to take it to earn money and I think that's the wrong reason to take anything. So I appreciate your offer but I would be taking it for the wrong reasons."' McNeill has been absent from football management ever since, contenting himself with the running of his lively, memorabilia-festooned pub near Hampden Park and his contributions to commentating on televised football and to newspaper columns.

Modern match-goers inside Celtic Park's South Stand can find themselves standing next to Billy McNeill in the queue for Bovril, soft drinks and pies, a captive victim, like his fellow Celtic supporters, of the high-price-low-quality catering inside Celtic Park. A season-ticket holder, he leaves his car, like everyone else, in the lap of the gods a mile from the stadium before walking up to the ground that featured in so many highlights of his life. It would be nice if the club made greater acknowledgement of McNeill and his fellow Lisbon Lions. It is certain that if McNeill was used by the club in an advisory capacity, his knowledge of the club's traditions could help those inside the club to maintain awareness of the standards required of Celtic as a football club rather than as a purely profit-making business. Many clubs with a lesser pedigree than Celtic give famous former servants greater recognition than Celtic currently give McNeill. No one would grudge Billy McNeill a permanent place in the higher echelons of the club but for the moment it is reassuring to see the articulate, expressive McNeill as part of the club's core support, still as passionate about his team as he was as player and manager.

EIGHT

Liam Brady – The Impossible Dream

Maseratis, BMWs and Porsches sit sleekly in the car park at Arsenal's training ground at London Colney, gleaming in the bright sunshine that bathes prosperous, leafy Hertfordshire on this hazy, sunny, midweek afternoon. Arsène Wenger, Arsenal's urbane French manager, is surrounded by half-a-dozen busy Japanese TV people as he reclines in a lightweight chair on the front lawn to carry out an interview for Japanese television. Dennis Bergkamp pads into the treatment room in sandals, Kanu ambles to his car and Freddie Ljungberg, in scruffy-but-trendy hat and jeans, discusses the design of his new football boots with a couple of fast-talking London lads. First-team training is finished for the day but some youngsters are still enjoying the acres of pristine pitches that surround Arsenal's three-year-old, ultra-modern, indoor training centre. Barrowfield it ain't – but Liam Brady, Head of the Youth Policy at Arsenal, has his mind on Glasgow's East End as he prepares to give his first in-depth account of his time as Celtic manager since his departure from the club in the autumn of 1993.

His arrival at Celtic Park in 1991 had appeared to herald a new era at the club. All six of his predecessors as manager had been former Celtic players who had stepped up to take on that role and all had been contacted secretly before being revealed to the public as the new Celtic manager. In the summer of 1991, however, the Celtic board, with public relations man Michael Kelly prominently in place, decided it was time to modernise the club's image. The new Celtic manager would not now be appointed on a nod-and-a-wink, old-boys' network basis. Instead, the process would, supposedly, be as transparent as possible.

A shortlist of four candidates to be interviewed was drawn up: Liam Brady, who had been a world-class player with Arsenal and Juventus and the holder of a record 72 caps for the Republic of Ireland; Tommy Craig, previously assistant manager at Celtic to David Hay and Billy McNeill; Ivan Golac, the Yugoslav who had been manager of a Partizan Belgrade side that had knocked Celtic out of the 1989–90 UEFA Cup in dramatic style; and Frank Stapleton, the former Arsenal, Manchester United and 70-times capped Republic of Ireland striker. It was a cosmopolitan selection: none had played for Celtic and only Craig had experience of Scottish football as a player, even then very briefly as a teenager with Aberdeen in the late 1960s.

The four men were all interviewed on the same day and the board made sure the parade of candidates was as public as possible. They rotated in and out of the main entrance door at Celtic Park, each arriving at reception like any other interviewee for any other job. There they were met by a receptionist who had a list of interview appointment times and who ticked off each candidate's name as they arrived, before asking them to take a seat and wait until the interview panel was ready. It could have been appointment selection at ICI or the civil service except that this was Celtic, supposedly moving into a new, progressive era, one rid of cronyism. Brady, for one, was not too impressed. 'I was interviewed first at Celtic Park,' he says. 'It was a day when they were holding interviews, which was a bit mind-boggling. It was a very public affair. They were ferrying people in and out of Parkhead in front of the media and in front of supporters and if I was in their position I wouldn't have gone about it in that way. It was a bit of a show.

'I then went back up to have a private interview with Terry Cassidy and Jack McGinn, with my solicitor. In the second interview I was asking a lot of questions – in the first interview they had been asking a lot of questions. They offered me the job, I accepted it, it was on the national news when I got back to London, and I was the subject of intense media attention. I think I got the job because the field of runners and riders didn't have great track records, without being disrespectful to any of them. Frank Stapleton was one of them; like myself he was keen to get into that management situation. I think

Tommy had the disadvantage of having been there and again, in a kind of overt political stance by the board, they wanted to move away from what had been to something new.

'I was enthusiastic about it. I couldn't have wished to get a better start in management. I didn't know entirely the ins and outs of the political situation at Celtic vis-a-vis the board at that time with people who were trying to oust them. I didn't know the extent of that. I didn't know the problems that they were going to have regarding a new stadium. All I really looked at was the club, its tradition and the playing staff and I thought, "This is a great start." I took it from there but I wasn't long in having my eyes opened!

'In my second interview I wanted to know what I had to work with as regards finance to bring players in. I wanted to know the players who were out of contract or whatever and I was told, "Take your time, get your feet under the table and sort it out in your own time. Have a look at the staff, speak to the players who are out of contract or who are talking about leaving." One player in particular, Paul Elliott, was still under contract but was adamant that he was going to leave. I had an assurance that I would get a chance to speak to the player. Within days, Brady discovered that a source inside Celtic Park had leaked it to chosen media contacts that Elliott definitely was to be sold. A furious Brady, who was tying up some loose ends in London prior to taking up the reins at Celtic, immediately telephoned the club to protest. He felt that he had been deceived. The new Celtic manager, instead of feeling he had the chance to assess in a relaxed way all the talent that was available to him, already felt undermined and a tense situation developed between him and several key people involved in the running of Celtic, including chief executive Terry Cassidy.

Although Liam Brady's appointment was presented as a fresh start, the public interview process had not been quite as transparent as it seemed. Brady, following his retirement as a player at West Ham United in 1990, had begun work with a Dublin sports management company, managing players. He had teamed up with an Irish agent who had been involved with the Irish players at the 1990 World Cup. One of those players was Celtic and Ireland goalkeeper Packie Bonner and Brady's first contact with Celtic had been in representing Packie in contract negotiations with Billy McNeill and Jack McGinn during the 1990–91 season. At the end of that season, Brady travelled to Celtic Park for Bonner's testimonial, ten days before Billy McNeill lost his job. Brady had enjoyed his year in sports management and although it had been interesting he wanted to have a crack at management. With Billy's departure things fell into place. Brady intimated to Packie Bonner that he would be interested in the job and when it became available his previous dealings with the club gave him a head start on his competitors.

It also helped that Liam Brady's pedigree as a player was of the highest class. He had made his Arsenal debut in 1973 at the age of 17 and had matured into one of the club's greatest players. It was his last-gasp, driving run from midfield that set up Alan Sunderland's winning goal in Arsenal's dramatic 3–2 victory over Manchester United in the 1979 FA Cup final, a year in which he was named English football's Players' Player of the Year. Brady had then stunned the Arsenal support by announcing that after one more year at Highbury he would join Juventus. He spent seven years in Italy, with Juve, Sampdoria, Inter Milan and Ascoli before finishing his playing career at West Ham.

His profile suited Celtic pefectly. Here was a Dubliner who knew all about Celtic's heritage but had developed into a well-travelled, wealthy, rounded individual, the epitome of the successful Irishman abroad. Brady was quietly spoken and intelligent, an aficionado of the music of Bob Dylan, a man who had always relied entirely on guile and style as a footballer. He had observed many high-profile managers at work but as he started his career as Celtic manager the matter up for debate was whether he could blend those observations and his experiences as a player into a successful brand of management. His ambition was to become a 'famous Celtic manager'. He certainly looked the part: no tracksuit for Liam, only the finest of suits, and whilst Billy McNeill and his predecessors had always sat on the bench in the dugout Liam chose to stand upright just in front of the bench to observe proceedings. 'I used to stand because in that dugout at Parkhead you are a bit low down and it's a wide pitch at Celtic. I wasn't modelling myself on anybody, it was just a question of feeling that you could do more about things if you were standing rather than sitting on your behind.

'I wanted to get in there, working with the players,' says Brady. 'I had about a month of watching videos and speaking to Jack McGinn, who was a tremendous help to me, and to Tommy Craig, who stayed with me. I brought Mick Martin in to help with the coaching and general atmosphere around the club and the rest of the staff stayed the same. Mick was first-team coach, I was manager and Tommy was assistant manager.'

The first two signings of the Brady era were to prove pivotal to the manager's fortunes. Prior to the early 1990s Celtic had lived within their means but now the decision had been taken to go into debt – Rangers had won three Scottish League titles in succession by mid-1991 – and considerable amounts of cash were released for Brady to muscle in on the transfer market, where Rangers had long been splashing out millions of pounds. It was a high-risk policy – these signings would have to produce success if the club was not to spiral into deeper and deeper debt through a combination of high transfer expenditure and increased wages for these pricey players. Brady quickly spent £1.1 million to buy Tony Cascarino from Aston Villa. The striker, a Republic of Ireland international, had gone to Villa from Millwall in the spring of 1990 for a £1.5million fee. At the time of that signing, Villa had been closely involved in the race to win the League Championship in England and Graham Taylor, the Villa manager, had signed Cascarino in the hope that he would produce goals for the team in the final run-in to the title. Cascarino had failed him, netting just twice in ten games and even then in meaningless matches at the very end of the season. Under Dr Jozef Venglos in the 1990–91 season, Cascarino scored just ten goals. He struggled badly at Celtic Park in the first half of the 1991–92 season – it seemed strange that a man who stood at 6 ft 2 in. and weighed 13 stone could possess so little physical presence. After just half-a-dozen appearances Cascarino was relegated to the substitutes' bench.

Brady's other major signing in the late summer of 1991 was one intended to strengthen the defence in the wake of the departure of Elliott to Chelsea. Gary Gillespie, an elegant, ball-playing centre-back, was bought from Liverpool for £925,000. A Scotland international, he had been injury-prone in England and would miss serious chunks of both of Brady's initial two seasons at Celtic.

Neither signing worked out well and both players' extended absences from their central roles destabilised the team during Brady's first season. Brady was also unlucky in beginning at Celtic minus the team's central playmaker, Paul McStay, a very good player who had damaged his knee ligaments in mid-1991 and subsequently missed the first two months' fixtures under the new manager. The spine of the Celtic team was severely weakened through the extended absences of those three players and Celtic, as a consequence, struggled. Three defeats – to Aberdeen, Rangers and St Johnstone – in Celtic's opening seven Premier Division fixtures left them reeling in the league. They toppled out of the League Cup at Airdrie on penalties. A first-round UEFA Cup victory over Germinal Ekeren was followed, disastrously, by a 5–1 defeat to Neuchatel Xamax in a second-round UEFA Cup tie. That thumping in a quaint corner of Switzerland was the worst defeat in Europe in Celtic's history. Charlie Nicholas, who had rejoined the club under Billy McNeill in 1990, suggests that Brady told his team that the Swiss were a weak side and that the manager threw caution to the wind in opting for a line-up that contained only three defenders. Brady has a different opinion.

'The team went out there and performed abysmally,' says Brady of the Xamax game. 'I wouldn't put that down to me. They were a team that were no great shakes but Packie dropped one in the first five minutes; there was a header from a corner-kick inside the six-yard box. Managers can't legislate for things like that. That was shortly after we had gone to Ekeren in the previous round when I had said something in the Scottish papers that Scottish people, and particularly the Scottish media, jumped on, which was that for a Scottish club to knock a Belgian club out of a European competition was, at one time, expected. Now they're on a level playing field and to beat Ekeren as we did, 2–0 at home, was a good result. There were a few things in the papers saying that we didn't really play well and they had a couple of chances . . . but the days of wiping the floor with a Belgian club were well and truly over and I said that publicly. Then we went to Ekeren and got a good performance and a good draw and I thought, "Well, we might have a chance of getting some distance in this competition." But we went out to Neuchatel. I had watched them play and didn't think they were better than us in any shape or form but we went out and really showed the frailties of a poor playing staff, I'd say. On the night the players let the club down badly. They went under and I told them in no uncertain terms that that wasn't acceptable. They went under and they didn't fight. They accepted defeat. There was not really anything I could have done about it on the night. I think I made as many substitutions as I could!'

Paul McStay had just been feeling his way back to match fitness at the time of that UEFA Cup debacle, but with the midfielder restored to the side Celtic went on a strong run and although they were well out of contention for the League title their good form took them to a 1992 Scottish Cup semi-final to face their nemesis, Rangers. A pattern to Old Firm matches under Brady had seen Celtic play most of the good football in those matches only to be stampeded into submission by Rangers' sheer physical power. That semi-final would be different in that Celtic could justifiably point to dreadful luck as the reason for their 1–0 defeat. Regardless, it meant that they would finish their first season under Liam Brady without a trophy. The pressure of being manager of Celtic at a time when Rangers were in a position to strengthen their side whenever they wished began to get to Brady. 'I'd be lying to say that it didn't affect me,' he explains, 'whilst they kept on winning the pressure just got greater and greater. They beat us in that semi-final and I took that very hard because I felt we had improved dramatically from the Celtic I had taken over and we were a whisker away from beating them in that Scottish Cup semi-final. The pressure just explodes when something like that happens. The fans clapped our lads off the pitch because they'd had a real go and they were a bit unlucky and we were on the end of an appalling refereeing decision when John Collins was taken down in the box and a penalty wasn't given. The fans go away muttering about the referee but saying that overall the team played well and had a real go and things like that but then a day later it sinks in that Rangers are in another final and we're not going to win anything and then the whole thing ferments. They were just too good for us at the time. They had the capability and financial clout that meant that if they got a player injured, as we had with Paul McStay, they would pick the phone up and get the cheque book out.'

Tony Cascarino had left Celtic for Chelsea in February 1992 in exchange for Tom Boyd. By the time of his departure, Cascarino had lodged himself firmly in the collective consciousness of the Celtic support; even at the 2002 Scottish Cup final against Rangers Celtic fans could be heard invoking his name in a chant, 'Cascarino is better than Flo' just to emphasise how big a flop they regarded Rangers' Norwegian striker to be. Brady had had his logic in signing Cascarino, 'I had played with him for Ireland and I figured that Celtic didn't have that kind of Hateley-type centre-forward. I figured that we were going to dominate 90 per cent of the games we played in and that we were going to get into positions where we would cross the ball a lot and if I could have somebody to get me 10 or 12 headed goals a year I was going to have someone who would bring something to the Celtic attack that they didn't have. As the goals didn't come for him it just got too much for him and I could tell that he was better off out of the team than in the team. It was quite obvious three or four months into his time at Celtic, when he had only scored a couple of goals, that he was feeling the pressure of that. I had an inkling that his wife wasn't happy and decided that we would get him moved on.' Cascarino, in common with Bonner, had been represented by Brady in his role in the Dublin-based players' agency where Brady had worked for a year but Brady is adamant that he did not gain from the transaction. 'When I joined Celtic as manager I severed all ties with the company,' he states.

Brady's judgement could have been questioned in the matter of signing Cascarino but he looked to have completed a better piece of business with the acquisition of solid centre-half Tony Mowbray for £1 million from Middlesbrough in November 1991. Unluckily for the manager, injury disrupted Mowbray's first season at Celtic Park. With hefty fees having been spent on three players with little return, Brady could with some justification feel that the fates were against him as he looked back over his first year at Celtic Park.

German entertainers do not often have a reputation as purveyors of smiles to faces of paying customers but in the autumn of 1992, there was a brightening to be found in many countenances at Celtic Park as Celtic defeated FC Cologne in the first round of the UEFA Cup. A 2–0 defeat in the first leg in Cologne had looked almost fatal to Celtic's chances of surviving into the second round but a performance of verve and vigour in the return at Celtic Park saw Celtic obtain a cheering 3–0 victory. With Collins and McStay on top form Celtic looked a more than useful attacking outfit and Brady's faith in attractive attacking football looked as though it was beginning to be rewarded. It was the first time Celtic had defeated a club from one of the major European footballing nations in more than a decade. The following round brought an aggregate defeat to another German side, Borussia Dortmund, but this was no disgrace. Dortmund were challenging for the Bundesliga title and with players such as Stefan Klos, Stefan Reuter and Stephane Chapuisat in their side, would reach the UEFA Cup final that 1992–93 season. Domestically it was different.

Brady's side had made a better start to his second season in charge than they had to his first one but three successive defeats – to Hearts, Dundee United and Rangers – over the Christmas and New Year period left them out of contention in the League. They had gone out of the League Cup at Aberdeen in September 1992, which left only the Scottish Cup to play for in the second half of Brady's second season. By then they had another new signing on board: Stuart Slater, a speedy winger who had cost a record £1.5 million from West Ham United. In common with Cascarino, Slater would struggle in Scotland. He teamed up with the now 33-year-old Frank McAvennie whom Brady had cheekily lifted from under the noses of Partick Thistle. The striker had returned to Scotland as a free agent after wanderings that had taken him as far afield as Hong Kong. Brady's hunch proved correct in this instance and McAvennie scored a number of goals in the second half of that 1992–93 season. Neither he nor Slater, however, could save Celtic from the ignominy of defeat at Falkirk in the fourth round of the Scottish Cup in February 1993.

'When you are lagging behind Rangers by a number of points come Christmas,' says Brady, 'and you get knocked out of the Scottish Cup by Falkirk, that's a bitter, bitter blow. It was around then that I thought I couldn't turn it round and, to be fair, I didn't think anyone could and I was proved right. Until the structure changed, nobody was going to be able to turn it round. I had been still convinced that I was doing the right thing and away I went and it was only, I suppose, halfway into the second season that I realised that it wasn't going to work.'

Brady toyed with the idea of resignation at the end of that 1992–93 season but the determination that had seen him through so many great battles as a player swayed him to stay. That summer of 1993, though, he took the decision to remove his former Republic of Ireland team-mate Mick Martin from the position of first-team coach. Joe Jordan, who had recently lost his job as manager of Hearts, was appointed assistant manager to Brady and Tommy Craig became youth development officer. Martin had always been ready with a joke and a smile; Joe Jordan was a much more fearsome prospect. The switch to a tougher regime was the last throw of the dice for Brady.

'Initially, it worked out brilliantly with Mick,' says Brady. 'He was exactly what I was looking for but, like everything else, as the success didn't arrive, the dissent in the ranks began to appear as it does very easily if you're involved with one of the Old Firm sides. Players and board begin questioning things. When you're winning everybody's patting you on the back saying "Well done", and the players were very happy with Mick and the training was good. We were getting a commitment from the players initially and it went well but as soon as you had a hiccup it was different. Mick did an excellent job all the way through. I just thought Joe Jordan was somebody that had done very well at Hearts, knew the Scottish League inside out, was the tough kind of character that I was looking for, a different face for the players, and that's why I asked Joe to become assistant manager. Joe was a very serious guy and I just thought he would bring a sense of focus and discipline that maybe I hadn't brought to the situation but to do that I had to make room or else the board wouldn't have stood for it. Now, to do that I had to make changes and that was a very difficult decision for me to take.

'In many ways I should have really resigned after the second season and said, "Look, it's time for somebody else to get into it." I suppose you're always hoping that things will change. It was either resign and say, "Look, somebody else needs to run this club and probably somebody with more experience, somebody who is able to cope better with all the goings-on off the field," or try and change it. We had a team that was nearly successful and you're always tempted by that. You're always tempted to believe, "Well, we could turn it round." It was probably the wrong decision; not the decision to get Joe in because Joe was a dear friend of mine and I respect him greatly. I felt that maybe, looking back, that the pressure came on from the board to make changes – they weren't happy with having gone two seasons and not having won anything. They wanted changes and things like that. I now regret not having said after the second year, "Get somebody else," shaking hands and saying, "I'm sorry that I haven't won anything for you but I've tried to run the club in very, very difficult circumstances and I think I've done it OK. Get somebody else in but a word of warning to you: unless you sort yourselves out nothing's ever going to happen here." I should have done that really and probably lacked the decisiveness and courage to do it.'

By 1993 the Celtic board were under severe pressure from 'rebel' groups whose purpose was to oust them from position. A businessman, Brian Dempsey, had become their sworn enemy after major shareholders Christopher White and Michael Kelly had voted against his proposed appointment to the board at the last minute in October 1990. Dempsey was soon joined in his struggle against the board by Fergus McCann, a Celtic supporter and Scot who had become wealthy after having emigrated to Canada in the 1960s. The two men spearheaded pressure groups who wished to oust the board from position and it was Celtic Park itself that would prove to be pivotal in their advances on power. The ground that Brady looked out upon during home matches comprised vast terraces behind both goals, a smaller, narrower terrace alongside the Janefield Street side of the ground – the 'Jungle' – and just one stand, affording only 8,000 seats. Brady's third season as Celtic manager, 1993–94, would also be the final season in which Celtic Park, in that form, would be able to host Premier League football. Under Lord Justice Taylor's 1990 report into football stadiums, which had been published in the wake of the 1989 Hillsborough Disaster, all Premier League grounds in Scotland and England would have to be all-seater by the beginning of the 1994–95 season. The Celtic board appeared paralysed by inertia as the need for action on this dilemma drew ever closer.

'The board didn't know where to go,' says Brady. 'They had this pressure from a group outside the board – Brian Dempsey and latterly Fergus McCann – who were very critical of them, extremely critical of the fact that they couldn't deliver a new stadium. The board had exhibited this pie-in-the-sky stadium project at Cambuslang that everybody recognised as being dead in the water before it had a chance. That was, I think, invented to demonstrate to the Celtic support that they were doing something but it was quite obvious to people with business acumen who knew the full story that it was a no-goer right from the off. You see, what was happening at the time was that that particular board were firefighting all the time to stop people from moving them out and taking over the club. That eventually had to happen.

'I had support on the board. I think I had support from those of the old school really: Jack McGinn, Jimmy Farrell, but none of them had any real power. The ones who were leading the board were the ones whom I didn't really see eye-to-eye with, such as Michael Kelly. To be fair to the board, to go two years without winning anything is not on at Celtic and they probably thought, "We haven't got the right manager. We need to get another manager." But as far as I was concerned, there was no manager ever going to succeed there in that climate because they weren't driving together in the same direction and they didn't have the money or the business clout. What bank was going to lend them money when they had a crowd of people trying to usurp them from their positions and they had a support that was totally fed up with them? The support wanted change as well. Which people were going to back that board, whatever scheme they had? We had a lot of support staying away. That affects the playing staff, of course it does. If you look at any of the clubs in England recently where you've had power battles within the boardroom the playing side inevitably suffers. Everton is a good example of that. They've been going through ten years of it really; Norwich, when Martin O'Neill fell out with the chairman there and the support turned against the chairman, and so forth. Once you get that happening it's very difficult to drive a team forward and to get a team united.

'Another thing that I found difficult up there was that we had good players but nothing special, but the media make them out to be something great because they play for Celtic or they play for Rangers. If you fell out with a player or you dropped him for some reason it was in the papers the next day: "I'm off to Bayern Munich" or something like that. You'd read the paper and say, "I wish." All these stories were created and there are a lot of forces within the Old Firm that, as a manager, and an inexperienced manager, I found very difficult. You'd wake up in the morning wondering what the press had in the papers and it would maybe be something like "Bayern Munich want Tommy Coyne" or "Gerry Creaney not signing a new contract". These were decent players but nothing special and the Scots papers knew that as well but it didn't stop them writing that Bayern Munich were going to buy Gerry Creaney or something.'

Brady's initial attraction for the Celtic board had had much to do with his stature within the British and European game. As with Graeme Souness, Brady's was a name well known outside of Scotland, which had made it easier for him to obtain the signatures of players following their careers in England. For various reasons, few of those signings had been successful and Brady is candid about that in his self-assessment.

'If I've made an excuse with regard to how difficult it was with the then current board I have to admit that my signings really didn't come off and on the pitch that was where I failed. I thought I ran the team well and our tactics were good and our preparation was good, training was good, all those things were all right. The thing that I didn't get right were the signings to help make the team better and I think that's where it failed on the pitch. Walter Smith made plenty of mistakes in his signings but I couldn't afford one. Stuart Slater was a big disappointment to me. I had played with him at West Ham and he was, I thought, potentially a very, very good player. He had speed, he had pace, he was direct. I was convinced he could score goals in an attacking team like we had at Celtic. The place was just too big for him. I'm sad to say that that move to Celtic probably didn't do his overall career any good at all because he never managed to shake himself out of that disappointment of going up there and not doing well. In the case of Gary Gillespie, the doctors had told me he was

OK. He had his medicals done, I asked them their opinion, and they said he was all right. I wanted to play football. I wanted to play from the back and a fit Gary Gillespie would have been exactly the right man for that job but he wasn't able to cope with the rigours of football week in, week out. With Cascarino, you could tell that he just didn't like the place, Glasgow, and the pressure of playing for one of the Old Firm sides and particularly the Old Firm side that wasn't doing as well as the Rangers side. You can turn a determined player round but if he hasn't got the determination you can't turn him round.'

The staff changes that Brady had made in the summer of 1993 had little immediate effect. Celtic could be found wallowing in mediocrity at the start of the 1993–94 season. They struggled to defeat an ordinary Swiss side, Young Boys of Berne, 1–0 on aggregate in the first round of the UEFA Cup and lost 1–0 to Rangers in a League Cup semi-final. Celtic's opening ten league matches yielded two wins, five draws and three defeats, leaving them sitting ninth in the 12-team league. Brady was still maintaining his dignity – something of massive importance to him – under extreme pressure. 'I thought I did a very good job as regards running the club in very difficult circumstances,' he says, 'when the club was the subject of much ridicule about how the board were going about taking Celtic forward. The players weren't convinced that the people running the club knew what they were doing or had any direction to what they were doing. I didn't wash the dirty linen in public. Some of the players did but I didn't and never resorted to that. I tried to keep the lid on a lot of things that were happening. There was a decent atmosphere there at the club and I felt that in very difficult circumstances I ran the club well. We had a bit of dignity. We weren't resorting to public slanging matches in the media, things like that, but I was basically trying to keep the lid on the whole thing all the time.'

That dignified stance and aversion to tipping off the Scottish press about the goings-on inside the club meant that he also lacked the option of using the press for his own ends but he feels that was not a disadvantage. He had little time for the Scottish media. 'I never really fancied them at all,' he says. 'I had very little to do with them. I never made any friends among them because that was one of the things I had never liked as a player: managers who had their pals in the media and who, even when they were making bad decisions, could do no wrong as far as this or that journalist was concerned. I had a couple of people approach me and I never got involved with them. I kept them at arm's length, I never did exclusives for them. I just didn't want to go down that road. I think that's the right way to do it. I don't think that worked against me because you live or die by your results. In the end, they can criticise you however much they want but if your results are good they can't do it really. They can only do it to a certain extent. The knives were out when we weren't winning and in the end they got their day, as happens with many a manager.' Brady laughs, relaxed, as he considers the memory of it. Time and distance have softened the blow.

The tenth league match of that 1993–94 season, a midweek fixture away to struggling St Johnstone on 6 October, had resulted in a 2–1 defeat and convinced Brady that it was definitely time to go. 'I was obviously upset,' says Brady. 'The realisation was there that it was not going to work. That is pretty upsetting. I was pretty down but if you feel down and are not able to shake yourself out of it . . . We murdered St Johnstone that night. We just kept missing goals. I thought someone else needed to come in. I went home and discussed it with my wife. I said I'd made my mind up and she said, "OK, no problem." I rang Kevin Kelly, the chairman, the next morning and asked him to come in early and just told him that I was resigning, that I was sorry it hadn't worked out. I said, "You won't get any problems with me going. I don't want any money. Good luck, I really want the club to be successful again and for things to turn round." And that was it. I think he was pleased that I was going and they didn't have to sack me.

'I went straight home and got on a plane to Ireland and played some golf. I didn't think I owed the Scottish press a sit-down press conference. I made my statement to the effect that it was time for somebody else to have a go. It was a very sad time but I felt a weight off my shoulders once I'd gone. I decided to go because of our poor start and because the players didn't seem to be going out and playing with any confidence. The pressure was on them as well as me and I think it's up to the manager to relieve that pressure. Having had two seasons without winning anything and then getting off to a poor start I couldn't relieve that presssure. I couldn't give them the confidence so I thought, "Well, it's time for somebody else to come in and see what they can do."

'There was a hell of an amount of difficulty there but I actually enjoyed a lot of the job. I enjoyed being out training with the players, I enjoyed picking the team, I enjoyed being in the dressing-room. When we won it was, in many ways, an even better feeling than when you were a player. We played football in the traditions of the Celtic club and the fans: when they got the football that I really wanted, they really loved it. I never had a real problem with the support. They weren't waving their handkerchiefs or chanting "Brady out! Brady out!" I think the people who were coming to Celtic Park week in and week out realised that I was working under very difficult circumstances and in a very difficult period in the club's history. I didn't strengthen the defence well enough with my signings to enable us to score one or two goals and win a game and I didn't really get it right in attack so that we would score more goals than the opposition.

'Looking back, the club was just too big for a guy who wasn't experienced in football management and going into a situation that was a minefield, really, with what was happening off the field at Celtic Park. At the time I didn't think I was too young for the job. I still didn't think that even after the first season or even in the second season. It was only when coming away from it that I realised the magnitude of the club. For a guy as inexperienced as I was it probably wasn't the right appointment.'

Brady was convinced that whoever succeeded him was willingly walking into quicksand. He did not speak to Lou Macari, the next Celtic manager, before Macari took up the post but Brady was slightly miffed by what he perceived as criticisms made by Macari on his succession to the post. 'Lou went in there and he was kind of blaming what he had as being down to me,' says Brady, 'and that he was going to have to sort out what I had left him. I thought, "I'll keep quiet. Wait till you see the people you've got to work with, Lou, and then you'll realise what you've got yourself into." '

Two months after leaving Celtic, in mid-December 1993, Liam

Brady took over as manager of Brighton and Hove Albion in the Second Division of the Football League. The club's severe financial predicament saw its officials hopping in and out of the High Court to try to stave off bankruptcy and Brighton were second bottom of their division but Brady took them to mid-table by the end of the season, stayed there in his second season and then saw his team fall back to the relegation positions again in the 1995–96 season. Brady left the club by mutual agreement in November 1995. His managerial career had drawn to a halt at the age of 39. Now 46, he no longer harbours any ambitions to go back into management. He has been to Celtic Park just once since he left the club, when he took his son up to see a match towards the end of Wim Jansen's time as manager. He sat with a couple of friends, not in the directors' box, and was pleased to see the club come so close to winning the title. He has never been back inside the boardroom at Celtic Park. The match, against Hibs, was one in which Brady hoped to see Jansen's side clinch the 1997–98 League title, but they failed to do it that afternoon. Once again, Liam Brady had found himself at Celtic Park at just the wrong time.

NINE

Lou Macari – Board Games

The Clyde Coast was a favourite destination for Celtic in the build-up to big matches from the time of Willie Maley onwards. It provided Lou Macari, a youngster in Largs in the 1950s and '60s, with the opportunity to watch his Celtic heroes, such as Billy McNeill, Bobby Lennox and Jimmy Johnstone, at close range as they trained for matches with Rangers or against European opposition. The young Macari, a Scot of Italian descent, would often be the only spectator, looking on with big-eyed intensity as the Celtic players honed their preparations. He later followed Celtic everywhere during the early 1960s, travelling the land on supporters' buses when Jimmy McGrory was manager and the team was struggling to win games.

Those experiences, which Macari had carried around in the back of his mind during the subsequent three decades of his playing and managerial career, bubbled to the surface when he was approached by David Smith of the Celtic board in the autumn of 1993 with the offer to become the now-struggling club's new manager. He remembered how Jock Stein had engineered the turnaround after the Jimmy McGrory era, when Celtic did start winning games and trophies on a consistent basis. At the 1965 League Cup final at Hampden, when Stein's Celtic were on the verge of beating Rangers for the first time in a Cup final for eight years, the 16-year-old Macari sat on the steps at Hampden Park, not watching the game but looking out into the car park. He was terrified that Celtic were not going to win, even though they were 2–1 in front, and sat with his fingers linked through one another, praying that the final whistle was going to go.

Macari is a friendly, chirpy individual whose determination and single-mindedness helped him to become a professional footballer. Those positive qualities can also, in certain circumstances, make him appear stubborn and wilful.

After leaving Celtic in 1973, Lou Macari had remained in England for two decades, and enjoyed a picaresque career as player and manager. He spent 11 years as a player with Manchester United and was a member of the Scottish World Cup squad that participated in the 1978 World Cup finals in Argentina. Macari was, after that tournament, banned for life by the Scottish Football Association as a result of critical comments he had made in a tabloid newspaper about what he saw as the SFA's lack of organisation for the finals.

Six years later, in 1984, Macari went into management with Swindon Town, whom he took swiftly from the Fourth Division to the brink of the First. A brief period in charge of Birmingham City was followed by seven months at West Ham United, during which the Football Association charged the Swindon Town chairman Brian Hillier and Macari with a breach of FA rule 26a4. The allegations were that Hillier, with Macari's knowledge, had bet £6,500 on Swindon losing an FA Cup fourth-round tie at Newcastle United on 30 January 1988, when Macari was the Swindon manager. The bet had been placed through bookmakers Ladbrokes at Cheltenham racecourse on the day of the match. Newcastle were 13–8 on to win and Swindon went on to lose the tie emphatically, by 5–0. Hillier was banned from football for six months and fined £7,500; Macari was fined £1,000 and censured by the FA for his role in the affair, which the FA described as 'minor and foolhardy'.

Macari maintained he was innocent of any wrongdoing, but resigned as manager of West Ham one week later as more Swindon-related bad publicity emerged, in relation to illegal payments to players at that club. The Football League had originally informed Swindon that they would be investigated on that matter in 1988, when Macari was manager. Swindon were eventually found guilty of 36 breaches of Football League rules, 35 of them relating to illegal payments to players, and as a result of that investigation, were denied the promotion they had won to England's top division under manager Ossie Ardiles during that 1989–90 season. Meanwhile,

Macari had launched an ultimately unsuccessful appeal against the FA's decision on the Newcastle v. Swindon bet.

Macari made a fresh start by moving on to Stoke City in 1991, winning them promotion from the Third Division in his first full season as manager and taking them into the First Division just one year later. He was on the verge of signing a five-year contract with a grateful Stoke when Celtic, having parted company with Liam Brady, came looking for Macari in the October of 1993. Macari's memories of the Celtic of his youth helped persuade him to accept their offer and, in that light, he was unable to see it as a bad job. His role as manager at Celtic was to be that of firefighter; it was hoped by the board that some managerial miracles from him would help to beat back the blaze of fury surrounding the club.

By the autumn of 1993 there was a growing restlessness among large sections of the Celtic support at the perceived incompetence of the Celtic board in meeting the dual challenge of competing with Rangers in the modern international transfer market and constructing an all-seater stadium to comply with the specifications laid down in the Taylor Report.

At the time Lou Macari took control as manager, Celtic were severely in debt. Macari's appointment looked a logical one in that he had a very good record of working on a shoestring and getting good results and performances in financially straitened circumstances. His own assessment of his abilities as a player was that he was not especially gifted, but had worked hard and sweated to become a success. That influenced his management style, which saw him place great emphasis on players' fitness. Macari, himself a teetotaller, deplored players who over-indulged in alcohol.

The team made a good start under Macari, winning his debut match, an Old Firm game at Ibrox, 2–1 and then losing just once in the league before the end of 1993. Celtic had moved into a position where the eternal optimists among the support believed they had a chance of challenging Rangers for the Scottish League title, but that optimism was undone on New Year's Day 1994 when Rangers raced into a 3–0 lead by half-time in the Old Firm match at Celtic Park. Some of the more impatient Celtic supporters, thoroughly frustrated by the board's refusal to make way for fresh people and ideas, launched missiles at the directors' box. The board, in November 1993, had turnéd down a solid takeover bid that had been spearheaded by Fergus McCann and Brian Dempsey, and the directors who were in place had shown no signs of making progress with Celtic's problems. That 4–2 Old Firm defeat heralded a difficult opening to 1994 for Celtic. The last lingering hopes of success in the League were destroyed by a disastrous January that saw Celtic slip to fifth in the league and get knocked out of the Scottish Cup at Motherwell.

Macari had been appointed because of his ability to work to a tight budget successfully in England's lower divisions and now, at Celtic, he began to use the same methods that had brought him his previous successes. That meant he trawled the bargain-basement English market, which he knew best, to bring in low-cost signings. Goalkeeper Carl Muggleton was bought for £150,000 from Leicester City; 33-year-old centre-forward Wayne Biggins arrived from Barnsley; Lee Martin, a skilful full-back who was out of favour at Manchester United, cost £350,000; ex-Aberdeen forward Willie Falconer came in for £350,000 from Sheffield United.

These signings were not designed to excite the support – they were the result of a manager working within a tight budget to obtain best possible value – but the sight of players such as the lumbering Biggins, who was never of true Celtic standard, served only to increase the discontentment of those who were aggrieved at the board and all its works. On a more basic, practical level, even the modest outlay that was involved in those signings, in combination with plummeting gates and associated revenues, led to Celtic exceeding their overdraft limit and on 3 March 1994, the Bank of Scotland informed the board that they were ready to call in the receivers. One day later, with Celtic on the verge of bankruptcy, the directors finally ceded control of Celtic to Fergus McCann.

McCann introduced a new way of running a football club under which every employee was to be regularly held accountable for their actions. Lou Macari was expected, along with managers of all other departments at the football club, to attend regular progress meetings to advise of his plans and his ongoing progress in football matters. This demand was resisted by Macari, as were other requests from Fergus McCann, now his managing director. On 14 June 1994,

Macari made a telephone call to McCann from the airport just before he flew out to the USA to take a family holiday and watch the World Cup. McCann told Macari he was dismissed from his post as manager of Celtic. He had been in place for less than eight months.

That dismissal prompted Macari to launch an action against Celtic later in 1994 for breach of contract. Three years later, presiding judge Lady Cosgrove considered eight weeks of evidence at the Court of Session in Edinburgh to make an 80-page judgement in which she ruled that Macari had indeed been in breach of his contract with Celtic. Lady Cosgrove described Macari as 'amiable but not particularly astute' and rejected his claim for approximately £400,000 [the equivalent of almost three years' salary for Macari] in damages from Celtic. Macari was said by her to have failed to have appreciated the change to the regime brought about when McCann became managing director.

Lady Cosgrove held that a contributory factor to Macari's dismissal was that he still lived in Stoke-on-Trent, in the north of England, whilst he was manager of Celtic. The judge had heard evidence from McCann that, within weeks of taking over at Celtic, he wrote a warning letter to Macari highlighting his failure to move to the Glasgow area. 'In that situation,' Lady Cosgrove ruled, 'the residence term was important and Mr Macari's breach of the clause [in his contract] was no technicality but was contributing to an unsatisfactory situation where he was absent from Celtic Park for much of the week. Looking simply at the clause and Mr Macari's failure to move his home to Glasgow I am satisfied that he was in material breach of his contract with Celtic at the time of his dismissal.' She decided that Macari had been guilty of 'a wilful and continuing act of disobedience of a legitimate and reasonable order of the employer'. On that basis alone, she continued, unless there were exceptional circumstances, Celtic had been entitled to dismiss him as manager. Lady Cosgrove commented that in her opinion McCann was 'a rather devious individual' and an 'uncompromising and somewhat arrogant employer who expected unquestioning compliance' and she rejected a counter-claim by Celtic that sought to recover some of the £250,000 the club had paid to Stoke City when it had recruited Macari in 1993.

'Obviously I am hugely disappointed at the outcome,' said Macari in February 1998 when Lady Cosgrove made her ruling. 'I will be meeting my legal representatives to study the findings to see if there are any grounds for an appeal.' A brief statement from Celtic summed up the official point of view inside the club: 'Celtic is very pleased with the judgement, which was as expected.'

Lou Macari went ahead with an appeal, which was heard in 1999 by three appeal court judges at the Court of Session: Lord President Rodger of Earlsferry, Lord Caplan and Lord Marnoch. They rejected Macari's appeal, leaving him saddled with the problem of what to do about an enormous legal bill. Lord Rodger said, 'I readily acknowledge that from the outset Mr McCann and his colleagues on the board wanted to replace Mr Macari as manager of the club. All that is, however, a far cry from saying that the instructions which Mr McCann issued were spurious, inspired by an intention of driving Mr Macari from his job. I am satisfied that, while the managing director was undoubtedly hoping that Mr Macari would be replaced, he was of the view that, in the meantime, the manager, who was being paid a large salary, should attend more often at Celtic Park.'

Jock Stein would often fondly recall Lou Macari the player rolling up through the car park at Celtic Park before training, with his nose stuck in the racing pages of the newspaper. His careful assessment of the odds had been matched on the pitch, where he had been a pocket calculator of a player who could assess a situation swiftly and surely; a goalscorer who relied on craft and timing to put the ball in the net. It had been very different for him as Celtic manager. Returning to Celtic Park had been the biggest gamble in Lou Macari's life and, with the odds stacked against him, it was a calculated gamble that had failed spectacularly.

TEN

Tommy Burns – Twists and Turns

Tommy Burns' trilogy of seasons as Celtic manager brought enormous life and colour to the club that he loves. The unfolding drama of those three years would make a perfect three-act play – a tragedy with the sympathetic figure of Burns at its centre. In the first act he would struggle against the odds and after numerous setbacks finally achieve success by winning the Scottish Cup just before the curtain closes for the first interval. The second act would establish him as a manager of the world, a well-loved success, as he produces a Celtic team in the club's finest traditions. The third act would then see his demise as manager as he is brought down with a crash before making a poignant exit. As Burns sums it up, 'I probably did about 15 or 20 years as a manager in those 3 years.'

The Tommy Burns era at Celtic proved to be a mass of contradictions. Multiple tensions underpinned his time as manager yet he restored to the team its traditionally free-flowing, attacking style in tandem with winning football matches. He brought the club its first trophy in six long years, yet soon after achieving that success he almost quit. As a local boy and a popular former player, he was a manager in the traditional Celtic mould, yet he ushered in the era of big-name, highly-paid, foreign players that paved the way for the multinational Celtic teams of the late 1990s and early 2000s.

David Low, the financier who put in a power of work to help Fergus McCann engineer the 1994 takeover of Celtic, liaised closely with the new managing director as he sought a manager for the club in the summer of 1994. Low explains how the special circumstances of the time influenced their choice. 'In taking over a football club there were a million and one things needing done. It is necessary to attend to a stadium and the team and that's just the big things. There is no way on earth that within a season or two we were going to be on a par with Rangers and swap League titles year to year with them. We were going to achieve little as far as I'm concerned.

'We're not going to achieve much within the next five years on the park because unless we deal with the stadium, unless money coming in goes towards building the stadium, you're not really going to have a future. You've got to build that stadium with 60,000 seats so that you're secure for the future. So you're going to have to have a good manager, a manager whom the supporters are going to be patient with, and you are going to have to have a manager who will work within a lesser budget than Rangers until the stadium is built and understand and accept that, somebody who is a good manager, somebody who is a Celtic guy, somebody whom the fans will be patient with. That's obviously Tommy Burns, who was doing pretty well at Kilmarnock.

'Tommy was a Celtic man with a good record so it seemed a good choice. I was asked my opinion and it was a choice I supported at the time and he became the Celtic manager; not because I recommended him, I think quite a few other people recommended him as well. Fergus and the board at the time were a board with a lack of football experience. Fergus had all his Canadian and American experience so he had to sound out people whose judgement he trusted. There were a lot of opinions taken at the time and the name that came up was Tommy Burns.

'Now the important thing about Fergus is that Fergus absolutely and utterly believes that certain people have skills and abilities and you employ people to do jobs based on those skills and those abilities. That applies to catering, finance, marketing and to football management. Fergus McCann would never dream of interfering in the manager's job in any shape or form. The object is to employ somebody whom you think is the best for the job and let him get on with it and to work in tandem with that person on an all-for-one and one-for-all basis. You all trust each other and you all share the same objective and that's the betterment of Celtic on and off the park.

'Burns and subsequent managers were employed on that basis and to demonstrate the principle I remember specifically that there was a game against Kilmarnock towards the end of the takeover season at Rugby Park, when Lou Macari was still manager, and Celtic were atrocious that day. I remember someone heavily involved in the takeover, who will have to remain nameless for the moment, was so annoyed he wanted to go storming into the dressing-room and give the players a really strong dressing-down and Fergus McCann went ballistic and stopped the guy doing such a thing.

'Fergus McCann's attitude was, "Yes, they were bad but what happens in the dressing-room is exclusively the province of the manager. You don't know anything about football management, I don't know anything about football management, the manager is responsible for the players and the results, the manager can sort out that dressing-room and if we've got anything to say about it we'll say it to the manager." I saw that very early on and that's a very important, very positive attitude, one that any board should have.

'Fergus McCann had two particularly strong principles with regard to football management. You want to employ a good manager and, as with employing anybody in any walk of life, you take advice, you take references. Fergus and I could never see the logic, if you needed a manager and had a shortlist, of asking other managers what they thought about the manager you wanted because it's an old boys' network, nobody ever says anything bad about anybody so you never get the correct picture. You always get a skewed, mason-style, old-boys' network-type assessment so if you want an objective analysis it's key to ask the right people the right questions. Managers consistently get jobs with big fat contracts on the wrong basis and more often than not get big pay-offs. That was anathema to Fergus.

'The other view Fergus had was never to let a manager near the money. Not because you can't trust them – managers are not, as a rule, dishonest but some are and there are a whole lot of bungs etcetera. It goes back to employing horses for courses. He had the US-style of management. You employ a first-team coach, not a manager, and he coaches or manages but when it comes to players coming in and going out, it is a general manager that does that and in the absence of a general manager doing that, Fergus would do that until we employed a general manager. Again, this is very American, very twenty-first century, very correct, because what does a manager know about contract negotiations? Why does a manager want to get involved in contract negotiations? You can answer that one yourself. Fergus and the board expected all managers to adhere to these principles.'

Tommy Burns' initial year as manager proved a severely testing one. He was 37 years old at the time of his appointment on 12 July 1994 and had had just two years' prior experience of management, at Kilmarnock, during which he had led the Rugby Park side to promotion to the Premier League. Burns' assistant at Kilmarnock, Billy Stark, joined Celtic along with him but Kilmarnock demanded compensation for the loss of their management team. The Scottish Football League fined Celtic £100,000 over their supposedly improper approach to Burns, a manager of another member club, an approach that broke the rules governing League clubs. The SFA, after a cantankerous dispute that dragged on for almost a year, also fined Celtic £200,000 for the removal of Burns and Stark from Kilmarnock after a tribunal had sat in judgement on the case.

It added a layer of difficulty to Burns' task of reconstructing the football club, but he focused on creating a good atmosphere at the club for the players. He also encouraged players to attend supporters' functions regularly in an attempt to improve relations with the club's followers. An added complication to his job was that the club had to play their home games in the 1994–95 season at Hampden Park because the terraces at Celtic Park had been demolished to make way for an all-seater stadium. Hampden was unpopular with the supporters; it was rarely full for Celtic's run-of-the-mill League games and consequently lacked atmosphere.

Burns, within days of becoming manager, transferred goalkeeper Carl Muggleton from Celtic to Stoke. Muggleton had been a Lou Macari buy from the lower reaches of the English League and Burns wanted to clear such players out of the club. 'A lot of these guys,' says Burns, 'were never good enough to play for Celtic in the first place so we weren't going to get the money, perhaps, that we had paid for them and nobody was going to pay them the money that this club was paying them. So it was a double-edged sword; nobody was going to pay top dollar for players that had failed here but when they were leaving they were still wanting the same money that they had had when they were here. So that was the problem. I was just wanting to cut my losses; I was not going to be bogged down and judged on somebody else's players.'

Celtic started the 1994–95 season brightly, beating Rangers 2–0 at Ibrox and easing into the League Cup final but then a sequence of draws and defeats saw the team create an unwanted Celtic record of going 11 League matches without a victory. That run was crowned in November 1994 with a shock defeat, after extra-time and penalties, to First Division Raith Rovers in the League Cup final. Celtic had played well enough in the opening stages before going 1–0 down in 19 minutes after poor defensive cover allowed Steve Crawford to open the scoring. Andy Walker equalised and with six minutes to go Charlie Nicholas made it 2–1 to Celtic. Three minutes from time, Gordon Dalziel, looking offside, headed a close-range equaliser after Gordon Marshall had spilled the ball into his path.

'After the first 15 or 20 minutes,' says Burns of that final, 'I think we became very nervous. I knew the players were very uptight about it in view of the fact that it was the first Cup final in four years. So all the pressure was on them; incredible pressure was on them from the support in view of the fact that it was Raith Rovers and the supporters expected the score to be 4–0 or 5–0 but you've got to live with that. Equally, we knew that we still had to go out and do the job and anything can happen in football, as it did.

'We did everything right except finishing – it was the old story. We kept missing them and kept missing them and then Raith went up the park and with literally their first shot at goal in the second half it hits Gordon Marshall's chest and it's in to make it 2–2. Then you think, "We're not going to come back from that." I think the players just suddenly thought to themselves, "It's been snatched away from us." One minute they were thinking, "After five years we've done it." Next thing, it hasn't happened for them and I just don't think we could get ourselves up for the extra-time, when Raith were possibly the better team. We looked like a team that had possibly resigned ourselves to the fact that we weren't going to get there. It was bitterly, bitterly disappointing because of the fact that they had played so well in the game. Over the 90 minutes they had played so very, very well. Yet, ultimately people will remember it as the day we got beaten by Raith Rovers. In saying that, you get up the next day and you've got to go and start again. You don't just lie down and cry about it. There is no point in being in football management or in any job if you can't react to disappointment.'

Three days later, prior to a League match with Hibernian at Easter Road, Burns went among the faithful who had travelled to Edinburgh to support the team. The Celtic support like nothing better than a manager who acknowledges their presence and importance. Burns' gesture was rewarded by those terracing troopers assuring him that they were still behind him as manager. 'I had been with the players and had done everything I could with them. They were warming themselves up. I sat and had a blether with the supporters and they were telling me not to be downhearted and to continue to give it a go. That was unbelievable for me to be in there among them and for them to cheer me up. We helped each other.'

Tommy was actively involved on the training ground and Billy Stark worked around about him and acted as a sounding-board. The chemistry between the two was good and after that defeat by Raith Rovers, Burns and Stark put their heads together to discuss the best way forward. The defeat had concentrated their minds and, if not quite a good thing, it accelerated the process of change at the club. They told a core group of half-a-dozen players whom they had identified as being useful professionals that they were going to be part of the club's advance forward from that point. Those players were told that a lot of changes were going to be made but that they would be the few guaranteed to remain at the club. Others would soon be departing

Two excellent performances in their replayed semi-final with Hibernian in April 1995 took Celtic into the Scottish Cup final, where they would again face First Division opposition, this time in the shape of Airdrie. There was again huge pressure on the players for the Airdrie match and before the final Burns stressed to the players time and again that they could be the players who could make history as the team that ended the lengthy sequence during which Celtic had failed to win a trophy. They responded with a gritty performance that was settled when two new signings, left-back Tosh

McKinlay and striker Pierre van Hooijdonk, combined for a memorable headed goal by Dutchman van Hooijdonk in a forgettable match.

Van Hooijdonk had joined Celtic for a £1.3 million fee from NAC Breda of Holland in January 1995 and he joined a team that played in fits and starts that season, finishing fourth in the Premier League, 18 points behind champions Rangers. 'Too many of them were far too inconsistent,' says Burns. 'We were entitled to expect better from that kind of quality of player. They would play well in one game and then you would have to wait another two or three games to see that kind of form again. Equally, we were aware of the fact that that wasn't something that happened only when we came to the club. That had been happening the season before and the season before and the season before. So we were looking at that team over that season to see what we needed. I think a lot of the time the inconsistency was down to the fact that they were playing in front of a crowd that was very frustrated and if, early in the game, things didn't go well for them the crowd would get on top of them and they would go into their shells. There wasn't a magic wand we could wave; they just had to play through that. They are all Celtic guys in the support but they can be as difficult as anybody else and once they get on your case they can make it difficult for you. We kept saying to the players, "You have to play through that. If you work hard and chase and work hard for each other they will appreciate the fact." You also had players with big reputations who were giving you one good game in four or five and thinking that because they were supposedly better players than the other guys they could get away with that – and they had been getting away with that for seasons and that was something else on which we had to stamp down.'

In the summer of 1995, on a blisteringly hot day, Tommy Burns sat in the airless, poky, windowless cubby-hole that serves as the manager's office at Celtic Park on the first anniversary of his appointment as Celtic manager. It was 12 months to the day since he had taken on that role, and although the Scottish Cup had been hauled in just a few weeks earlier, the manager's frustration showed itself clearly as he described his relationship with Fergus McCann. 'It has been very volatile, up and down.' As he looked to the future that summer's day the outlook was not, as far as Burns could see, entirely bright. 'Knowing the way he is and the way I am, it won't be always smooth. He will always be wanting to get in his tuppenceworth and I'll always want to get my tuppenceworth in but sometimes that's a healthy thing.'

Burns had spent that summer looking for top-quality international players of an impressive standard. It was a real departure for the club to change policy in the direction of bringing in foreign players of flair and experience. It was an ambitious attempt to attain consistency and to make progress by drastically improving the technical capabilities of the squad. It was exciting for the support to know that Celtic were now looking to import top-class talent from abroad. Burns had, in that 1995 close-season, initially identified the Russian World Cup player Dmitri Radchenko, an attacking wide player, then Marc Degryse, another World Cup attacker, this time with Belgium, before targeting French international winger David Ginola. All three signings fell through after they had failed to reach agreement with the club over contractual matters although there did not always appear to be genuine intent on the part of the players involved to actually come to Celtic. Ginola, for example, had found out Celtic's terms before using them as a benchmark to negotiate a deal with Newcastle United.

Burns expressed frustration that none of those players had been snared by the club and questioned why so many players were slipping through the club's net – although the manager did concede that their demands were extravagant. 'It's a wicked old world, football, now,' Burns commented that summer of 1995. 'It's dog eat dog and the money that's going about just now is crazy. It's no longer a game; it's big business. I don't feel comfortable about doing that, to be honest with you. We never made big money here as players and we were very successful players here but that's it. It's sink or swim and you've got to go with the flow. Otherwise, you can set your standards lower and bring in players and try to make your progress gradually.'

The missed transfer that really made Burns angry that summer involved a player with a much lower profile than those other signing targets: Gordan Petric, a tough, functional Yugoslavian centre-back. Burns had wanted the player but instead Petric moved to Rangers that summer. 'That was very hard to take,' says Burns. 'At the time, we were in a training camp and I said to Billy Stark, "That's it, I'm resigning. I'll go back and say 'That's me finished.' I'm not putting up with that." Billy Stark said to me, "That's one way to look at it. The other way to look at it is that we stick it out. We're here to try to stop this nine-in-a-row thing. If another guy comes in, it's going to take him a year to get things set up the way he wants and by that time Rangers will be even further down the road to the nine-in-a-row. So I think there is more about you than to walk away." I gave it a little bit of thought and then I said to him a bit later, "You're right."'

During that first season, McCann and Burns had agreed that the managing director would handle all transfer business. 'After the first year that I was there,' says Burns, 'I was quite happy to agree on that, provided it was done when I wanted it to be done.' McCann felt that financial prudence was essential because an overall balance had to be struck between the cost of building the new stadium, strengthening the first-team pool and erasing the overdraft of £5.3 million. The club's first public share issue, in January 1995, had been oversubscribed and had raised £13.8 million whilst a rights issue had raised £12.3 million, of which £9 million had been invested by McCann. The early results of McCann's careful financial planning were indisputably visible in August 1995 when the new North Stand was opened at Celtic Park. The club had spent close to £18 million on that first of three phases of stadium reconstruction and this hugely impressive, two-tiered stand held almost 27,000, which, in conjunction with the South Stand, created a capacity of almost 35,000. These two stands faced each other, with enormous gaps at each end of the stadium, ready to be filled, at a commensurate multi-million pound cost, in each of the next two years. The support responded to this homecoming by scrambling for season tickets and as the 1995–96 season began, Celtic had a record 26,000 season-ticket holders. The ground would be full to its temporary capacity for every game. The ribbon was cut to open the new stand by Rod Stewart, prior to a friendly with Newcastle United, who included Ginola in their line-up. Celtic also had a new signing, McCann having authorised the spending of a club record £2.2 million on German international Andreas Thom at the very end of the summer of 1995.

Van Hooijdonk, tall and dangerous in the air, worked well with the diminutive Thom, who shuttled around at speed. Paul McStay and John Collins in midfield provided the forwards with good service and the addition of the two continentals provided a real impetus for Burns' side. The 1995–96 season would see them playing some great football with a great level of consistency. Everyone involved drew a lot of satisfaction from seeing a team play the game the way Burns wanted it to be played, at a high tempo, with a good quality of football and winning a lot of games in sumptuous style. Burns thoroughly enjoyed himself that year as Celtic and Rangers fought it out for the Premier League title in the closest Old Firm duel for the championship since the 1978–79 season.

Morten Wieghorst, Burns' seventh signing, was bought for £600,000 from Dundee to stiffen the midfield in December 1995. This brought the overall outlay to £7 million. His signings had all proved successful ones, and the manager had the full confidence of his players. Despite that, the team, good as it was to watch, just lacked that little bit of penetration required to beat Rangers. The Ibrox side knocked Celtic out of both domestic cups and beat Celtic once in the League. The other three Old Firm matches in 1995–96 ended in draws. Celtic finished the season undefeated in the League away from home for the first time since the 1916–17 season and set a new Celtic record by going for 31 League matches unbeaten. Their season's tally, unfortunately, contained 11 draws, so although Celtic lost just once in the League whilst Rangers lost three times, it was the Ibrox men who took the League title by four points.

It had been an altogether smoother ride for Burns that season but it was not without its frustrations. He had attempted to bring in Portuguese striker Jorge Cadete in February 1996 and the player had even been introduced to the crowd before a match with Partick Thistle that month. The injection of Cadete, Burns had hoped, would give Celtic the additional spurt required to go on and take the title. Instead, Cadete would not make his Celtic debut until April 1996, by which time Celtic's hopes of winning the League were fast slipping away. It was later admitted by the SFA that their chief executive, James Farry, had acted negligently in processing the necessary documentation for Cadete's transfer. That not only delayed the player's League debut but prevented him playing in a semi-final of the Scottish Cup between Celtic and Rangers, which Celtic lost 2–0. The Cadete episode resulted in an independent commission of inquiry ruling, in 1999, that the SFA had acted negligently. The SFA paid Celtic compensation and Farry was sacked for gross misconduct. The slow-grinding wheels of justice did nothing for Tommy Burns, who was deprived of the services of a proven goalscorer at a crucial stage of the 1995–96 season.

'Then we went into the final year,' adds Burns, 'and, with the nine-in-a-row thing, by that time it was a case of handling pressure.' Burns was also introduced to the difficulties of dealing with competing continental egos. His squad was now top-heavy with quality attacking players: van Hooijdonk, top scorer in Scotland with 32 goals in the 1995–96 season; Thom, his skilful, productive partner that season; Cadete, a direct, fast striker, who was now ready to be a regular starter; and Paolo Di Canio, an Italian winger who had been acquired from AC Milan during the summer of 1996 for a very reasonable fee of £1 million.

'With Cadete coming in,' explains Burns, 'that produced another ego thing because van Hooijdonk and Thom had become the fans' big favourites. Then Cadete coming seemed to take a wee bit of the glory away [from them] and definitely created a wee bit of friction there; they would be vying to see who was the most popular. Then at the start of the next season we brought in Di Canio and he instantly became a fans' favourite. So there were a lot of big players there. They were all great players but they felt they were big enough and strong enough to say things themselves if they thought they weren't getting looked after particularly well . . . and the press are always looking for big-name players to have something to say about any situation. So I would be trying to keep the lid on it and keep them happy and then they would come out and say something against Fergus McCann. As a manager I was trying to stop the nine-in-a-row and to keep the players happy. I didn't want people outside to perceive the club as being in turmoil. I was then accused of not being able to keep the players under control and being too emotional on the sidelines and upsetting the players that way and not being able to handle the dressing-room, which was rubbish.'

Van Hooijdonk was demanding that his contract should be reviewed in light of his good performances for the team. 'To be fair,' says Burns, 'McCann did look at van Hooijdonk's contract and made him a counter-proposal, which he wouldn't accept. Things were too far gone by then because van Hooijdonk had started to mess us about a bit. He thought he should be playing all the time and started to do other wee things that were causing us problems. He was doing things like coming back late from internationals, taking another day. I had told him he could play in a testimonial match for his pal in Holland, which he did do. I found out that he should have been insured by the club so I told him just to watch what he was doing in the game, as it was only a bounce game. It was later pointed out to me just what the consequences could have been if he had been injured. So I said to him afterwards, "Look, we got away with it this time but make sure you don't do anything like that again." Then he went away and did the same thing again. He played in another testimonial, despite me telling him not to do so. Then the press, being the press, found out about it and that then caused a problem between him and I, which, ultimately, ended in us selling him on to Forest for £4 million.

'The club needed those players. We could never have reached the levels we did or have gone and challenged for the League with the group of players we had. They lifted the team and people enjoyed watching them. If anything, the problem they caused me was trying to play the four of them in the one team. There were some games in which we could get away with that. There were other games, at the top level, where we couldn't get away with it. I think they all had something to offer positively going forward but it was defensively where playing them caused us a problem. I remember playing Hamburg and playing the four of them. I realised five minutes into the game that that was a mistake because we were already a goal down and Hamburg were causing us all sorts of problems. When they attacked we were four players down. As you go along you realise the need for balance in a team – it is all about getting the right blend. All those dressing-room things came to a head. The van Hooijdonk thing became a problem but we addressed the problem very quickly – we just moved him on for £3 million more than we paid for him. So that was very good business.'

That home leg with SV Hamburg resulted in a 2–0 defeat and the result was repeated in the away leg, knocking Celtic out of the 1996–97 UEFA Cup in the first round proper. It equalled Celtic's highest-ever aggregate defeat in Europe, which had been set one year previously with a 4–0 aggregate defeat to Paris Saint Germain in the European Cup-Winners' Cup. Celtic had by then also toppled out of the 1996–97 League Cup, losing 1–0 to Hearts in between the two Hamburg ties but they were again competing closely with Rangers in the Premier League. That season's Old Firm matches would hold the key to the destination of the 1996–97 Premier League title and in the first of the four League fixtures Celtic had been desperately unlucky to lose 2–0 at Ibrox. By the time of the second match between the big two, Celtic held a narrow advantage at the top of the table. After eight minutes centre-back Brian O'Neil slipped and gave away possession to Brian Laudrup, who strode on to score. Van Hooijdonk missed a penalty, as did Paul Gascoigne for Rangers, but this time Rangers had had more of the play and had missed a number of chances. Celtic had defended high up the park, leaving lots of space behind the back four and making them vulnerable to the break, something at which Rangers, with Laudrup in their ranks, were expert.

Celtic still hung on to top spot after that defeat but a 2–2 home draw with Hearts on the final day of November 1996, in which Di Canio became Celtic's tenth sending-off of the season, saw Celtic slip back to second place. They lost the third Old Firm League match, at New Year, by 3–1 and the decider, in March, by 1–0 at Celtic Park. Rangers had clinched nine titles in succession, equalling in number, if not in style, the feat of Jock Stein's 1966–74 Celtic side. 'That must be one of the worst Old Firm games ever seen,' says Burns of that March match. 'There was just so much pressure on the players. We lost a horrendous goal; there was a misheader and then a miskick on the goalline yet before that Di Canio smashed the ball off the bar from a free-kick. If that had gone in, the whole thing would have changed for us. Football depends so much on luck.'

When Celtic then lost to First Division Falkirk in a replayed Scottish Cup semi-final, Burns could see the writing on the wall. He had signed a three-year contract on becoming manager in 1994 and had received no indication at any time that this would be extended when it expired in the middle of 1997. 'I was never in the business here of doing what I always felt was best for me,' says Burns. 'I was trying to do what I thought was the best thing for the football club and if that meant upsetting McCann or telling him something to his face at a board meeting then I was quite happy to do that. I was never the most important issue here; the most important issue was that the club moved forward.'

Burns, at the very beginning of 1997, had chanced upon some internal documents that indicated he would be leaving the club. A variety of people had all had their say about what they believed his faults to be, such as that he upset the players through his antics on the sidelines, that Burns was unable to handle the dressing-room and that he played favourites in the team.

'The favourites thing was another thing,' says Burns. 'You've got players there that you can rely on; maybe not the most spectacular players but they've got this club at heart and you know what you're going to get with them. You need that type of player here. Grant was one of them, McStay would have been another; but they were main players a far as I was concerned. I had been fined a couple of times by the FA for saying things to referees or to linesmen. The people that said those things had had ample opportunity to see it from my point of view; they had sat in and listened an awful lot of times to the problems I was having. Even now, if the exact same thing happened I would still be as emotionally involved and as passionate about the football team. If I felt there was somebody that didn't share that or was trying to hold it back then I would still tell them the same thing although I would maybe do it in a different way now.

'I can remember going into a board meeting just prior to leaving and giving them the best summing-up of reasons that I could as to why they should keep me on because after those three years of being here, with all the experiences that I had lived through, then I was surely much better equipped for the job than I had been when I first came in. I was much better equipped for the job. I knew exactly who would be going, who would be staying, how we would be generating money, a number of different things.' That impassioned plea failed to salvage Burns' position as the Celtic manager.

Burns admits that there were many occasions when, through his inexperience as a manager, he did the wrong thing, such as 'talking back to McCann and saying things to him in board meetings. With someone like him, there was only going to be one winner. There were certainly a lot of times when I was at fault for what I said, when I said it and how I said it. That's right but I was driven to that.'

Nine days after the 1–0 defeat in the replay against Falkirk, Burns arranged a meeting with McCann on a Friday evening. 'He paid up the remaining weeks of my contract and made me an offer of some money and in hindsight I should probably just have taken the money. I just refused it and left. I refused the money because I felt it was derisory, considering the contribution we had made over the years in taking the club from where it was to the level we were leaving it at and the quality of players we were leaving and how the season-ticket base had been built up.' The settlement was a lump sum in the nature of tens of thousands of pounds. 'That was stubbornness,' admits Burns. 'Very quickly, later on in life, you realise that, well, that's just football. If they don't want you, then, fine, that's it, OK, take the money and move on. It's just a job like everything else. That's it but I looked on the job of Celtic manager as a labour of love.' Burns had also been offered, by McCann, a position in charge of the club's youth development but, feeling that he had more to contribute to management, Burns declined the offer.

As Billy Stark thinks back to the three-year period he spent as Burns' assistant at Celtic Park, he summarises, 'I don't remember generally the job being too big for Tommy. I think, definitely, if you can get together years and years of experience before going into a job like that it must help you. Obviously we didn't have that so you could then question whether if it had come five years later we would have done much better. I don't know about that. There were circumstances such as the year at Hampden and the stadium being built that would have made things really difficult even for an experienced manager. I think Tommy handled it really well. There are lots of things I am sure he would change in terms of the politics of the thing and how to deal with certain things and I think that is where experience would really tell. I think he would certainly do those things differently. Still, I never, ever think that it was a wrong decision for us to go to Celtic Park at that time, even allowing for all the things that we had to go through. I would never look at it that way.

'I loved every minute I was at that club as player and manager. I would say that the politics brought more pressure on Tommy than having to win League championships and be successful as a manager. I think Fergus in years to come will be looked upon as the right man at the right time and I wouldn't grudge him that. I think he did a great job; he was what was needed to get the job done. He did it the right way, of course he did, when you look at where Celtic are now. Some people suffered because of it and I think his view of Celtic was not comparable with Tommy's. One thing I will say about Fergus is that he never interfered in any shape or form in terms of the football side, other than if the money was there to buy a player or not, which obviously you wouldn't construe as interfering. Those are decisions that have to be made. I think it was Tommy's passion for Celtic that really cost him, with the wee bit lack of experience in dealing with directors of football clubs. I think that's where he would play it differently now because I think Fergus never forgot that first year.'

Tommy Burns was Celtic's longest-serving manager of the 1990s and his 1995–96 team, despite failing to win anything, is fondly remembered by Celtic supporters. Tommy's teams may have been less than solid defensively but the manager felt that after Celtic's moribund period he had to focus on fast, flowing football to revive the interest of the support. 'Tommy's style was playing football,' says Jackie McNamara, an attacking full-back in that side. 'It was great. I think anyone would say that we were brilliant to watch. Although he got criticised a lot for attacking, and sometimes we got caught on the break, I think it was always worth watching us. It was brilliant to play in, to get forward and then get back. The pressure Tommy was under, to stop the nine-in-a-row, was immense. He was so passionate about the club and that obviously made him a bit fired-up. I think if everything had been normal, and there had not been so much pressure, Tommy would have been a lot more quiet and laid-back. I thought he was magnificent as a manager here.'

Five years on from his departure, it was good to see Tommy Burns back at Celtic Park as player development officer, with the vital task of piecing together a youth development system fit for the demands of the early 21st century. He had spent just more than a season as manager at Reading after his departure from Celtic, but his time at the Madjeski Stadium was not a particularly successful one and he was dismissed by Reading in mid-September 1999 before returning to Celtic, at the request of Kenny Dalglish, in the spring of 2000. Burns was also, in early 2002, appointed assistant manager to Berti Vogts, the new coach of the Scottish national team. Vogts is the figurehead, with Burns the man with responsibility for the players' preparation on the training field. Mental scars were inflicted on this emotional man by his turbulent period as Celtic manager. Even now, discussion of that era can make Tommy Burns choke with anger. His successor as Celtic manager proved to be a very different type of individual.

ELEVEN

Wim Jansen – Going Dutch

Johnnie Wilson looked down from the stand at the San Siro stadium in Milan and marvelled at the skills of one man as Celtic faced Feyenoord in the 1970 European Cup final. The Celtic scout's attention had not, unfortunately, been captured by the doings of anyone in the green-and-white hoops. Nor had his attention been engaged by Ove Kindvall, Feyenoord's speedy Swede, or by the crafty midfielder Wim van Hanegem. The object of Wilson's attention was one Wim Jansen, a midfielder with an unhurried, simple style who grabbed the game and pushed and pulled it in any direction he chose as the Rotterdam side seized hold of the first major trophy in Dutch football history.

Jansen was a regular for both Feyenoord and the vivacious, exciting Dutch national team throughout the 1970s, helping Holland to reach the final at both the 1974 and the 1978 World Cups. Although the midfielder had played a prominent part in both of those finals and had since added some extensive coaching experience to his impressive CV, when he arrived in Scotland to take charge of the Celtic team in 1997 his qualifications were doubted severely by the media. He had won respect in Belgium and Holland for his coaching there in the '80s and early '90s, working alongside Dick Advocaat at Dutch side Dordrecht between 1988 and '91 after a year in charge of KSC Lokeren of Belgium. He had been joint head coach of Feyenoord with Wim van Hanegem from 1991 to 1993 and the same duo had coached the Saudi Arabian national team in the year prior to the 1994 World Cup before both were sacked abruptly. His most recent appointment before becoming head coach at Celtic had seen him spend two years as coach of San Frecce Hiroshima in the Japanese League, a post which he had left in December 1996.

To the Scottish press, Jansen was an unknown and his appearance helped contribute to the jesting in the media that followed the announcement of his appointment. Atop his head perched a curly late-'70s hairstyle that, by July 1997 when he was appointed Celtic manager, looked odd both because it was well beyond its fashionable wear-by date and because Jansen was now 50 years old and comfortably middle-aged. Although it appeared to be a perm, his hairstyle, like much else about Jansen was not what it seemed: it was curled by nature. His craggy looks and copious locks gave him the appearance of an absent-minded professor or a bouncy, benevolent bachelor uncle; to those disposed to be cruel, as many of Celtic's critics were, he could be portrayed as a man in the lay-by of life.

The appointment of a foreign coach at Celtic thoroughly confused the Scottish media. The press had had no idea who was getting the job because the club's new general manager Jock Brown and Fergus McCann had made it a priority to ensure there were no leaks before the appointment was announced. On the morning of the day Jansen was announced as coach, *The Scotsman* had confidently devoted its entire back page to the exclusive news that a Portuguese coach, Artur Jorge, was to be installed as the new manager. So when Jansen walked through the door at his introductory press conference, the situation was so confused that one press person exclaimed incredulously, 'Robert Prytz – the new Celtic manager – what's going on here?' Prytz had been a perm-sporting midfielder for Glasgow Rangers in the early 1980s.

None of the furore over Jansen's appointment or the barbs aimed in his direction by the media ruffled him in the least. This was small beer in comparison to some of his previous experiences.

Jansen had been at the epicentre of controversy in 1974 during the World Cup final between Holland and West Germany. A penalty was given against him after he had missed his tackle on German forward Bernd Holzenbein. Holland had been leading 1–0 and the penalty enabled the Germans to equalise and go on and win the trophy. The Dutch were convinced that Holzenbein had dived and English referee Jack Taylor admitted years later that the decision against

Jansen had been wrong. Jansen was again a key component in the Dutch national team when they reached their second final, once again against the hosts, this time Argentina, in 1978. The atmosphere before the final in Buenos Aires was so vicious that Jansen and his team-mates had feared for their lives in the event of winning the match, which they lost 3–1. At club level, Jansen had switched from Feyenoord to Ajax late in his career, a move that brought extreme wrath and some violence down on his head. So a few cheap, paper-weight jibes were unlikely to trouble him too much as he began his career at Celtic.

To the Celtic support Jansen was the manager, but his official title, significantly, was that of head coach. Fergus McCann had made two major decisions relating to the management of the football team that summer. He had put in place a new structure that had seen the appointment of a general manager to work with a head coach. The general manager would be expected to carry out numerous and varied administrative duties, such as producing a plan for the long-term development of what was now termed the 'football division' of the club, dealing with contractual matters relating to players and staff, negotiating with players' agents, and the supervision of staff, including the head coach. The head coach would be responsible only for the coaching of the first-team and selection of the team.

McCann's other key decision had been to switch to a foreign coach. Continental European coaches were comfortable with the general manager-head coach axis, which was almost alien to the British game. 'He didn't want anybody in the head coach role who was influenced by the British football culture,' says Jock Brown, who had been chosen by McCann to take on the role of general manager. Brown was, at that time, best known as BBC Scotland's football commentator but had also specialised in sports law and negotiation at a legal practice in Glasgow. His combination of legal and football knowledge had convinced McCann that Jock Brown, the brother of the then Scottish national coach Craig Brown, had the correct qualifications to be general manager.

'Jock Brown was in my opinion a sound appointment,' comments David Low, the man whose financial advice had helped McCann gain control of the club. 'I mention Jock Brown because he is relevant to

Jansen. Jock Brown is not the most perfect guy in the world but he had all the requisite experience to carry off the general manager's job efficiently and professionally. He was doomed to failure for all the wrong reasons, for all the usual reasons. This is what the critics would say: he's a Hun, which he's not. Then there's all the back-biting from all the journalists he used to work with, "Look where he's ended up and who does he think he is?" So he's doomed for that second reason.

'Also, Jock Brown did like getting involved in football things, footie evenings, footie banter, mucking about with the football guys, talking about football things and I'm not saying he interfered – because he didn't – but there is a snobbishness amongst the football fraternity. There is an unspoken ranking system whereby the most respected people in football among the football mafia are those who played for their country and captained their country. So Jock Brown's contributions were never accepted and never sought. In short, if you don't have the support of the fans, the media or the manager you're on to plums!'

Brown believes that McCann's new set-up was a good one, but he felt it needed some fine-tuning before it hit the road. Even as he had considered whether to accept the offer of the job of general manager he had questioned some of McCann's specifications. 'He was utterly determined that the head coach, as he called him,' comments Brown on McCann, 'would only do pre- and post-match interviews and nothing else and the general manager in his terms would be the connecting party and the spokesperson on the football side for the football club. That isn't workable because the press in this country are not prepared to deal with anybody except the guy that picks the team.' Brown was aware this would cause problems and, along with public relations officer Peter McLean, argued the point with McCann prior to taking up his position. McCann was not for changing and was insistent on his specified conditions.

Even as Brown had prepared to get to work in late June 1997, his premonition had begun to take solid, sinister shape. A mischievous newspaper story quoted a prominent member of the Celtic Supporters' Association as stating that Brown was, in his opinion, 'Rangers-minded', hardly the best media plug for his new career at

Celtic. Brown had then run into trouble from two other directions.

On his appointment, one of his initial tasks was to help McCann decide on the most suitable head coach. Jansen, at that stage in June 1997, was one of four candidates for the post. McCann demanded that utter discretion should be maintained during this time and that no leaks should be made to the press as to the new coach's identity. This had led to much frustration on the part of the press and Brown, part of whose remit was to deal with the media, bore the brunt of the blame from pressmen when Jansen took up the post of head coach on 3 July 1997 without their prior knowledge as to his identity.

Brown was also presented with the difficulty of both Paolo Di Canio and Jorge Cadete failing to appear for pre-season training that July of 1997. Both men eventually provided sick notes from their doctors whilst remaining in Italy and Portugal respectively after the summer break. It soon became clear that both were determined to prise hugely improved financial deals from Celtic if they were to return to the club. Di Canio returned to Celtic briefly before hightailing it back to Italy, determined not to return to Scotland. Brown initially decided to play tough, announcing that Di Canio was not for sale, for fear that caving in to the player's pressure for a transfer would set a poor precedent. After there was no sign that Di Canio would return from Rome, Brown eventually decided that the player had to leave the club but publicly did nothing to indicate clearly such a thing in black and white to the press.

Eventually, Di Canio moved to Sheffield Wednesday on 6 August 1997 in part exchange for Regi Blinker but the manner in which Brown conducted relations with the press during the month before Di Canio's transfer infuriated them. He had relished jousting with journalists as they tried to find out what was happening with Di Canio. They had formed the impression from Brown's press conferences that the Italian was not for sale and, as with the appointment of Jansen, reporters had had no advance knowledge of Di Canio's move. They were further infuriated when Brown, the lawyer, stated that Di Canio had been 'traded', not sold. He based that statement on the fact that Blinker had moved to Celtic Park as part of the deal that took Di Canio to Hillsborough yet it was clear that Wednesday, in addition, would have had to have paid Celtic a sizeable fee since Blinker would have been a mere makeweight in the deal. It was not, at the time, Celtic policy to reveal transfer fees but they would have received a substantial sum for the talented Di Canio; the *Rothman's Football Yearbook* lists Di Canio as Celtic's record transfer fee received at £4.7 million. That episode ensured that Brown made long-standing enemies amongst the press from the earliest days of his career as general manager. Their determination to discredit him helped them to discredit simultaneously the new management structure at Celtic Park.

The new set-up meant that Jansen would have no input or interest in players' contracts. Traditionally, the managers of Celtic had been involved in contract negotiations and managers such as Willie Maley, Jock Stein, Billy McNeill and David Hay had used players' pay and bonuses as a means of motivation. This was no longer possible by the late 1990s, when Celtic were recruiting foreign internationals who would not deign to join any club unless they were receiving many thousands of pounds a week. Jansen, as a foreigner, was nonplussed by his absence from any contractual negotiations – it did not make a great deal of difference to him because Jansen was used to employing other methods to motivate players. The new head coach was given a boost when the club let it be known that no less a figure than Johan Cruyff, Jansen's illustrious former Dutch international team-mate, had contacted Celtic to congratulate the club on their choice of Jansen as their new head coach. Cruyff had once stated that Jansen was one of only four men in the world to whom it was worth listening on the subject of football.

Murdo MacLeod was brought back to Celtic during that summer of 1997 to act as reserve-team coach and was quickly promoted to the position of Jansen's assistant: the head coach had specified he wished to have someone alongside him who knew the Scottish football scene. After a poor pre-season and two defeats in Celtic's opening two League games, Jansen's appointment was being questioned loud and long in the papers. The ability of Jansen to control and assess matters swiftly, which he had displayed in the 1970 European Cup final, helped him to turn that situation around quickly.

'When a new coach comes in,' says Murdo MacLeod, 'he will get respect right away because he is the coach but within two or three weeks the players will be judging him and the respect will either remain or he will maybe lose a wee bit of respect, depending on what they think of the guy. I think when they watched Wim in training, right away players were saying, "This is different. This is difficult." He worked in wee sessions with 3 v. 3 in a box, for example, at full pelt before resting them. Five-a-sides would be played at full pace. The players realised what he was talking about and they responded. They would play five-a-sides and he used to stop it all the time if players were not doing what he was wanting them to do. In the first two, three, four weeks he stopped five-a-sides all the time and they must have got fed up with the whole thing. Gradually, over time, he didn't have to stop the five-a-sides because the players started doing what he wanted them to do in games. The five-a-sides were always very competitive and the players, I'm sure, must have enjoyed them.

'He very rarely had the players doing hard running although now and again he would have a wee, short session where the players would be doing sprints in different directions. It was clever because the players did·work hard in their training sessions where it would be 8 v. 8 or 9 v. 8. Everybody would be moving, it would played at a good pace and there was no walking about.' It meant that ball-work was hard work for the players and that they built up their fitness through working flat out with the ball in their training sessions while simultaneously honing their control, passing and teamwork.

'Players were not allowed to walk about,' adds MacLeod, 'they had to keep moving all the time. You will see some teams' strikers lose the ball and you will then see them standing – Wim hated a striker standing even when the ball wasn't close to him. He liked them to be moving all the time because defenders find it hard to mark somebody that is moving all the time. Defenders are watching the ball all the time and they are quite happy for a striker to stand in front of them and wait for the ball and then when the ball comes and the striker makes a run, the defender makes a run.' Instead, as Jansen correctly understood it, if the striker is moving all the time, he pulls defenders around and creates space for team-mates. The most obvious proof of the success of that theory could be seen that 1997–98 season in the shape of Henrik Larsson, whom Jansen had identified as the first player he wanted Celtic to sign in the summer of 1997. Larsson had a clause in his contract stating that he could leave Feyenoord if another club offered a £650,000 fee for his transfer. That modest sum secured the Swedish international's signature for Celtic and Jansen began the business of converting Larsson from being an attacking midfielder into a potent goalscorer and goalmaker. Jansen had initially spotted Larsson playing for Helsingborgs in the Swedish League and had brought him to Feyenoord but after Larsson had been two months at Feyenoord, Jansen left the club following a disagreement with the chairman.

'He wasn't a shouter,' continues MacLeod as he looks back to Jansen's time as head coach. 'He was an organiser, a tactician. I think the players knew that Wim knew what he was talking about, knew how to set up the team, knew how they should play every game. Wim knew his players well and he would go round and speak to them all individually before a game. He would also speak to players through the week to tell them what he wanted from them and they then knew they were playing on the Saturday. It would be a shock to the players if, after speaking to Wim in depth during the week, they were not in the team when it was officially announced on the Saturday.

'The team changed the way they played with every game. It would be slightly different every time and the players would play in slightly different positions. A lot of people wouldn't notice it. As an example, rather than having a player always sitting wide in a particular area, he would maybe bring him in 10 or 15 yards. Lambert was once used as centre-half against Dunfermline. He dropped back off. If a team played a wide left player Tom Boyd would then play against him and Mahé would then be given the role of getting forward into midfield on the left. If a team played somebody wide right, Mahé would then go to left-back. Everything would be shifted around a wee bit depending on circumstances.

'At half-time he would let them come in and settle down for a couple of minutes. Nothing would be said and he would let everybody settle down. He would organise a couple of things but there would be no shouting and bawling. A couple of times he would have a go at someone for saying something out of turn although generally he did like players voicing their opinions; he really liked it when players talked to him, he liked that feedback. They knew their jobs because he would have talked to them all week about what was expected of them. So if anybody wasn't doing their job he would tell that player he needed more from them.'

Paul Lambert, who had signed from European champions Borussia Dortmund in November 1997, became extremely close to Jansen and would often be pulled about to fill in spaces and cover for team-mates. In the key area of midfield a lot of teams found it difficult to pick players up because Jansen had a fluid system there, where he deployed Morten Wieghorst, Lambert and Craig Burley, who had joined Celtic from Chelsea during the summer of 1997. If Lambert moved position slightly, then Wieghorst would also move and Burley would move. Burley delighted the support that season by often getting into the box late to score. Wieghorst had a great season supplementing the more eye-catching talents of Burley and Lambert. Another great strength of Jansen's management style was that he maintained a settled line-up throughout the season, allowing the players to grow deeply familiar with each other's style of play. The Dutchman also had a very good eye for a player. In his first few games he had tried out most of those players who were available to him and had quickly identified those who were not good enough for his requirements. Those looking on with a practised eye were in general agreement with his decisions.

Soon Celtic were on a roll. Eight straight League victories were accompanied by an exciting UEFA Cup run that ended at Anfield on 30 September 1997 with a 2–2 aggregate draw in the second-round tie with Liverpool, who progressed at Celtic's expense only on away goals. Most importantly, a 3–0 win over Dundee United in the League Cup final at Ibrox on 30 November gave Celtic their second trophy of the 1990s.

On the pitch, performances were improving but there had been an early sign that things were not going well behind the scenes when David Hay was dismissed from his position as assistant general manager and chief scout in late October 1997. Hay had been chief scout during Tommy Burns' time as manager and had been involved closely in the signings of Pierre van Hooijdonk, Paolo Di Canio and Jorge Cadete. After Burns' departure Hay had been acting general manager in the period prior to Jock Brown's appointment.

Following Jansen's appointment as head coach, Hay had also played an important part in liaising, in tandem with Jock Brown, with Henrik Larsson's agent after Jansen had made it clear he wanted to sign the Swede from Feyenoord. The same agent had dealt with Celtic over Pierre van Hooijdonk and felt aggrieved by his treatment in his dealings with the club so was hesitant about dealing with Celtic again when they wanted Henrik. Hay had helped Brown to smooth the waters over on a trip to Holland to see the agent. It also helped that Henrik liked Wim Jansen and wanted to work with him again.

It was an ongoing dispute over pay that had resulted in Brown taking the decision to dismiss Hay, who then took his case to an industrial tribunal. Hay lost that case in June 1998 but in late 1997 his dismissal gave the press another stick with which to beat Brown. Jansen was angered by Hay's dismissal and his relationship with Jock Brown quickly deteriorated to the point where Jansen would no longer speak to Brown.

A steady sequence of results in the League during early 1998 pushed Celtic five points clear of Rangers by March but that month a newspaper story appeared revealing to the public a one-year 'break clause' in Jansen's three-year contract. The head coach confirmed that the report was true but declined to say whether he would be leaving Celtic at the end of the 1997–98 season. By that point the degeneration of Jansen's working relationship with Brown was obvious to all inside the club.

Celtic had made some good buys that 1997–98 season, investing £12 million in players such as the powerful centre-back Marc Rieper from West Ham United, Larsson, Burley and Lambert but when Jansen asked for a budget for new players during the second half of the season one was not forthcoming. Jock Brown suggested that Jansen should instead put forward the names of any players he wished to sign. Jansen responded that he could not put forward any names unless he knew the type of money that was available and, consequently, the type of player he could aim to buy. Neither Jansen nor Brown was willing to budge from their position. They reached stalemate and further friction was generated inside the club.

April 1998 saw Celtic's five-point lead wiped out by a home draw with third-placed Hearts and a 2–0 defeat by Rangers. By then, Wieghorst was absent through injury and he was missed badly. A week after that setback at Ibrox Celtic won 4–1 at home to Motherwell with Harald Brattbakk, a newly signed striker from Rosenborg Trondheim, scoring all four goals and hitting the post twice. That day, Rangers were losing at Aberdeen. Celtic went into a three-point lead but that was reduced to one point after Celtic's 0–0 home draw with Hibs and the following week saw another draw, at Dunfermline, which could have been fatal to Celtic's championship chances had Rangers not lost again on the previous day. So it was a turbulent, bumpy approach to the closing stages of the League season and the team was helped considerably by inefficiency on Rangers' part. Celtic entered the final day of the League championship requiring a victory over St Johnstone to take the title. Goals from Harald Brattbakk and Henrik Larsson in a 2–0 triumph gave Celtic their first League title for ten years and prevented the terrible prospect for the Celtic support of ten titles in a row for Rangers.

Wim Jansen was a reserved, shy individual who gave very little away. He was uncomfortable in the company of anyone who did not kick a ball and disliked dealing with the press. If he was out for dinner he would have a couple of glasses of wine and then stop. He was a very disciplined man, a very shy and retiring man but a very determined person. He lived a frugal life and had amassed a considerable amount of money through his coaching work so it was not imperative for him to stay in a job if he felt uncomfortable in it. His Celtic team having won the League title, this cautious, careful man now thought deeply and carefully about his next move.

Two days after winning the League title, Celtic were in Lisbon for a friendly match with Sporting. Players and officials were in residence at the splendid Hotel Palacio, where the Lisbon Lions had stayed prior to their European Cup victory. Jansen chose those surroundings to announce that he would be quitting as head coach of Celtic. It was not much of a shock – such a prospect had been highly possible since March, when it had been leaked that the three-year contract Jansen had signed allowed him the option of leaving after one year. Jock Brown believes that that had been a tactic designed to put pressure on the board to give Jansen an enhanced contract. He had specified that he only wanted a one-year contract when he had met Brown back in the summer of 1997. The club had agreed on a compromise of a three-year contract with a break clause whereby Jansen or the club could terminate the contract after one year.

At that Hotel Palacio press conference, Jansen claimed that he had wanted to quit Celtic just two weeks after his arrival because of ongoing clashes with Jock Brown. 'It would be wrong,' said Jansen, 'to stay when I do not share the views of the people in charge of the club. It is not the right thing to do . . . My relationship with Jock Brown was bad from the beginning to the end,' added Jansen, 'and it was not the best way to continue at the club for me. I cannot work with him and our relationship has been getting worse and worse. There was no base to work with. This is the reason I am going because the important thing is you have to work together. How can I plan for next season when I don't know if I have £1 million or £20 million to spend on players?'

Fergus McCann retorted that Jansen would have been sacked if he had not resigned. McCann commented: 'You can't have one man in a club saying, "I am Celtic Football Club." This is a team effort and everyone is a part of it. This League title was not won in one year or by one man.' Jock Brown and McCann had long anticipated Jansen would quit. 'We had no doubt at all he was going,' says Brown. 'Then wee Fergus, of course, being a diplomat, said that if he hadn't gone we would have sacked him anyway, which is true. There is no doubt about that. He was going because by that time Fergus didn't think he was right for the job, notwithstanding winning the championship. Fergus thought we had made a mistake by October and I wasn't prepared to accept that. I thought that was too soon. There was no question of making a change at that time.'

Much of the friction that had arisen that season had developed because of different interpretations of the titular roles inside the club. Jock Brown, as general manager, was superior in rank to Wim Jansen and when Brown perused his job description it was clear that he could be held responsible for the overall progress of the team. His job function laid out Brown's duties as: 'Overall responsibility for club's football activities in all respects – performance, personnel, budgetary, staffing, within objectives approved by the board. Accountable to the managing director for meeting job objectives as to team success and overall financial budgets.' It went on to state that Brown was responsible for the supervision and direction of the head coach, the chief scout, the manager of youth development and other football personnel.

It seemed inevitable that there would be some blurring of the lines in terms of who was most responsible for Celtic's successes that season: Brown or Jansen. Brown, the lawyer, who lived by words, could look at his job description and see that he would be held responsible for the successes of the team. He was entitled to believe that his overall input had been essential in such matters as bringing in players identified by Jansen and David Hay who had been vital to winning the title, such as Rieper and Brattbakk. More traditional football types believed that the titles in the new set-up were almost irrelevant and that the most vital work was that which was done in the dressing-room, on the training field and on the touchline on matchdays by Wim Jansen. It had, after all, been Jansen who had channelled the talents of the players into a winning team.

Jansen returned to Glasgow for a flying visit on the eve of the 1998–99 season. On the opening night of the second run of the musical *The Celtic Story* at the Pavilion Theatre on 31 July 1998, he made a surprise appearance on stage at the end of the show to wild applause from the Celtic supporters present. Those Celtic supporters had, for hugely sentimental reasons, required the prevention of Rangers passing the nine-in-a-row mark, no matter how unsentimental the methods used to achieve that goal. Wim Jansen had been their smiling, unsentimental friend, using a clinical, tactical approach that was in contrast to the all-out attacking style traditionally associated with Celtic. He remains the only Celtic manager to have left the club at the end of a League championship title-winning season, which was entirely in character with this efficient eccentric.

TWELVE

Jozef Venglos – The Good Doctor

It is a truth universally acknowledged that the Scottish national team does not do too well at the World Cup finals. The 1990 finals in Italy, to take only one example, saw the team lose their opening match 1–0 to Costa Rica, the underdogs' underdogs, and a country making its first-ever appearance in the finals. Scotland failed to reach the knockout stages of that tournament, as they have done on all eight occasions on which they have reached the finals. Czechoslovakia, in contrast, coached by Dr Jozef Venglos, swept aside the Costa Ricans 4–1 in the knockout stages of Italia '90. Only a hotly disputed penalty, won for West Germany with a typical surge to the turf by arch-diver Jurgen Klinsmann, gave the eventual winners their 1–0 victory over Venglos' Czechoslovakians in the quarter-finals. It was the type of World Cup record that Scots have only been able to dream about and if someone had managed to lead a Scottish team to that level they would have been declared a national hero for the remainder of their lifetime. Yet when Venglos was appointed manager of Celtic in the summer of 1998 the reaction to his arrival was a mixture of disbelief and abuse.

The less than gracious welcome that Venglos received was fuelled to a considerable extent by a rumbling press campaign to discredit Jock Brown and Fergus McCann. McCann's forthright, brusque style had made him enemies during his time as Celtic's managing director and Brown, as his general manager, was pilloried in the press. One year previously, Brown had joined Wim Jansen on the steps of Celtic Park to hold high a Celtic scarf with the newly appointed Dutchman and acknowledge the cheers of the Celtic fans gathered at the ground. One year later, Venglos took to the same steps with a scarf, on his own. This time, around 200 supporters chanted 'Brown Out'. The whisperings against McCann grew into sideswipes and snipings and reached their crescendo on 1 August 1998, when the managing director unveiled the League championship flag prior to that season's opening League match with Dunfermline Athletic. As McCann sidled into view, it seemed as though approximately half of the 60,000 present were cheering his unveiling of the flag whilst the other half were booing and jeering the man himself. The urbane Venglos looked on, baffled. The kindly Slovakian admits that he had been unaware of the strains and conflicts that were besetting the club at the time of his appointment and, most unfortunately, Venglos, as the most highly visible representative of the McCann regime, became the whipping boy for the anti-McCann agenda that was prevalent amongst certain elements of the press.

Dr Jozef Venglos had a university doctorate in philosophy and physiology and he could speak seven languages. He was a well-travelled, sophisticated individual, having worked in his native Czechoslovakia, Turkey, Portugal, Australia, Malaysia, England and Indonesia as a coach. He had been assistant to Vaclav Jezek when Czechoslovakia had won the 1976 European Championship and had later been manager of Czechoslovakia for 76 matches, twice taking them to the finals of the World Cup and once to third place in the European Championship. It was an impressive pedigree but he was best-known in Britain for the year he had spent at Aston Villa. His appointment as manager at Villa Park had been a daring one as he was the first individual from outside the British Isles to have been entrusted with the management of one of England's top-division clubs. At Villa, Venglos introduced mineral and vitamin supplements to the players' diets. He also cut out the half-time cup of tea because he believed that if tea was taken while a player's adrenaline levels were high it acted as a depressant on the muscles. 'Gentleman Jo', as he was known in the environs of Villa Park, was well-liked but after a season that ended with Villa in 19th position in England's top division, the Villa chairman Doug Ellis' nerve failed him and he terminated his coach's contract.

The experiment was perceived to have been a failure because of Venglos' style but Gordon Cowans, Villa's most outstanding player of that era, begs to differ. 'The appointment of Jo Venglos was a total shock to us all. Nobody, honestly, knew him. He was really up against it, being the first foreign manager, coming in with his ideas on how to play the game and with strict ideas on the way players should live – for example, he didn't particularly like people going out drinking. I liked his ideas and the way he wanted to play the game but trying to put that over to us British players, with the mentality we've got, was very difficult. I think that's the reason it didn't work. I think we were very set in our ways. Yet now you see so many foreign managers coming in, changing things and doing well.

'Maybe if he had had another year he might have done better but in the first year we struggled. You can't really knock Jo Venglos for what he did because I thought he had some very good ideas and I agreed with the way he wanted to play the game. So in the end you've got to look at the players and think, "Did they let him down?" And I think in the end we probably did by not really giving him the chance to instil those ideas into us and play the game the way he wanted us to do. He was a lovely fellow, a really, really nice fellow. It was hard on him that it worked out the way it did.'

It was during the 1998 World Cup in France, where Jozef Venglos was working as a member of FIFA's technical committee, that he was first approached to become Celtic's head coach. Four years on, he was again to be found in what is to him his natural footballing environment, as he drank in the top-level international action in Japan, again as a member of the technical committee of FIFA, at the 2002 World Cup. The happy members of the Japanese crowd were just beginning to drift away from the Yokohama Stadium after watching co-host nation Japan's first-ever World Cup finals victory as Dr Jo turned his mind away from the action he had just seen and diverted his attention to recollections of his Scottish sojourn. 'I was at the World Cup in '98 in France,' he says, 'and Jock Brown, as general manager, came to me and spoke about the possibility to go to Celtic. I didn't know the full situation, generally, in the club, but the chance to be manager was very nice and a demanding job and an honour for any coach. I told him I'd think about it. Then we spoke once more and I said it would be a privilege to come. We had another meeting in Vienna, then another one in Amsterdam.

'I had always respected Scottish football. In central Europe we have very fine football but it is different in its style from what there is in Scotland and going to Celtic was a chance to experience Scottish football. I had always respected British football; the atmosphere and the spirit of fair play.' Venglos could recall direct experience of Celtic: he had been a player with Slovan Bratislava when the two sides had faced each other in a 1964 Cup-Winners' Cup tie. He had enjoyed the excellent atmosphere at Celtic Park for that encounter and also, years later, that of Hampden Park, when he was coach of the Czechoslovakian national team that lost 3–1 to Scotland in a key World Cup qualifying match. Lubo Moravcik, Dr Venglos' fellow Slovakian, was in full agreement with Celtic's choice when he heard that Venglos had joined the club. 'I was not really surprised that he was made coach of such a big club as Celtic because I know his qualities,' says Moravcik, who would later become just one of several significant signings made by Dr Venglos. 'I think he has been at many clubs in Europe and he had a lot of success with Czechoslovakia during his career as national coach. I think he is respected all over the world because he was working also for FIFA and UEFA. I think he has got a very good reputation. So he deserved to become a coach at Celtic – it wasn't something he only achieved through luck or something like that. It was something that he deserved.'

The contract offered to Dr Jo was for one year only. McCann's five-year plan was due to reach its conclusion in March 1999 and Venglos was to guide the club through to the point where McCann's successor as the figurehead of the club would decide on how he wished the club to proceed. Venglos at the time of his appointment had been combining his work for FIFA with the post of technical director at Slovan Bratislava. The good doctor had no qualms about going to Glasgow for just one year. 'Yes, I told them it's OK,' he says, 'because they told me they wanted to make a transition after McCann had come and had started to build the club with stronger economic powers and I said it's OK. Everything was OK. I was pleased with the club but when I came, Rangers were stronger, using more money to buy players, but I had nice players and quality players, so it was not a problem.'

By the time Venglos' appointment was formally announced on 17 July 1998, pre-season training was over and Celtic's European Cup qualifier against St Patrick's Athletic of Ireland was only five days away. A bonus row over payments for the Champions League qualifiers was brewing and that created a negative atmosphere among the players that lingered for several weeks. The new coach had no connection to this – it was a matter for the executives but it was less than ideal. Venglos was also hampered in that he had little time to impress his ideas on players and no chance of bringing in new players before the action got under way. 'I had much experience of working with players,' he says, 'but you need time to get to know people. It's better to know these people when you have a little bit of time and to know them step by step but after the World Cup some players had injuries so the beginning was not easy. It was a special year because 10 players from Celtic had played in the World Cup and it was very important to give some of those players a rest. So the beginning was not easy.'

A frustrating 0–0 draw with St Pat's in front of 57,000 at Celtic Park got Dr Jo off to a slow start but that result was made irrelevant when the Celts won 2–0 in Dublin the following midweek. A 5–0 spanking of Dunfermline on flag-unveiling day was an encouraging beginning to the Premier League fixtures but that August of 1998 Celtic tumbled out of the European Cup following a 3–1 aggregate defeat by Croatia Zagreb. Venglos' gradual familiarisation with his players, which ought to have taken place during June and July, was actually taking place as Celtic were launched into vital competitive fixtures and key players were absent, most notably Danish international centre-back Marc Rieper, who had returned from the Danes' run to the World Cup quarter-finals with what would eventually be a career-ending toe injury. He managed only a handful of games before conceding defeat in his battle for fitness. Rieper was the most serious absentee but the team was perforated by absences through injury during the opening half of that 1998–99 season although Venglos still retained hope that he could lead Celtic to the title. 'When you are manager at a club,' he says, 'always the ambition has to be the highest one and that is to win the League and I was the same.'

Eric Black, who had been appointed head of youth development by Jock Brown in 1997, was to remain in that position but would also act as Venglos' assistant. 'I had met him once, prior to him taking over as head coach at Celtic,' says Black, 'at a coaching course with the SFA, and I had been very impressed by him. To meet him first-hand, the first thing that struck me was how humble and modest he was for somebody that had achieved so much in the game. I think he was a very shrewd individual. I think he had weighed up everything about the club within his first month. He had weighed up the whole history of the club, the expectations of the fans, the expectations of the directors, how they operated.

'I did a lot of the coaching on the pitch and he would get involved in that as well. There were particular things that he wanted done and wanted to be involved in. I was there for him to bounce ideas off me. He was very sure about what he wanted and the type of players he wanted and the way he treated people was second-to-none. I have never seen anybody as considerate with players and he was very adept at dealing with players and their mentality through looking at the types of individuals they were. He was magnificent at that.

'He was very methodical in his team talks. It was mainly just information about the other team and a structure about how we were going to play. He didn't alter the structure that often. He was quite happy to keep it and believed in getting as near to a regular starting eleven as you can on a regular basis. So there wasn't any real need to repeat certain things – a lot of the players were good players who knew their positions and knew their roles within the team. So his team talks were good but eventually I think it became repetition because people knew their roles. Then he would just speak about the opposition and how we could maximise his knowledge of them.'

That autumn of 1998, pressure was building on Jock Brown from the press and Venglos bore the brunt of it. Disgraceful stories attacked Venglos' character and portrayed him as a bumbling oldster out of touch with the modern game of football. The more gullible supporters who read such stories on a daily basis eventually began to believe they contained a kernel of truth. The problems Venglos had with players recovering from injury and his short settling-in period were ignored as the tabloids opened full fire on the coach. 'You know the press,' says

Venglos. 'You have two kinds of press: constructive criticism and others who are always thinking of other things. That was no problem. As a coach you have to live with that. I can say that I was trying to be professional in my work but some people in the press were not. I didn't always read these things. I would read the press that produced constructive criticism. Every coach and every player needs that. When Lubo came, they did not behave nicely. They said I was his uncle and so on. It's a pity that they didn't know a player who had played in the World Cup and in the national team many times. They also started to speak about my English. It wasn't fair play.'

Lubo Moravcik himself registers annoyance at the press reaction to his signing by Venglos. 'I think the press tried to put pressure on him and me; they were suggesting things like I was his son because he had brought me to Celtic but it was never like that. He brought me in because he was thinking to do something good for Celtic; not because it would help me or help him. Whenever he did anything it was always for the benefit of the club, not for his own pleasure. The press in Scotland are always trying to create some sort of story. I was very happy that what they had said before I played was proved not to be right once I had played some games.'

The introduction of Moravcik from MSV Duisburg in November 1998 had cost Celtic a minuscule amount of money. His arrival detonated even more vicious criticisms of the club in the press because of the size of his transfer fee – the sum bandied around in the papers was put at £350,000 – and because Moravcik was then 33 years old. Celtic in general and Brown and Venglos in particular were ridiculed by the press because of the player's age and because he had been purchased so cheaply. Had they known more of the truth, their criticism would have been even more fierce: Brown had negotiated the price down even lower because he had seen that the relationship between Moravcik and the German club's coach had deteriorated so badly that the player's transfer fee would only be a token one. Venglos, for his part, knew that Moravcik was a master professional and that although he was in his thirties the player was in excellent condition and had a style of play that was not entirely reliant on speed and strength.

Minutes before the Slovakian made his debut, against Dundee,

Jock Brown's departure from Celtic was announced by the club. Brown had done his job professionally in pursuing Moravcik's transfer and prior to leaving the club had been in Stockholm acquiring the signature of Johan Mjallby from AIK Stockholm. The announcement of Moravcik's signing had been rewarded with hysterical press vilification of Brown's capabilities in his capacity as general manager and a few days later the press got their wish when Brown left the club; a sizeable number of supporters had been so influenced by the press that Brown knew he had to be sacrificed to appease them. The general manager had never recovered from the poor relations that had developed with the press from the beginning of his tenure at the club. He was not replaced.

Moravcik made his debut against Dundee and onlookers with a trained eye could perceive the immediate influence he had had on his team-mates as Celtic smoothed their way to a 6-1 victory. Venglos' methods were beginning to bear fruit. 'I found that there were nice players and a nice organisation at Celtic,' he says, 'and in our matches from October we started to play quite good combination football and the supporters appreciated it. There were exceptional players at Celtic, such as Lambert and Larsson, and we began to show what we could do, in combination, as a team. Lubo came and after one or two games everything was OK.'

Moravcik had been rusting in a rut at MSV Duisburg; the coach Heinrich Fink was making him play as a holding midfielder in front of the back four. Now, at Celtic Park, he was reunited with a coach who understood his qualities and the player was free to prompt and probe from an advanced attacking position. A fortnight after his Celtic debut, Moravcik took the field for an Old Firm match. Johan Mjallby, the Swedish international centre-back signed by Dr Jo from AIK Stockholm for £1.5 million, made his debut in that match. Venglos decided to field Larsson and Venglos' fellow Slovakian as Celtic's attacking duo. The coach's tactics worked perfectly: Larsson was pushed on to the Rangers back line with Moravcik in a withdrawn role, floating in the area between the front of midfield and the penalty area. It meant that the Rangers central defenders were constantly torn between holding their positions in central defence or moving out to try to clamp down on Moravcik's mercurial talents.

Whenever the Rangers men stayed static, Moravcik had much space in which to work; when they came out, they were pulled out of position and left glaring gaps in their defence. The result was a 5–1 victory for Celtic, in which Larsson and Moravcik each scored twice. It was Celtic's biggest winning margin against Rangers since the mid-1960s and the days of Jock Stein.

'You have to play football as a team,' states Moravcik, whose introduction to the Celtic team had given the players the confidence that they now had a special individual alongside them, one who could unlock any opposition system or tactical plan. 'You can't play attacking football if you don't have the players for attacking football but if you've got attacking players you make sure you use them in the best way you can. In football, someone has to recover the ball, someone has to defend, someone has to attack, and Doctor Venglos always has good attacking players in his team. I think he's also intelligent enough to have in his team the type of players who will run after the ball to get it for the team. He knew that he had got good players in midfield and that he also needed one player who could do something different. That is why he brought me: because my quality was maybe something different from the quality of Paul Lambert or Phil O'Donnell or maybe Burley. He brought me because he knew that with me alongside them we could make a very good team. He always looked for players who would complement each other and do a job for each other.'

Subtlety permeated Venglos' approach to coaching. 'He doesn't have to shout,' says Moravcik. 'Through his work with players, they can see immediately that he is doing the right things. Naturally, that means that players respect him. He is very intelligent and is good at explaining what he expects from the players. Players understand immediately what he requires from them. He is a gentleman and a good man who respects everyone and who helps his players. Players try to give him back what he gives to them. I had had three years' experience of working with him in the Czechoslovakian team and, when I came to Celtic, it was really a pleasure to work with him every day; it was a rich experience for me. It only confirmed to me how good he was as a coach. In Slovakia he was named Coach of the Century, our best coach ever. I think that means something.'

That victory over Rangers, on 21 November 1998, sparked off a 20-match sequence in which Celtic lost just once. The players were receptive to Dr Jo's ideas and the resultant football was, at times, breathtaking in its expansiveness. Even an injury to Moravcik in February 1999 at Motherwell, which ruled the Slovakian out for the remaining crucial League matches that season, failed to halt Celtic's progress and they stayed hot on Rangers' trail. 'If you are missing top players,' says Venglos, 'and that season we were missing many top players, it's difficult to maintain the balance within the team because you are giving a chance to young players. After two or three months the players were responding to me with a beautiful passing game that was attractive to the supporters.'

Venglos stressed to the players in training that when they played the ball forward their first thought should be a forward movement, as a third party to the move, to support the ball or run off the ball. Players were encouraged to train in small groupings of three and four and to think in terms of playing in groups of three and four on the field during a match. That way they would be supporting each other in mini-groupings on the pitch as they moved forward. It was a very modern idea and highly relevant to the way in which modern football is played by top international sides, where players go forward in units in close support of one another. Venglos' aim was to rehearse these things in training so often that players would automatically carry them out in matches. The players were initially puzzled by some of Dr Jo's methods but they quickly started to respond and started to think automatically that as soon as they passed the ball they would need to make a forward movement to support the team-mate in possession. Such plans worked best when the players were playing one-touch football and as the season progressed it was possible to see a very impressive style of passing play evolving.

An atmosphere of calm was generated by Venglos in advance of a match. He would privately ponder his plans for each game, sometimes over a glass of wine, in the confines of his flat in Glasgow's West End, mulling over the permutations available to him as if he was tackling a game of chess in a Bratislava cafe. Having chosen his options, Dr Jo would then give his team talk approximately an hour and a half before the game, sometimes in the team hotel. He would always be in and around the dressing-room before kick-off although he would go out for a short while before returning to speak to the players briefly before they took the field. At half-time he would be very calm and precise in telling them what he wanted changed. He was almost serene and was never a bawler or a shouter. He would always put his ideas across to the players in a decent manner.

'He was tactically very astute, a very intelligent man,' states Eric Black. 'I remember one incident in a Rangers–Celtic game where he put Simon Donnelly on as a man-marker on Barry Ferguson, which worked. Simon played from midfield and then when we won the ball he was in a position to go and cause problems. It was the first time I had ever thought of anything like that; putting an offensive player on somebody to man-mark them. Normally you would put a defensive player on a creative player to try and stop them playing. We had a creative player performing a dual role, which was something I had never considered before, I must admit. It was great to see. There is no doubt he was ahead of his time. He was excellent tactically and on physical conditioning: he would take into consideration such things as how a player's nervous system and motor system worked when they were on the pitch.'

A 1–0 defeat at St Johnstone in late April brought an end to Celtic's run and left them needing to defeat Rangers in the final Old Firm League match of the season, which took place on Sunday 2 May. On a wild night at Celtic Park, Stephane Mahé was dismissed, somewhat harshly, by referee Hugh Dallas and a disputed award of a penalty two minutes before half-time put Rangers 2–0 up at the break. Rangers added another goal in the second half for a victory that enabled them to clinch the 1998–99 Premier League title. It was misleading to seize on those dying days of the season as the reason for Celtic failing to win the title; the most serious damage had been done early on in the season through the handicaps set in Venglos' way during the weeks immediately after his arrival at the club. Most significantly, his late appointment as manager had the knock-on effect of his signings arriving at the club only once the season was well underway rather than before it began, as would have been the case had he been given some breathing space prior to the season. Mark Viduka, whom he had signed from Croatia Zagreb in early

1999, had signed and subsequently disappeared, going walkabout in Australia when his goalscoring ability was required at Celtic Park, in another unfortunate episode for Venglos. That was the latest in a series of interminable delays that had stalled the introduction of Viduka until February after Doctor Jo had, in August 1998, initially identified him as the striker he required. When Viduka did arrive he was still not fully fit, which meant that Celtic had spent the opening six months of the season with only one outright first-team striker, Henrik Larsson. Such a situation would have been a major handicap to any manager and his team. Venglos' major signings – Mjallby, Viduka and Moravcik – each in their different ways proved to be excellent ones for the club.

'It was probably as good a standard of football as I have seen at Celtic,' says Eric Black as he thinks back to that time. 'He hardly had any money at all to try and build a team and the players he did buy proved they were top buys. Given another year or two I don't doubt that he would have been a very successful Celtic manager. He didn't win anything but that was a lot to do with certain circumstances: he was trying to build a team and that can't be done immediately. I felt, looking at the way the team was playing, that there were a lot of positive signs. I would have liked to have seen him carrying on, bringing in one or two players and allowing things to develop.'

Moravcik comments, 'He didn't really have an easy situation when he came. I don't know why Jansen left but it was really strange because after a successful season he left and Doctor Venglos came and I think most of the supporters and most of the players didn't understand what was happening. That made it a bit of a difficult time for him with the expectations of the job but after a couple of months – and it's a little bit logical that he would not achieve success immediately – the team started to play very well. He brought in good players: Johan Mjallby, who is still playing; I played a long time for Celtic; another guy, Marko Viduka, was the best player in Scotland one season. He couldn't really bring in the players immediately and because of that, success came a little bit later. With things not being easy for him at the beginning, we lost contact with Rangers but after that we played very well, I think, and we performed really well in some games. We played nice football, attacking football; players were confident and playing well.'

Venglos says of his time at Celtic, 'It was a great privilege and a great honour for me to have been a part of the great history of this great club. I was able to work with very good players, some very top players, which they have proven, like Henrik in the World Cup, and Lambert and Lubo Moravcik. Secondly, I had the possibility to compare the organisation of the club with those I had worked at before. The club, when I left, were very nice to me and I have excellent feelings towards the Celtic supporters. I like them very much. They like football and understand it and I feel that when I was at Celtic it was a stage where I felt the club was improving during that year.'

Dr Jo signed off as manager after a dreary Old Firm Scottish Cup final. Viduka was unavailable and Moravcik was only just back from a three-month absence through injury. Neither side played well and although Celtic had a couple of chances, a dull but even game went Rangers' way when Rod Wallace scored the only goal of the match shortly after half-time. Fergus McCann had by then quit as managing director and Allan MacDonald had taken over as chief executive, with plans to install his friend Kenny Dalglish in a new role for Celtic – director of football. 'I knew that Kenny Dalglish was coming,' says Venglos, 'and that was understandable. Kenny was a great personality in the history of Celtic. He was experienced and I said, "OK it's time for me to go." I had no objection to going.'

Lubo Moravcik is sorry that the players were unable to obtain the best possible leaving present for Dr Jo. 'Unfortunately, I think the League was already lost at the beginning. My one regret from that season is that we didn't win the Scottish Cup. I think Doctor Venglos deserved to leave with this trophy. I think he had taken the decision before the end of the season to finish after the season. He didn't really talk to me about that but I was feeling that he had worked hard for Celtic and that he had felt the pressure. He is a guy who really takes on full responsibility for everything; he is not someone who says, "I don't care". For him the season was not easy but even though we were a few points behind Rangers, he never said, "Oh, it's finished." He was always working hard to get closer to them and he believed right up until the end that we could do that.'

A newly-created post of European Technical Advisor was offered by Celtic to Dr Jo and he maintained close links with the club through his youth academy in Slovakia. It is typical of Dr Jo's courtesy that he sent a fax with his congratulations to Martin O'Neill when he won the League for Celtic and the doctor attended Celtic's Champions League matches against Ajax in Amsterdam and against Juventus in Turin during the 2001–02 season. Their performances pleased him.

Doctor Venglos remains engrossed in football and when, early in 2001 he was in Japan, lecturing on the game, J-League club JEF United Ichihara took note of his presence in the country. When Venglos returned home to Slovakia he received a call asking him to take over as coach. With Japanese thoroughness, those calls continued for one year and eventually Venglos capitulated and agreed to give it a try. One of his first signings, in the summer of 2002, was to be Lubo Moravcik, on a free transfer from Celtic. Lubo was pleased to discover that this time there was no one demanding a second opinion on the good doctor's judgement.

THIRTEEN

John Barnes – A Green Recruit

A massive model of the Yellow Submarine rests on the Liverpool horizon as a monument to the success of four of the city's favourite sons. It peeks over John Barnes' shoulder as he describes how he, like the Beatles, found his 'sea of green' only to discover himself washed up on its shore by tidal waves of opposition – and not only from the blue meanies. He is, appropriately, sitting in Paradise Street in the heart of Liverpool as he looks back over his times at Celtic.

Barnes had been 35 years old in the summer of 1999 and his illustrious playing career had been drawing to a close when he made it known to friends that he was looking for a position in coaching or management. One such friend was Kenny Dalglish, his former manager at Liverpool, under whom Barnes had bloomed into a world-class winger. Early in 1999, Dalglish, in association with Glaswegian pop singer Jim Kerr and other backers, had put forward the idea of Fergus McCann selling his shares in the club to their consortium. This idea was rebuffed by McCann, who was determined to sell his shares to the Celtic support but after the departure of McCann from the post of managing director in the spring of 1999, his successor as the club's executive figurehead, Allan MacDonald, had brought Dalglish to the club by appointing him as Celtic's director of football. Dalglish now needed a head coach to deal with first-team matters. He rang Barnes and asked him if he would be interested in the job. A meeting followed at a hotel in London where Barnes met Celtic chief executive MacDonald and Dalglish to discuss the vacancy. Barnes did not take long to accept their offer. He knew it was a big job but had no doubts that he possessed the capability to make a success of it.

'Football isn't rocket science,' says Jamaican-born Barnes, who became the club's first black manager. 'Football isn't difficult at all but unfortunately you have people who have misconceptions about football and about who should be doing what. I didn't think it was too big a job for me but other people would think it was too big a job for me, which would undermine me. Kenny, at 35, did the Double in his first year as manager at Liverpool. Going up there was slightly different but football is football.'

On his arrival in Glasgow, Barnes found that that perception was not shared by everyone. 'I felt that a lot of people thought I shouldn't have been there,' he says. 'That's what I was up against from the start. There was a lot of negativity towards the situation because I was going to be there. There wasn't hesitancy on my part but there was a bit of apprehension as to how much support and how much backing I would actually get, not necessarily from the club but from the press, from the fans, from everybody. So that was the only apprehension I really had. I thought that if the football went OK it would not be a problem. Rangers were the better team at the time – they had a bigger squad and they had spent more money – but I knew that Celtic would be in the top two and I felt that with a little bit of luck we could maybe win the League.'

Barnes was aware that questions were being asked about his inexperience as a manager and was prepared for criticism if his team failed to produce good performances. He was, though, more puzzled when he made a reasonably successful start to the season only to find that it still brought condemnation down upon his head. The team were frequently playing attractive, flowing football, as had been evidenced in their opening League game, in which Aberdeen were simply outpassed to the point where they were bypassed as Celtic ran up a magnificent 5–0 victory. Celtic won nine of their first 11 League matches, thumped Ayr United in the League Cup and progressed smoothly past Cwmbran Town and Hapoel Tel Aviv in the opening two rounds of the UEFA Cup.

'I was still getting a lot of stick,' says Barnes, 'and that's what I found hard to take. I was still being questioned about every decision I made. I think we had scored more goals than Rangers and conceded fewer although they were four points ahead of us. I thought, "If this is the situation when we are doing OK and there are still these question marks, still these doubts, and I'm still being undermined, then it's going to be a very difficult job." I felt that I could do the job if everything remained equal but, as I found out, up in Scotland it is different to England, where Man United, Liverpool and Arsenal, for example, can all be successful. One will finish first, one will finish second and one will finish third but they will all be successful. Up there in Scotland, with Celtic and Rangers, whoever wins leaves the other team in the doldrums. There is no middle ground where you can say you are going in the right direction. It's either you're number one or you're a complete failure, basically. So that was the difficult thing.'

Barnes' approach to the job was to take training every day – along with Eric Black, who had remained as Celtic's assistant head coach – take in another match approximately once every week and supervise the team on Saturdays. He would go in to Celtic Park at around 9.30 in the morning and stay at the office after training until around four o'clock and take a day off on a Sunday. Kenny Dalglish would attend most training sessions and would join Barnes in looking at videos of players who were potential signings for the club. Dalglish might even take a player aside for a word or two at the end of a training session.

Barnes had set up home in a luxury Milngavie flat that was situated opposite a sprawling estate, which had a farmer's cattle field to the rear and which sat next door to the local fire station. Alarm bells were soon ringing for the Celtic manager. Henrik Larsson sustained a fractured leg in the 1–0 away UEFA Cup defeat at Olympique Lyon in late October and that ruled the prolific goalscorer out of action for six months.

It meant that Barnes plunged into November 1999 facing a difficult home second leg against Lyon followed by three tricky away fixtures, minus the one man who could always be expected to bring in the goals. The 55,000 Celtic Park crowd for the Lyon match had their spirits dampened when an early goal for the French club left Celtic requiring three goals to take the tie. They failed to score one and, on a damp squib of an evening, tumbled out of the tournament. That heaped even more pressure on Barnes as he faced his Old Firm debut three days later. Celtic went 2–1 ahead but Paul Lambert had several teeth knocked out after a heavy collision with Jorg Albertz in the Celtic penalty area that cost the team a vital spot-kick. Lambert had to leave the field, following which Celtic slid to a 4–2 defeat that left them seven points behind their Glasgow rivals. Barnes' critics rounded on him after that setback, which had made Celtic's chances of taking the title now very slim. Only one week of November had passed but Rangers, still unbeaten in the Scottish League, were beginning to look unstoppable. Barnes felt with some justification that his team had been in position to get a victory at Ibrox prior to Lambert leaving the pitch as a result of his injury and a win that day would have left Celtic just one point behind Rangers. That didn't matter to the manager's critics. They took the chance to use both barrels as they opened fire on him.

'A lot of people in the press thought I shouldn't have been there,' says Barnes. 'Maybe some people at the club thought so too, I don't know. The noises within the club were quite positive but you can never tell. At press conferences I found that, being an inexperienced manager, every decision I took, in terms of the way I wanted the team to play, in terms of team selection, everything was being questioned. We would win 4–0 and the first question would be, "Do you think you were a bit lucky because they could have had a goal?" Or "Do you think you were a bit lucky because they hit the post?" It was all negative even when we were doing OK. So I felt I had to become very defensive because if I wasn't I felt I would have been slaughtered. As it turned out, I was slaughtered anyway.

'I felt that if I had been as honest as I would have liked to have been, it would have undermined the situation even more, particularly when Henrik Larsson broke his leg. When that happened I felt, "It is going to be hard for us now." Without Henrik and without Paul Lambert when he got injured, I knew it was going to be difficult for us but I couldn't say that to the press because not only would that be disrespectful to the players but it would also undermine our title challenge if there was going to be one. So I said that we still had a chance and that we had players who were good enough to compete but obviously we didn't. So that was that.'

It had been unfortunate for Barnes to have lost Larsson at that stage but his next move was a disastrous one. He brought in Ian Wright, the former Arsenal player who was then on the verge of his 36th birthday. Asked what Wright would bring to the team, Barnes responded, 'Goals'. A more accurate response would have been, 'Offsides'. Nine times on Wright's debut, the ageing striker was caught offside against Kilmarnock – it was clear he could no longer rely on the exceptional pace of his younger days to get past defenders. Wright had been winding down his career at West Ham United and Nottingham Forest but he was no longer required by either club when he arrived at Celtic, reputedly on an astronomical weekly wage. It made no sense at all and, as he was a friend of Barnes, it looked like nepotism at worst; desperately poor judgment and a lack of imagination at best. The more prescient among the Celtic support feared for the future. They were correct. Wright scored an easy goal in the 5-1 victory over Kilmarnock that marked his debut but he made just four starts for the team and proved much more of a liability than an asset. Barnes now admits it was a gamble that went wrong.

Barnes had spent a Scottish record £5.75 million on signing Eyal Berkovic from West Ham United in the summer of 1999. The Israeli's ball skills were unquestionable but the fee – with wages to match – seemed exceedingly extravagant for a player who was reputedly difficult and had a history of conflict with his own team-mates. A lightweight, creative playmaker, he was used as an attacker in tandem with Lubomir Moravcik, another lightweight creator. This required Craig Burley to act as a defensive midfielder alongside Paul Lambert. Burley did so but with a great degree of reluctance. The player felt that he should have been given an attacking role similar to the one he had enjoyed two seasons previously in Wim Jansen's title-winning season and after the Rangers defeat Burley was moved on to Derby County. 'At any football club,' says Barnes, 'especially up in Scotland where it's a two-horse race, you need everybody to be together. All it takes is for either fans, directors or players to be affected negatively and that could really undermine the whole situation.

'So some players were then reading things in the press and they would feel those things were true. Football is such now that you can't have factions. Everybody really has to be pulling in the same direction. Unfortunately, negativity sells in this country and the only thing that you can do to combat that is to win. So if you're winning and you're on top, fine. If you're second and you're doing OK, you're still second and there's a lot of negativity. So the press could undermine the situation because there was an unhealthy relationship between players and the press. There were a lot of stories getting out. There are a lot of stories at football clubs and nothing is supposed to get out but at Celtic there were a lot of stories getting out that shouldn't have been getting out – there was an unhealthy relationship between certain pressmen and players. We had a big meeting about it with the players but no one said anything. It is a situation that can undermine not only progress but undermine success and I felt that the press were a big part of that.

'When I was dealing with the press you could feel the hostility. The thing is, we smiled at each other and in many respects, because I became very defensive, although I was being very polite, I suppose they felt the hostility coming back from me as well. They could feel that I wasn't giving them what they wanted so we were basically paying each other lip service. I knew they were waiting for any little thing to try and trip me up. So it was a strained relationship because I'm not that sort of person at all. I am laid-back and relaxed and I really get on with everyone but I found it difficult up there, I did find it difficult. The only thing you could do was win matches. Dick Advocaat would have been getting it if I was winning because if you're winning then the other one gets it.

'I felt that the press gave my signings a hard time,' adds Barnes. 'Even when we started doing not particularly well, the press's criticisms were not aimed at the Celtic team as a whole. It was "Petrov shouldn't be playing" or "Petta shouldn't be playing" or "Berkovic shouldn't be playing". I felt that that gave the other players a bit of an excuse because it was never suggested that it was their fault. It was always going to be the signings that I had made. So therefore you were caught in a situation where Bobby Petta couldn't perform. Even when you put him out there he couldn't perform because the whole 60,000 were getting on his back, as they did, unfairly as far as I was concerned. It really meant that he couldn't perform to his true ability and as you can now see both he and Petrov are two of the best players they have had in the last couple of years.

'If a club has had seven managers in ten years, as Celtic had by the time I arrived, the players can get a little bit complacent because what that's actually saying to the players is that if it goes wrong it's not their fault. So therefore they can get a little bit complacent about the situation rather than taking on responsibility themselves. They can say, "We're going to get a new manager if it doesn't work out. We'll be here because we've got a four- or five-year contract. When the new manager comes in, if we respond to him we respond to him. If we don't we don't. We can really choose as to whether we can respond to him or not." At first, the players' response to my ideas was fine but then, of course, once the press started questioning the system, that was when the players started to question things as well.'

Lubo Moravcik was one of the players who felt less than comfortable with the system of play that Barnes imposed on the team. 'I knew his system. Before the season I thought John Barnes didn't want me. I asked him if I should leave because he was the new coach. I told him that he was the new coach and had never seen me play. I asked him what he thought about me. I said that I wanted to play football; I didn't want to stay and watch from the sidelines. I had one year left on my contract and I said to him that if he didn't want me I would prefer to leave and go to another club. He said, "No, no, I want you to stay and this is going to be your position, a left-sided attacking midfielder." I accepted what he said and knew what he wanted me to do. I had played in that position many years previously so it wasn't something completely new. I was happy. If I wasn't happy and had said I wouldn't play in his system, he might have said, "OK, you can go", but I accepted what he wanted. I couldn't later go and criticise him and ask why I was being played on the left side when I wanted to play in behind two strikers because I didn't say that before the season, but when I analyse it, the system for the players that he used for the games wasn't the best one. It wasn't bad because we won many games and we played well but it wasn't the best system.

'I will tell you something about Barnes,' he adds. 'He didn't create the system to suit the players that he had. He made the system first and thought he would get the players to fit into his system. I don't think he was right to do this. He didn't have the players for this system; this is my opinion. I think you have to look at your players and adapt your system to the players that you have. Martin O'Neill has got his system but he brought in the players who could play in this system. Barnes, I think, made a mistake because he brought in the players who weren't good for this system. He was using 4–4–2 and the players could not play in the positions in which he wanted them to play. He played me on the left, like Giggs. I'm not Giggs! He played Berkovic on the right, like Beckham, but he's not Beckham.

'He brought in Olivier Tebily, for example, who is not Laurent Blanc. Tebily is a good player, he has played well for Birmingham, but to bring in a player who is unknown and give him this responsibility is giving him a very hard job. If you want to be successful you have to be very clever in what you do. Football is not one game or ten games: football is over the whole season. John Barnes' system couldn't work with the players he had. It's not the system that is important; it is the players who are important. It may have worked in 10 or 20 matches, but Martin has been successful for 2 years, not 1 time or 20 times. Sometimes, with John Barnes, we would play very well and win 7–0, sometimes we would lose 2–1.

'Barnes was also unlucky because the best and most important player for Celtic, Henrik, got an injury very early in the season and it is very hard to replace him. I think it was that that meant the season wasn't really successful. John Barnes is a very nice guy, I've got nothing against him, he's a really good guy. He worked well with us and was very clever at explaining things to us. You would listen to him in the way you would listen to any coach but you eventually reach that difficult moment when you can see whether he is wrong or not. If everything is OK and you are winning, you can't see the faults but when the team is in trouble, that is when you see what is wrong. In my opinion he should have kept the team from the previous season, seen what was very good and kept it and maybe brought in better players, because we had been doing well at the end of that season. Instead, he said, "These are my ideas and I will do everything in the way that I want to do it." Of course, he has every right to do things the way he wants them because he has got the responsibility but in my opinion the way he did it was not the right way.'

Barnes himself began to feel the pressure of being at the centre of the cauldron of emotion that is Celtic. 'Everyone felt that they could influence the situation because I was an inexperienced manager,' he says. 'No one would be saying anything directly to me but you would hear little whispers inside the club about directors saying, "What about this player playing in a different position?" or "Why doesn't Vidar Riseth play centre-back instead of right-back?"' As things got tougher, one director helpfully approached Barnes to offer him the opinion that one player should be playing in a certain position although this director was then quick to stress that this wasn't his opinion but the opinion of someone else that he was simply passing on to the manager. The manager was looking for backing and support but instead found people chipping away at his position.

'It was a situation where it was backs to the wall,' says Barnes. 'I had a lot of meetings with Kenny and a lot of talks with Kenny. Kenny was probably a little bit disillusioned with the whole situation himself. I was his appointment so he was under pressure as well because of the way that the press were reporting things to be. So Kenny and I had a bit of a siege mentality. We would talk to each other a lot about the situation. We were just hoping to keep on Rangers' coat-tails for as long as possible, as we did up until Christmas.'

November of 1999 had been a tough month for Barnes but he was handed one piece of luck close to its end. His team went down 3–2 at Motherwell but were provided with a reprieve when Rangers unexpectedly lost 2–1 at home to Dundee on the same weekend. The Motherwell match also saw Mark Viduka begin a run that saw him score in ten successive League games and December proved a warming month for Barnes as his team gradually adjusted to the loss of Larsson. 'Paul Lambert and Henrik for me were the two most important players,' says Barnes. 'I knew from Paul's time at Dortmund how disciplined he could be and I wanted a disciplined team. I wanted a team to play in their positions, to understand their positions, and Paul Lambert understands that. He understands how to play that holding midfield role better than anyone in Britain probably, as he proved at Dortmund. So I loved Paul Lambert.'

Lambert returned to action in December 1999 and Celtic began to find form, scoring 14 goals in three League games prior to facing

Rangers at Celtic Park two days after Christmas. Celtic's final fixture of the 20th century saw them play some clever football and go ahead through Viduka after 18 minutes but the game ended in a draw after a Rangers equaliser from Billy Dodds. Barnes was named Manager of the Month after the team's improved performances in December and if his team had defeated Rangers in that fixture, as they could easily have done on the balance of play, he might just have bought himself a little bit of credit, even with some of his detractors. Celtic would then have entered the new year four points behind Rangers. Instead, Celtic were still seven points behind their title rivals as they entered the Scottish Premier League's month-long winter shut-down, a break that prevented the team maintaining the momentum they had built up in December. That winter break was, in Barnes' opinion, to prove the breaking of him as Celtic manager.

A trip to the Algarve in Portugal in January 2000 was intended to bring the team together. Instead, it provided the impetus to tear it apart and to destroy Barnes' hopes of remaining in his position. Mark Viduka was unhappy in Scotland. He felt that it was too easy for him to score goals in the Scottish League and wished to try his luck in England or Spain. He looked south and saw his Australian international team-mate Harry Kewell winning massive recognition at Leeds United, of a type Viduka was denied in the smaller arena of the Scottish League. He was in contractual talks with Celtic and as the new millennium began Viduka was in an unsettled state of mind, as he had been a year previously when he had mysteriously gone missing immediately after signing for Celtic. He roomed with Lubo Moravcik, who was then negotiating a new contract with the club. Both men were considering their futures at the club as Celtic took off for a spot of sunshine in winter.

'Lubo expressed his unhappiness in training,' says Barnes. 'Lubo doesn't say much. He's not one to shout and rant and rave but you know in training when Lubo is not happy. He did not particularly disrupt training but he does not train well if he is not happy, as with Mark. They are temperamental and they roomed together and both of them were unhappy contractually. I suppose if the club had given them what they wanted with the contract situation everything would have been OK. I suppose a lot of people felt it was because of me that they were not happy. I don't know, maybe it was, but I think it was more to do with the contractual situation.

'When we got back from Portugal things weren't right. There were arguments in the camp – the players weren't happy with each other. They had had this split between the players I had signed and the players who were already there so it wasn't a happy camp by then and you really do need everybody to be together to win football matches. Players were arguing with each other over little things in training. Some of the players maybe weren't happy with Eyal Berkovic as a person so then when he lost a 50–50 challenge that became a great big deal. Mark wasn't happy; Lubo wasn't happy with the contractual situation. So it was just an accident waiting to happen.'

Barnes believes that he had, in the football vernacular, now lost the dressing-room and he traces that back to the Portuguese trip, which was supposed to be a team-building and bonding operation. It turned out to have the opposite effect. With a lot of time on their hands, the players had got together and talked and a number of grievances had come to the surface. 'We didn't come back from that Portugal trip with any kind of togetherness,' admits Barnes. 'It was a team-building exercise and we used to go out to restaurants and we had a laugh, we had a joke. The problem wasn't when we were all together; the problem was when players were by themselves. The players would go off to their rooms together and there were a lot of things going on, over which I had no control, not footballing matters as such. There were a lot of political matters going on, which was the big problem.'

Lubo Moravcik agrees that he was having ongoing discussions with the club over his contract but states that this had no effect on his game. 'I asked what was happening with me; whether I should look for another club or whether I was going to stay. They said they wanted to keep me. I said that was OK but that that meant we would need to speak about a new contract. It took a little bit of time to sort it out because players always want more than the club expects to give. That means it is never a discussion that lasts for only one day. Look at Beckham, he talked over his contract for one year! That wasn't the same for me but it took a bit of time.

'Maybe subconsciously I would have been thinking about it but once I am involved in a match I never think about things like that. I would never go into a match thinking not to score a goal because I want to be hard with the Celtic; never, never, never in my life. If I play football I do so to enjoy it and make people happy because the people who come to see us don't care whether or not Lubo has a problem. I tell you, my father was someone very important in my life. He died and the next week I played football because I couldn't lock myself in a room and cry all year. The problem was still there but you put it aside for the time you are on the pitch. It was important for me to carry on with my football. So to do something on purpose on the pitch, what can be meant by that? Nothing, because you don't play for the directors of Celtic. You play for Celtic because of its fans and because it's Celtic. You don't play for John Barnes. You play for yourself, for the fans and, after that, the coach and maybe the chairman. So my problems out of football never influenced my football. I would never play against the coach because I would never play against me.

'It is not my problem if some players didn't want the coach or something like that,' adds Moravcik. 'Honestly, I don't care about that. I have never been a player to do anything against a coach even if I didn't agree with him; never, ever, ever. If he asked me to play I would play. If I was not happy I would tell him why I was not happy but I would never go to anyone and say that the coach had to be changed because he was not good enough, honestly. If I am not happy I say it directly, and I say why; I don't go behind anyone's back. When I had trouble in Duisburg, I said to the coach I wouldn't play any more. Why wait and say that the coach is not good and that the coach should be changed? I wasn't happy at Duisburg and I said so and I left.'

The introduction of Ian Wright to the Celtic team had been a gamble but Barnes took an even bigger gamble on the player Rafael Scheidt, a Brazilian centre-back whom he signed for a reported fee of £5 million late in 1999 without having seen Rafael play. 'Well, we didn't know what was going to happen with Stubbsy,' explains Barnes. 'So we were looking for another centre-back and I had seen him play two or three times on ESPN football. It used to come on at about four o'clock in the morning and they showed Brazilian football. I always thought he had a funny name but he was a Brazilian international and there was a chance of us getting him and getting a Brazilian international for £5 million was something that I didn't see as a risk. He was a ball-playing centre-half, very similar to Alan Stubbs; very good on the ball, very strong, good in the tackle. He wasn't a typical Brazilian centre-half, excellent on the ball and unable to defend, because he seemed to be a good defender. He's a strong boy who would tackle. He would still take the odd chance because he's Brazilian.

'He played maybe 45 minutes in a friendly we had over in Portugal; good on the ball, good tackler, good passer. We didn't go and see him play but we watched a few videos of him and he looked like a good footballer. So we signed him but he never played. He got an injury in his first game and then he got his appendix out. There were a lot of stories about him because of his name and then he got injured so regardless of how good a player he is maybe he couldn't have performed for Celtic. Maybe he's not a bad player but maybe he couldn't have played for Celtic because of the circumstances.' Barnes was lampooned in the press for spending so much money on a player who failed to make any impression at Celtic Park during the months he spent at the club. 'By then the whole situation had been undermined,' says Barnes, 'whereby I felt that any players I signed, of which he was one, were getting stick. I had gone a month after he had signed so I didn't see a lot of him. A lot of managers sign players without having watched them in the flesh but unfortunately if you are inexperienced and you do it, people give you a lot of stick.'

Barnes has assembled a defence of his actions in not going to watch the player in action and instead relying on televised evidence of the player's talents. 'If you go and watch a player and he plays badly,' he asks, 'do you not sign him and say he's crap? If you see ten videos of a player you can see that player much more because you're not going to South America to watch them play ten times. With the cameras now, you can have a camera trained on one player and you can see much more from videos. You can rewind to see his position, you can slow it down. If you go and watch a game you can think a player is in a bad position but when you see it again on replays you can say, "No, that's not as I thought." So I much prefer watching videos. It's not necessary to go and see a player.'

Injury again deprived Barnes of Lambert's services in the new year. The team now began to suffer as a makeshift defensive midfield partnership of Regi Blinker and the young, willowy Colin Healy – a burglar's idea of perfect home security – patrolled the rear midfield perimeter like a couple of friendly labradors. The team returned from their break to draw 1–1 at Kilmarnock and then lose 3–2 to Hearts in a hair-tearing display for the fans at Celtic Park. That sequence made for a quick-step that saw their title hopes dance away into the night. Three days after that, on 8 February 2000, Inverness Caledonian Thistle rolled up at Celtic Park for a third-round Scottish Cup tie. The match had originally been scheduled for ten days previously but, with the fans outside and awaiting the opening of the turnstiles, the game had been called off after high winds had left loose a piece of roofing that was deemed to constitute a danger to the supporters. It is tempting to consider whether things might have turned out better for Barnes if the match had been played on its original scheduled date but he dismisses the proposal out of hand. By then, he felt, the situation at Celtic was spiralling out of his control. Barnes believed he could see the players' unhappiness in training, that training wasn't sharp and that there was a clear lack of togetherness, but he expected that once the Caley game started, things would click into place and his team would get the necessary victory.

The possibility that Barnes could have done something on a one-to-one basis with his players to pep them up and draw out the best from them is dismissed by him. 'These are individual characters, so what you do is you prepare training and if players aren't willing to go ahead and do that, what you can do is you can make it worse: you can drop them and fine them and whatever but that would make the situation even worse. It's really up to individuals who are professionals who will say, regardless of whether they are happy with you or not, that they are a professional player.'

It is never a good idea to entrust people, in any walk of life, to simply do their job to the best of their ability because they are being paid for it, a maxim that applies to professional footballers as much as it does to any other profession. Man-management must be applied: players have to be prodded, pushed, coaxed and cajoled to give of their best, each in their own particular way. Barnes' willingness to trust in the players' professional pride was a flimsy strategy that highlighted his managerial inexperience.

'As I say,' he adds, 'the biggest over-riding factor with Celtic, for me, apart from anything else, was the fact that if you have seven managers in ten years the message that sends to the players is, "It's not your fault; no problem. So therefore if you lose, no problem, we'll just get rid of the manager." Once that gets into the mentality of the players, you've lost. It reached the situation where some players wouldn't talk to you or tell you the truth.'

For the Caley match, strikers Mark Burchill and Viduka were supported by Moravcik and Berkovic. None of those four was likely to win an award for tackler of the year and that placed a heavy responsibility on Blinker and Healy. The Celtic back four that night of Tom Boyd, Vidar Riseth, Olivier Tebily and Stephane Mahé, were the type of quartet that would get an opposing striker's goals party going with a swing. 'We had a horrendous injury situation at that time,' explains Barnes. 'So we had a real lightweight midfield and I felt that we didn't really have any option because we didn't have anybody else to play. Lambert was injured, Burley had already left and Petrov and Wieghorst were unavailable to us. So none of our defensive midfield players were available to us. Colin Healy was the one who was holding but we were very lightweight in midfield and I thought that they would cause us problems in midfield because we hadn't got any really defensive midfield players. Nevertheless we were Celtic, we were playing at home and I expected us to have most of the possession.' After 25 minutes Celtic were 2–1 down. 'I couldn't see it happening before the game,' says Barnes of the possibility of an upset, 'but after the first half an hour you could see it.' The score remained the same as the referee blew for the end of the opening 45 minutes.

The team traipsed in to the dressing-room at half-time, disconsolate, down and angry. Tempers were running high and when it was suggested to some players by members of the coaching staff that those players could be putting greater effort into their performances certain individuals simply exploded. Goalkeeper Jonathan Gould started to vent his fury on Eyal Berkovic, shouting the odds about Berkovic's lack of tackling on behalf of the team – Gould might have done better to examine the standard of his own goalkeeping. Fury spread around the dressing-room like a forest fire and the most serious blaze occurred when Mark Viduka, eyes wild, rounded on Barnes' assistant head coach Eric Black. The frustrated Australian, incandescent with anger that had been building up for months, appeared not to be content to restrict his attack to mere verbals – and as the bulky striker stepped towards Black in a furious manner others became alarmed at what they saw as the possibility of serious violence and intervened to restrain him physically from reaching Black. The thwarted Viduka then pulled off his boots, threw them away and refused to take any further part in the match.

'We were down at half-time,' says Black, 'and there was obviously the incident at half-time, in which yours truly was heavily involved. I made a decision at that time to try and provoke something – which I did! It didn't quite work out the way I had thought but never mind! I just tried to provoke a reaction because I thought Marko was the one player that could have changed the game for us. I just suggested that he was the one that could get us out of it.' Black's challenging words to Viduka in the dressing-room, in the midst of a heated atmosphere, provoked the striker but the moody Australian responded negatively rather than positively. 'I think you have got to try and provoke things at times to get the best out of people,' explains Black. 'I tried to provoke something in him and it didn't work in the way that I had hoped it would work and he responded in a way that I didn't think he would do. He reacted in the way that he felt was right. I think he decided that it was maybe best for him not to go out in the second half: that was a decision Marko made, not anybody else. I don't have any regrets about doing what I did. I would do it again if I thought it could save a game. I think you've got to do that.' Ian Wright replaced Viduka and ten minutes after half-time the situation worsened when Celtic conceded a penalty to go 3–1 down. There was no way back from that – there was no further scoring and Celtic had gone out of the Scottish Cup in shocking fashion.

'I will tell you something,' says Lubo Moravcik. 'Everything happened very quickly. We lost against Hearts at home when we had been 2–0 up. Three days after that we lost to Inverness. There was no time to think about what the atmosphere around the club was like. Until these games, I had never really seen there being any problem. When you play against Inverness, you have to beat them so it was nothing to do with the system. We didn't play well. I think the problem was that at half-time we lost our heads a little bit. The argument with Marko Viduka was a very stupid thing because even after being down at half-time we should have beaten them easily. After half-time, I think, because of what had happened at half-time, the team lacked concentration and in football you have to keep your concentration. This kind of thing never happened with Martin O'Neill. Even in a game where we wouldn't be playing well Martin would always come and keep our spirits up.

'This argument made us lose concentration and we lost that game against Inverness at half-time. We could have gone out and gone for that game but, no, the concentration was away. That was the only bad thing I experienced during that period; nothing bad had happened before. This was a problem that John Barnes should have kept under control and he didn't. If you've got a situation like that, the coach must just say, "Shut up! Nobody speak! Shut up! It is me who is speaking. If you concentrate when you go out there, you will beat them, I'm sure. So relax." Instead, everyone started to argue and you can't go back after that because then it's not under control and the boss is there to control everything. John Barnes didn't calm down the situation. He didn't have the experience to know how to do that because he had never been in a situation like that but Martin, Doctor Jo, Alex Ferguson, McLeish, have all had experience of that sort of situation.

'Barnes wasn't a bad coach but he didn't have experience at the crucial moment and I think that cost him his place at Celtic. That is my opinion. When Marko and Eric started arguing, John Barnes should have stopped it. Everyone tried to calm down the situation but it's not a situation that is there for everyone to calm down; that is the job of only one person, you know what I mean? After the situation calmed down, he said, "Now, let's go!" But by then it was a little bit late. If we had won the game, nothing would have happened because of that argument – but we didn't. Still, as they say in my country, "Everyone is a general after the war." '

The players, perhaps surprisingly, had the day off the following day. Barnes and his staff came back in and went home without any discussion of their futures. Kenny Dalglish was on his way back from La Manga in southern Spain, where he had gone to take in a youth tournament. Switching on Sky Sports, Barnes saw Celtic supporters milling around outside the ground and he recalls the moment when he felt sure his time was up at the club. 'I saw a fan say that he had been in and he was assured by someone there, a director or the chairman or Allan MacDonald or somebody, that something was going to be done, blah, blah, blah. No one had said anything to me up until that point – I had been at the club until four or five in the afternoon and no one had said anything to me one way or another. So Kenny came back and our meeting finished up around midnight and I said, "I'll go" and it was sorted out the next day. I couldn't have stayed on because I felt that I had been undermined throughout my time.' He realised his position had become untenable. That midnight meeting at Barnes' Milngavie flat also resulted in the departure of Eric Black and Terry McDermott, whom Barnes had brought in as 'social convener'.

'The fact that I was an inexperienced manager and people didn't want me there was my biggest problem,' states Barnes. 'I didn't take it personally at all because I knew that another inexperienced manager would have gone through the same thing. It was hard to deal with, but I didn't take it personally, as you shouldn't take anything in football personally, no matter what happens, because everyone wants success and if they don't feel that you're the right man for the job or to get success then it's nothing to do with John Barnes; it could be anyone.'

It is clear to Barnes that he did not receive enough of the one thing he felt he required more than anything else to be manager of Celtic. 'You need respect,' he says, 'and whatever it takes to get you respect that's what you need. If you're coming from a position of strength you get the respect. Unfortunately, in football these days it isn't enough that you are employed by the club to manage them and that therefore the players should respect you as they are also employees of the club and you are there to manage them. That should be enough for them to respect you. Once upon a time, players had to prove themselves to managers. Now it's the other way around. For managers to feel under pressure to prove themselves to players is ridiculous.'

Moravcik thinks the timing of Barnes' dismissal was all wrong. 'I don't agree with sacking the coach during the middle of the season. I don't think he deserved that because we didn't do anything really wrong. For me, that game was almost like an accident. It was really crucial for him.'

Barnes, following his departure from Celtic, contented himself with his television work for ITV but he craved a return to management almost from the moment he had been dismissed. His description of the type of club he would like to join says much about what he learned during his time at Celtic. 'I'd be looking for a smaller club than Celtic!' he says. 'I don't know how much smaller but a smaller club, one where people want me not so much because of a Kenny Dalglish who wants to bring me – I want to know that they want me there and I would be the man in control; I would have the support of the directors first and foremost, which would then give me strength in the dressing-room with the players. So I would be much more aware of the political climate at that particular club.

'I wasn't aware of the politics involved when I went to Celtic,' Barnes continues. 'I soon became aware of it but I wasn't aware of the political situation at the time. I was of the belief that all you are concerned about is the football but unfortunately these days as a manager, as a technical director, as a coach, as anybody going into football apart from players, you do have to be aware of the political climate that you are getting into and I was not aware of that, I wasn't even interested in it, naïvely so. I just felt that you would go there and you would try your best for the team and you would all be together and all pulling in the same direction for the club but in football at the highest level it is very political, and probably a little bit more so in Scotland than in England or anywhere else. I can see now why they say that your first job shouldn't be at a big club, not because of anything to do with what you feel or what you have to offer but to do with other people looking in and other people thinking that you're not the man for the job. If you go to any big club, the only way that you can have success at that big club as a young manager is if you are successful straightaway and continue to be successful because as soon as you go through a little bit of a hard time you are completely finished.'

The departure of Barnes saw Kenny Dalglish take charge of team affairs. It was not a role the ex-Celt appeared to take on with much happiness. He was still seething at the treatment his protégé Barnes had received and his simmering anger with the press would boil over openly in the forthcoming months. On his return to the club in the summer of 1999 Kenny Dalglish's brief as director of football was to take a long-term view in terms of youth development and to provide advice to Barnes as and when required. Barnes was in sole charge of first-team selection and training. 'As to whether people thought that Kenny would have something to do with the first team,' says Barnes as he looks back, 'and were therefore happy for me to come along as long as Kenny was going to be dealing with the first-team, I don't know, but that was not the situation. That was not the way it was explained to me. That was not what I required to come. I don't know whether other people thought that, and maybe they did, and that's why they felt that Kenny should have been doing more but I wouldn't have come under those circumstances.'

Dalglish had enjoyed huge success as a manager in England. He had won the double of League and Cup in his first season as Liverpool's player-manager, 1985–86, and remains the only player-manager to have achieved that feat. His second championship-winning side at Liverpool, in 1987–88, equalled the record for going unbeaten from the start of a season through 29 games. It was also one of the most entertaining sides ever to have won the English title, thanks to inspired Dalglish signings such as Barnes and Peter Beardsley. One more FA Cup and one more title followed before Dalglish resigned dramatically and unexpectedly in February 1991. Later that year he became manager of Blackburn Rovers and led them to a swift promotion to the Premier League and to the title in 1994–95, albeit through no-frills football. It was an impressive record but a later spell as manager of Newcastle United had been brief and considerably less successful. By the time he joined Celtic he was ready for a less hands-on managerial role.

'Allan MacDonald loved Kenny,' says Barnes, 'and, really, because Kenny wanted me, Allan just backed him to the hilt. Maybe there were a lot of directors, I'm sure there were, who were opposed to the idea at first, or even during my time there, but nevertheless Allan MacDonald really stuck his neck out because of Kenny. When I was at Newcastle I used to get involved with some of the coaching and things like that, with the reserves, and I used to speak to Kenny about football and he liked the ideas that I had and he felt that I was able to do the job. I picked the team. I had the philosophy, the strategy. I said what went on. I was given the title of head coach but you could also call me the manager. If you look in Europe at the moment, Ottmar Hitzfeld is a head coach but in this country we call him the manager. If you want to call me head coach, fine, but whoever picks the team, puts the training on, gives the team talk, sorts the tactics out, that was me. So I don't care what you call me. Now that they are bringing in more of a European mentality they are giving people titles. I was called the head coach but in the old days you would say that I was the manager. Kenny would go to board meetings. I think I went to one – I wasn't there long enough to go to too many board meetings! Kenny was the one who would really liaise with the board and Kenny was there for the development of Celtic as a club. So what happens is there is a technical director who stays at the club regardless of whether the manager comes or the manager goes. The technical director is there; he has nothing to do with the first-team as such. Obviously with me being inexperienced and Kenny being Kenny then if I wanted to go to Kenny I would but Kenny would not be doing anything down at the training ground.'

Barnes is keen to clarify that he considered himself to be the Celtic manager in everything but name but the title of head coach would appear to have created some uncertainty, not so much as to Barnes' role but as to his authority inside the club. The particular traditions of British football and the role of football club managers are hard to erode – people expect one man to be in charge on the football side of a club. A variety of individuals with varying degrees of influence in and around Celtic were clearly confused by exactly how the managerial hierarchy would work. Those who found the director of football/head coach axis too difficult to comprehend wanted to know with whom the power lay and expected it to lie with one person alone. The simple equation that they worked out for themselves was to measure Dalglish's managerial experience against that of Barnes and come to the conclusion that Dalglish was the man pulling the strings or if he wasn't then he ought to be. It is an assumption that may have undermined Barnes' position inside the club.

'I would go to Kenny and talk to him,' he explains. 'Maybe the directors wanted more from Kenny in terms of him being down at the training ground and having an input but that's not what technical directors do. If they had said to me when I first went that that was what was going to happen – that I'd be Kenny's number two as a coach with Kenny being the manager of the team – then I wouldn't have gone to Celtic. That's not because of anything against Kenny but I was in charge of the first team and Kenny was technical director but as time went on and really because of the negativity from the press and the stick that I was getting, even in the early days when we were doing OK, I suppose that's when some of the directors felt, "Well, maybe Kenny should have a little bit more of a say" type of thing. Kenny never said that at all. Kenny never wanted that but you read between the lines and you heard little whispers from people asking what Kenny's doing and whether he should be down at the training ground. So I felt that that was when they thought Kenny should have more of an input.'

The departure of Barnes meant that Dalglish would now have a great deal more input as he took over as caretaker manager. It started well for him with a 3–0 victory at Dundee on a snow-driven afternoon four days after the Caley defeat. As the players left the field, Dalglish went to each one and thanked him for his efforts. He then raised both arms to the sky in a salute to the supporters before following the players into the dressing-room. A sweet, headed Moravcik goal the following midweek gave Celtic a 1–0 victory in the League Cup semi-final with Kilmarnock and in March 2000 Celtic played competently in their 2–0 League Cup final victory over a very poor Aberdeen side. As players and management strolled round the track in celebration afterwards, the fans chanted Tommy Burns' name but not that of Dalglish; Burns had been recruited by Dalglish that month to assist with the team. A week later at Ibrox Celtic capitulated to a 4–0 defeat, their second loss in the League to Rangers that March. It had been one of the most unusual seasons ever at Celtic Park and its bizarre nature was underlined in mid-April when, in a 2–2 draw with Dundee, supporters witnessed one of the most odd own goals seen at the ground when goalkeeper Gould appeared to have held the ball during a Dundee attack only for the ball, as if it was alive, to squirm out from under his body and squeeze into the net. Celtic's season was by then long over and the team finished a record 21 points behind Rangers in the Premier League.

Team-mates at Celtic remember Dalglish the player as being self-contained – if he decided not to do something then that would be it; he would simply say that he wasn't doing it and there would be no persuading him otherwise. He was characteristically inscrutable as to whether he wished to continue as manager after that season. Tommy Burns had been brought back to Celtic by Dalglish in March 2000 to help out and Burns believes that Dalglish weighed up seriously the possibility of taking on the manager's role on a longer-term basis. 'I wouldn't say that he was never interested in it,' says Burns. 'I think that he thought long and hard about it. The one thing about Kenny is that he doesn't rush into anything – he would look at the whole thing. I believe that, in the end, he felt he didn't need all the hassle of the whole thing because of all the stuff in the press.'

Dalglish, ever since his days as a player, had always had a healthy suspicion of the press. On his return to the club, more than 20 years after his departure as a player, he discovered that the Scottish tabloid press had become ludicrously hysterical, aggressive and unreasonably strident. At one point Dalglish, irritated in the extreme by their criticisms of him, arranged for the Friday press conference to take place in Baird's Bar, a 'Celtic' pub in the rough and ready Gallowgate district of Glasgow, a couple of miles from Celtic Park. It was a less than comfortable environment for journalists as they found themselves being eyed suspiciously by lunchtime drinkers while they went about their business of questioning Dalglish. 'I don't know what the story is behind that,' says Burns, 'whether some of them were bad-mouthing him or whatever. I think those two or three months gave him an insight into what it would be like as the manager there week in, week out, answering the questions. I think he decided he didn't need that at that stage of life.

'The one thing about Kenny is that he has never really changed; he is still the same way. There are no airs or graces about him. He has been a phenomenal footballer; probably the best the country has ever had. He has had great success as a player at club level and as a manager he had fantastic success. He doesn't feel the need to kow-tow to anybody or to tell them what they want to hear. He just says it like it is and if they don't like it, then that's it. That might just be an 'aye' or a 'no' or a 'mibbe'.

'I don't think he has got any real respect for 95 per cent of the journalists; not so much because they've never played the game but because they've never been in a position where they have had to taste the sawdust of the arena. They have no concept of what it's like to be a manager under pressure and to deal with players, supporters and directors. They've got no understanding of that; they just come out with stupid headlines, people react to that and managers are left to try and cope with that fallout.' Dalglish might have made a useful manager of Celtic if his mind and his heart had been set on doing it properly. His knowledge of football is unchallangeable but he had failed to endear himself to the Celtic support when he took over from Barnes and the run of results towards the end of the season meant that the possibility of him continuing as manager was a slim one. His final days as Celtic caretaker manager did offer some optimism for the future as young players such as Stephen Crainey and Simon Lynch were given first-team experience.

Even as Dalglish was winding down as caretaker manager, Allan MacDonald was conducting a very public search for a new manager. His choice was Guus Hiddink, a Dutchman who had won the European Cup with PSV Eindhoven and Real Madrid but who was dismissed early in May 2000 by Real Betis of Seville after a run of 13 matches that had seen Betis win just once. Hiddink was ready to join Celtic as manager and had already spoken to MacDonald and his representatives about players and budgets for the 2000–01 season. It was at that point that one man intervened to veto the appointment of the Dutchman and change the course of Celtic's history.

FOURTEEN

Martin O'Neill – Uncommon Sense

A furious Dick Advocaat looked around the Rangers dressing-room and exploded into anger, telling his players that too many of them spent too much time playing golf and attending to their lucrative, non-footballing sidelines. His outburst rebounded off the walls and knocked him off his managerial feet; soon his players were firmly united in dislike of their manager because of his behaviour under pressure. It was October 2000 and Rangers had just lost 2–1 at St Johnstone, a result that saw them plunge to fourth position in the Scottish Premier League and nine points behind Celtic. Advocaat, who had brought five trophies out of six to Ibrox in the previous two years, was furious because he knew the game was up – and how! Martin O'Neill was in town and Celtic had become full of competitive fury.

Earlier that year, Liam Brady had answered his phone to find Celtic's majority shareholder Dermot Desmond, the new powerbroker at the club, on the line. John Barnes had left Celtic Park and Desmond was anxious to tap into Brady's knowledge of the game to help him decide on a suitable successor. He asked Brady for a name and asked him for the reasons for his nomination. Brady's suggestion was Martin O'Neill because of O'Neill's desire to win and because of his clever, steady progression up the managerial ladder during the previous decade from Wycombe Wanderers to Norwich City to Leicester City. Brady was one of various people whom Desmond was asking for their opinions and the glowing personal tribute paid by the former Celtic manager helped inch Desmond towards his eventual choice of O'Neill.

By that summer of 2000, O'Neill had been at Leicester for almost five years. He had taken them into the FA Premier League after his first season as manager and had led Leicester to the League Cup twice. It was an impressive record for a club with modest resources and several major clubs had tried and failed to lure O'Neill away from Filbert Street. There had, however, been numerous signs that Leicester might be unable to keep him and in the summer of 1999 Leicester were anxiously seeking O'Neill's signature on a new three-year contract during the weeks in which Celtic were deciding whom to appoint as their new manager. It was not until 11 June 1999, the day after John Barnes had been announced as Celtic's new head coach, that O'Neill finally decided it was time to put pen to paper and commit himself to a new three-year Leicester contract, reputedly worth £600,000 per year.

Leicester had been the latest stop for Martin O'Neill in a football career that had stretched back three decades to 1971, when the 19-year-old O'Neill had left his native Kilrea in Northern Ireland, leaving behind both Northern Irish League side Distillery and his university degree in law to join Nottingham Forest. O'Neill was a midfielder in the Forest team that, under the management of Brian Clough, won a surprise English League title in 1978. Even more surprisingly, Forest went on to win the European Cup in 1979 although O'Neill, to his chagrin, was not selected by Clough for the final. He did win a European Cup medal in 1980 when his team-mate John Robertson scored the only goal of the final against SV Hamburg.

The alert, observant O'Neill could not fail to learn from Clough's style of management, even though it was at times eccentric. More significantly, O'Neill felt unwanted by Clough at Forest. He could recall only three occasions on which he received praise from Clough or his assistant Peter Taylor in the six years O'Neill played for them at the City Ground. In O'Neill's opinion, Clough and Taylor could have extracted 20 per cent more from the Irishman if they had given him the type of encouragement he required.

Clough, in turn, was suspicious of O'Neill because the word-happy player was never afraid to voice his opinion on any issue. If the players had a collective grievance, the articulate O'Neill would be their elected spokesman to deal with Clough. O'Neill dreaded those meetings even though he projected a confident air and he would also dread Clough's arrival at training sessions, fearing, often correctly, that Clough would, given any old excuse, pick on him. The treatment dished out to O'Neill was markedly different to that received by John Robertson at Forest. The easy-going Scottish winger was well-loved by the Clough–Taylor management team to whom, in turn, the player owed almost entirely his success at Forest and, later, in the Scottish international team.

On the arrival of Clough and Taylor at the club in 1975 Robertson was verbally assaulted by Clough and Taylor for his frying-pan-based diet, his drinking, his smoking habit and his overweight, scruffy appearance. They smartened and sharpened up his attitudes to the point where he became one of the central points of the Forest attack and Clough had real affection for the easy-going Robertson. The manager was more wary of the mentally sharp, opinionated O'Neill and for a while early in Clough's career he pondered whether to keep the player in his team. It is difficult to avoid speculating that the outspoken Clough saw something of himself in the young man from Kilrea. As such, Clough may have seen O'Neill as a threat to his autocratic running of affairs at Forest.

O'Neill had moved on to Norwich City – after a brief period at Manchester City – by the time he captained Northern Ireland during their successful 1982 World Cup in Spain, at which they reached the second round before being undone by the great Michel Platini-inspired French side. Sixty-four Northern Ireland caps belonged to O'Neill by the time he ended his playing career at Notts County in the mid-1980s. He began learning the art of management at non-league level and Wycombe Wanderers were a non-league club when O'Neill joined them as manager in 1990. He twice led them to victories in the prestigious non-league FA Trophy final at Wembley and in 1993 they won the GM Vauxhall Conference to gain entry to the Football League for the first time in their 109-year history. Their progress under O'Neill was relentless, as they won promotion to the Second Division after their first season in the League. Norwich City prised the young, curly-haired O'Neill away from High Wycombe in mid-June 1995 after a series of clashes with Norwich chairman

Robert Chase. O'Neill resigned six months later and was appointed manager of Leicester on 21 December 1995.

By the time Martin O'Neill was announced as the new Celtic manager, on 1 June 2000, it had become de rigueur for the new manager to make a brief appearance to acknowledge those assembled outside the main entrance at Celtic Park in anticipation of the news. It had by then become an annual event – this was the fourth successive year in which a new man had been introduced in this way. O'Neill grasped the opportunity with assurance and panache. Wearing a dark suit, he strode purposefully through the reception area to the dais outside the main door to meet and greet the support. His expression serious, O'Neill awaited the dying down of the usual cheers then, with left arm outstretched and palm raised, he signalled he was about to speak and, like any experienced pro, he made sure he got himself onside before proceeding any further. 'First of all, thank you very, very much for waiting in the rain – I really appreciate it,' he said. Again he made sure he enjoyed the applause as he closed his left hand to wait for the expected cheers to subside. 'It's an absolute honour for me to be the manager here, I'm telling you that now,' he continued. 'It's an absolute honour. I will do everything I possibly can to bring some success here to the football club. Thank you.' It was brief, brisk and beautifully diplomatic. O'Neill had obtained his release from his Leicester contract after exercising a clause therein that allowed him, during the close season, to talk to clubs interested in obtaining his services.

Lubo Moravcik remembers well the impact O'Neill's decisiveness and clear-headedness made on the players in the weeks after his arrival. 'When he came,' says Moravcik, 'immediately I had contact with him. He said things straight. There was no speculation that we might go one way, or another way, or another way again. He had his clear ideas; he was very clear about his system, about players, about working during the game, after the game. Everything was clear and if someone was not happy he did not do anything stupid.' Eagle-eyed supporters might have spotted, in a home friendly against Bordeaux in July 2000, Stephane Mahé disputing an issue when O'Neill, from the touchline, reminded the player of the position to which the manager wished Mahé to stick during the match. A hard glare from O'Neill soon had Mahé shuffling into place.

That summer of 2000 Lubo Moravcik returned for pre-season training slightly later than the other players and he had put on a bit of weight during the break. At that point O'Neill was juggling with his playing options and his way of dealing with Moravcik emphasised his maturity as a modern man-manager of players who are economically independent and highly opinionated on their role in the team. 'I never in my life have been scared of a coach,' says Moravcik, who has never had any fear of confronting a problem or a manager and whose attitude emphasises the contrast between the players of the present and the players of the past. 'He can't kill you. You can respect him or care about what he thinks but you can't be scared. I have never seen a coach kill a player or a player kill a coach so why would you be scared? So I wasn't scared the first time he told me he was not happy with me. He said to me I was fat and that I needed to lose one stone. He said that to me because he had made me a wing-back and I said he had made a mistake in doing that because he didn't know me. I knew then that if I wanted to be happy in what I expected to be my last season at Celtic I would have to go to see him and speak to him and try to explain to him why I was heavy and what I had to do to get better fitness – and I did. I also had to make it clear that I was no wing-back.

'I went to see him and I said, "Excuse me, but this is not my position. My position is here or here and now it is up to you whether you accept what I offer you because I want to work for you and I want to be successful with Celtic because I like Celtic. He was very nice towards me because he knows I am someone who speaks straight. He told me, "OK, you came back for training a bit later and your fitness is not good enough. Now I will let you get fit and we will take things from there." I agreed with him that part of the reason I wasn't doing well was because I wasn't fit. I needed two weeks extra pre-season, he gave me it, I played very well for him and everything was OK. So he does listen to players and talks to players. He apologised to me for playing me at wing-back. He said, "Sorry, I didn't know you and because of that I put you in that position." It was not my position and he accepted my suggestion and he told me I now had to work hard to get back to fitness. I said I would do it and, when my fitness came back, he gave me my chance to show him I was right and I took that chance. I was very happy to work with him. Maybe if I had been younger and the coach had put me in the wrong position I would have just told him to get lost; that's the sort of thing younger players do. I didn't do it because I knew he had made his mistake because he didn't know me.'

The cerebral O'Neill, university-educated and quietly spoken, becomes transformed on the touchline. With his all-black tracksuit tucked into his socks, almost like a character from the bridge of *Star Trek's* USS Enterprise, he pecks, bird-like, at the bottle of water that, like a comfort blanket, always has to be set down on the ground alongside him. He is a very focussed, intense man, which is essential for a manager of Celtic, a man who thinks about football every waking moment. His intensity during a match is exceptional. One League match at Celtic Park found the startled Hearts manager Craig Levein visibly taken aback when he turned round from looking pitchwards to see a frantic Martin O'Neill scrabbling about in the Hearts technical area to retrieve as speedily as possible a ball that had gone out of play.

That intensity was highlighted in one of the most extraordinary matches ever seen at Celtic Park, when Rangers arrived at the ground on 27 August 2000 for O'Neill's first Old Firm derby. O'Neill's team hammered out a statement about their new-found resolve under their new manager as they overwhelmed Rangers, tearing into them with fire as they raced to a 6–2 victory. Three of those goals had arrived in the opening 12 minutes as Celtic peppered the Rangers defence with pressure. As the goals flew in, O'Neill leapt several feet into the air with joy whilst Advocaat, looking staid in his club suit, was a picture of gloom in the background. Rangers had been unable to cope with Celtic's fast, furious attacks that day but it was not a typical Celtic performance during the opening months of O'Neill's charge; the massive commitment to attack that Celtic had displayed from the kick-off differed from the generally cautious approach instilled by the manager. As such, the all-out attacking approach had completely wrongfooted Rangers. Once Celtic had established their three-goal lead, they were able to relax and let Rangers come on to them before hitting their opponents on the break with huge effectiveness, as shown to best effect by Larsson streaking clear to nutmeg Rangers centre-back Bert Konterman and loft a beautifully weighted chip over goalkeeper Stefan Klos' head for the fourth goal. Paul Lambert, one of the goalscorers in the 6–2 Old Firm game, commented immediately afterwards, 'The manager has instilled an unbelievable air of confidence in us. He makes you play better and he makes you want to win; he's got an awful will to win and he has really transmitted that to the players.'

O'Neill's initial priority on his arrival had not been to produce the most attractive football team but to produce a team that wins football matches and he had succeeded seriously. As a player at Nottingham Forest during the 1970s and 1980s O'Neill had been nicknamed The Squire by his team-mates because of his university background and gift of the gab, which complemented his habit of never being without a copy of the racing aristocracy's bible, the *Racing Post*. O'Neill may have loved a bet as a player but as a manager he appeared to be no lover of risks. His priority was to ensure that his team's goal was protected with maximum security to provide the team with a strong base. O'Neill's way of doing that was to enlist defenders who were bigger, stronger and quicker than most of the forwards against whom they played. That immediately reduced the chances of his team losing goals. O'Neill played three mountainous defenders in a 3–5–2 system that featured two wing-backs, two sitting midfielders, a roving midfielder in front of them and two forwards; one tall, strong and powerful in the air and the other, sharp, quick and mobile. It was identical to the system O'Neill had used at Leicester City and while supporters of the Midlands club were willing to accept any route to success, O'Neill's methods went, to a large degree, against the grain of the Celtic tradition.

Celtic started that 2000–01 season with a back three of Joos Valgaeren, Tom Boyd and Alan Stubbs; Valgaeren, a Belgian international, had joined the club at a cost of £3.8 million, signing from Dutch club Roda JC Kerkrade. Jackie McNamara and Stephane Mahé were used as the wing-backs; Paul Lambert, Stilian Petrov and Eyal Berkovic started the season as the central midfield trio; Chris Sutton and Henrik Larsson were the front pairing. Sutton, signed in mid-July 2000, had cost a Scottish-record fee of £6 million from Chelsea, where he had been badly out of favour. The player had spent just one season at Stamford Bridge after moving to Chelsea from Blackburn Rovers in a £10 million transfer, the third highest deal between British clubs. The striker had played 28 games for the Blues and had scored just twice. An indication of how badly he was out of favour at the London club is that he was omitted entirely from Chelsea's 2000 FA Cup final squad and, on the day of the match, as his team-mates prepared for the final with Aston Villa, Sutton had flown off on holiday with his family.

The Englishman proved an instant success under O'Neill's guidance, scoring the winning goal in the first game of the season, away to Dundee United, and the 6 ft 3 in. Sutton formed a potent partnership with Larsson. Sutton's ability to win the ball in the air allowed him to head knock-downs into the path of the speedy, skilful Larsson, and Sutton also provided Celtic with real physical presence up front. Larsson and Sutton had each scored twice in the 6–2 defeat of Rangers.

O'Neill had won himself much credit with the victory over Rangers but after a couple of months the patience of the Celtic support was becoming stretched by the safety-conscious, often cautious approach of their team. Two home matches on successive Saturdays in October 2000, against St Mirren and Dundee United, were tedious in the extreme but O'Neill's methods, which saw his players competing hard for possession, obtained results. That, more than anything, ensured the supporters remained on his side as he settled into the manager's job at Celtic Park that autumn of 2000.

'I think he's doing a super job,' says Liam Brady. 'He's a very intelligent man and he seemed to grasp quickly what Celtic was all about, possibly in a way that I didn't. I was maybe a little bit of a dreamer about playing football in a certain way. I was a bit idealistic but probably naïve along with that idealism, you know. I thought we could go out and play beautiful football and win trophies. I think Martin has come up the hard way. He has a lot of experience and knows that when he went into that situation at Celtic he wanted strong personalities, strong characters that would fight every inch of the way and I think that's what he has surrounded himself with, as he did at Leicester City to keep them going so well in the Premier League. He moulded that team more or less straightaway and then added the quality whereas I thought we would go out and play everybody off the park. I think that's where he has shown his particular grasp of the situation. My teams would lose games where it became a scrap. Martin always wins.

'I know Martin well. Martin was manager of Wycombe when I was manager of Brighton and we had a few drinks together plenty of times after a game and I know him from playing against him. He was in the Forest team when I was playing for Arsenal. Martin is a good lad. I like Martin a lot. He worked his way up. He was patient enough to wait for the right thing to come and intelligent enough to turn down the things that he didn't really see as being right.'

O'Neill's approach to his players is to simply provide them with the occasional prod in the right direction. He puts the occasional small pointer in their minds as to how best he feels they can go about winning football matches, and that, ultimately, is the main aim of everyone at the club. O'Neill's cleverness also helps him in dealing with those in the boardroom although all those involved at that level are aware that, with O'Neill having been personally selected by major shareholder Dermot Desmond as manager, the manager is not a man to be manipulated or messed around with in any way. O'Neill's philosophy when dealing with his players is to try to keep everything as simple as possible so that their minds are clear and they are feeling confident every time they trot across the white line on to the turf.

'Martin knows, in my opinion, all the time what he is going to do with the team,' says Lubo Moravcik, 'whether it's 0–0, if they are 1–0 down or 1–0 up, 2–0 down . . . he always has players on the bench who may be able to change something or keep the score as it is. If it was 2–0 to us he would maybe bring me on for pleasure but other than that he would always keep me for a situation when he needed me. He's not young – he's 50 – but he has been working hard to get this chance and I think he was ready, mentally, and with his experience, and with everything that he has been learning during his career, to get this chance. Success does not happen instantly, it is not easy to get but he has got it because he has proved over the years that he is good. It is for that reason that I do not want to become a coach to a team right away because I know how hard it is. I think it is better to be prepared before you get to a club like Celtic because if you make a mistake at a small team in the First Division or Second Division it's OK. People will simply say you were not lucky for this or that reason but if you make a mistake at Celtic or Manchester or Liverpool, everyone knows, everyone remembers it, everyone speaks about it. You know how it is. I think to go and accept a job like that you have to be very, very strong.'

The key to O'Neill's favoured 3–5–2 team formation lies in its defence, as opposed to the Celtic tradition of overwhelming the opposition through attacking power. If a team attacks the modern Celtic from the wings, Celtic have their three commando-type central defenders ready to combat crosses, as opposed to the two they would have in a 4–4–2 system. When the two Celtic wing-backs funnel back, it means that Celtic have five players strung across the 18-yard box, which makes it difficult for the opposition to thread balls through towards goal. Those five can also be supplemented quickly by the two defensive midfielders who have most frequently been Paul Lambert and the £5.75 million signing from Leicester City, Neil Lennon, in the opening two years of O'Neill's time at Celtic. Additionally, when the two wing-backs drop back to defend, it brings the opposing team's players up the pitch and into the attacking areas of the field. Once Celtic win possession, the two wing-backs can use their pace to attack the space that has been left by their opponents pushing forward. When every player is fit and available it makes for a highly effective, even an attractive, counter-attacking style.

Early in the 2000–01 season, O'Neill had found the two players who could excel for him in the wing-back role. Wide left was Dutchman Bobby Petta, who had been signed by John Barnes but who had suffered unfairly the rough edge of the supporters' tongues as the team struggled during the 1999–2000 season. Wide right was Didier Agathe, a Frenchman signed by O'Neill for just £50,000 from Hibernian early in the 2000–01 season, because the Easter Road side's manager Alex McLeish had signed him up only on a short-term contract. Bobby Petta was quick and skilled whilst Didier Agathe possessed outstanding pace, ball control and strength. They provided much of the flair in a team that features a rich blend of technically gifted players who can pass the ball around and others who can make life difficult for the opposition through their imposing physical build and fitness. 'With the system that Martin uses,' states Lubo Moravcik, 'sometimes we don't play very well but we win games – and this is most important.'

Pre-match procedures under O'Neill are all designed to keep the players relaxed and confident. O'Neill will read the team out an hour before kick-off. He will then leave the dressing-room and come back in only in the immediate approach to the match. Sometimes he will sit with the players for the final 20 minutes before kick-off; sometimes he might come in only for the last ten minutes before they are due to go out and will just say one or two small things to them before they take the turf. He won't give them a big speech; he believes that they are top players and that they know what the job is all about, which is, first and foremost, to win the game. At half-time, again O'Neill will provide the players with only one or two small pieces of advice. He will not talk for the full 15 minutes but will give the players small pointers about things they can try in the second half and leave it at that. O'Neill believes that the players won't take in that much at half-time anyway. He is a good talker and makes the right points at the right times with real simplicity, knowing that good players will take it in.

'Martin is very clever in the way that he speaks to players because he doesn't speak for a long time,' explains Moravcik who was another of the prime entertainers in O'Neill's side that first season. 'In a few words he tells you what he wants and expects of you. This is very helpful for everyone. Just one example: if he says, "Give balls wide to Didier or Bobby" and that's all he says to you, then you say to yourself, "This is easy." You know, it helps you. This is as easy a thing as you can ask a player to do, to put the ball wide. He is trying to make your duty as simple as possible. You know that if you do that the coach is going to be happy. Obviously you are not going to do that all the time but you know that if there is nothing else on for you and you do that – put the ball wide to Bobby or Didier – then Martin is going to be happy. So what he is doing is trying to help you and take the pressure off you, because if he tells you, "Now what I want you to do is to dribble past four people and send the ball into the top corner, you would say, "What! You are expecting me to go out there and do that?" You would then be thinking that if you didn't do that then he would not be happy. You would lose your concentration because you would be wondering what you had to do to make him happy. Instead, he just gives you one simple instruction so you think it's easy and it builds up your confidence. It's psychologically important.

'You know, Martin and Doctor Venglos are very different but they are very similar in that way; the way they speak to players. Doctor Venglos told me exactly the same sort of thing when I started to play for the national team in a big, big World Cup qualification game that we had to play. He said, "If we don't have the ball, I want you to go back into your area of the pitch and try to defend in the best way you can. Try to win the ball. Don't go to the right or anywhere else, just stay in the space where you have to work and work hard to try to get the ball and help your friends. Once you've got the ball, do what you want. I know you are good with the ball but when you are without the ball you have to work as well. So that's all you have to do to make me happy. The rest I trust you with because I know you are a good player." So I concentrated on when we didn't have the ball and worked hard in the way he said because he knew I wasn't good enough to play in defence but that I would be able to help the team if I did as he said. So Doctor Venglos is like Martin – he trusts his players. That is it exactly. Martin tried to help players with simple things. He knows that Alan Thompson is able to take the ball and shoot and score fantastic goals so Martin doesn't need to tell him to do that.

'So Martin is telling players things that are simple. Yes, they are simple things, but he is telling people to do them. It is psychological and I honestly learned such a lot from Martin. I told Martin before I left, "Thank you because I was learning many things, many, many things", such as just how important something can be even if it looks very simple. Something can look very simple but it is very important to mention it and to bring it to someone's attention. It is just the same as with Doctor Jo: it is simple to go and defend but you have to tell the player to do it and make his situation comfortable for him and trust him.'

Between matches, O'Neill rests his players up. If they are playing games twice a week, training is not as intense. He just keeps them ticking over. Players that aren't playing have to do a bit extra but the players who are involved in midweek and weekend matches are not trained too hard in between fixtures. It has worked for him because he has a lot of good players at the right age. Steve Walford, the first-team coach, supervises the training and John Robertson, the Uddingston-born former Scottish international winger and Nottingham Forest team-mate of O'Neill who is now Celtic's assistant manager, helps Walford. Martin O'Neill will attend training sessions, watching all that occurs with his habitual concentration, but he doesn't get involved in the mechanics of it; he simply looks on. He turns up on a frequent basis but is not there every day and all goes smoothly whether he is present or not. Londoner Walford, a former Arsenal, Tottenham Hotspur, Norwich City and West Ham United centre-back, who appears not to have been adversely affected by his nickname of 'Wally', sets up the training sessions and lets them flow, often through letting the players enjoy five-a-side or seven-a-side matches. Most of the time during the season the players are recovering from matches and Walford and Robertson let them enjoy themselves in training and don't do a lot of coaching.

'I don't think it matters too much to the players whether the manager is at the training ground every day or not,' is the opinion of Lubo Moravcik. 'For example, Doctor Venglos was at the training ground every day and everyone respected him because that's his style of work. If someone has got a different style I don't think it makes any difference to the players. So it does not really matter whether the manager is at the training ground or not because his quality is based on something different. If he is at the training ground, that's fine; if not, that's also fine. I will tell you something: if you want to get success as a manager you need to have a good team of people working with you. Steve Walford and John Robertson are also a part of the success. Martin is the boss but he's got good guys around him and Wally was also brilliant on the training ground. We worked very well with him – it was a real pleasure. John is a little bit different to Wally; John is more a guy who tries to help everybody with their mental attitude. He would talk to you and help you that way. I think in that Martin has been very clever because he brought in the right people and they are people he trusts. So because of that he doesn't need to be at the training ground every day because he has around him people who are doing exactly what he wants. If he didn't trust the people he was working with, then he would not be able to be absent from training at any time. Martin has a lot of things that he has to do; I don't think he is sitting somewhere doing nothing when he is not on the training pitch!'

The effectiveness of O'Neill's style was proven in 2000–01 as Celtic powered to their first Treble of League Cup, Scottish Cup and League title since 1969 and the days of Jock Stein. A Larsson hat-trick won the League Cup final against Kilmarnock and a mere three Premier League defeats meant that the form of the previous season was reversed and that it was Celtic who ended the season out of sight of rivals Rangers. The gap at the top was 15 points and the 97 points Celtic had accumulated was the record total for Scottish champions, seven points higher than the previous best. The Scottish Cup final saw Hibs, who had proved a potent third force in Scottish football over the season, brushed aside with maximum efficiency as one goal from McNamara and two from Larsson gave Celtic a 3–0 victory at a sunshine-strewn Hampden Park. Larsson's 35 League goals had been a vital ingredient in bringing home the title. The Swede had returned to action refreshed and with a healthy appetite for the game after his lengthy absence following his leg-break the previous season. His goals gave him the Golden Shoe award as Europe's leading goalscorer for the 2000–01 season.

Taking the Treble had been a superb achievement in O'Neill's debut season. Now he had to maintain the momentum. Winning the Premier League title had provided Celtic with a ticket to the 2001–02 Champions League although conditions of entry to the group sections were that the team had to negotiate a two-legged third-qualifying-round tie, for which Celtic were unseeded. It threw up the tough prospect of an encounter with Ajax Amsterdam, but the pace and skill of Petta and Agathe, allied to a compact midfield and the cleverness of Larsson and Sutton up front gave Celtic a 3–1 lead after the first leg in the Amsterdam Arena. O'Neill's side had bucked the trend again by attacking Ajax away from home and that performance of controlled power – their finest away result in Europe for two decades – took them into the group stage even after they had been outplayed by Ajax at Celtic Park in the second leg and had lost 1–0 to the Dutch side. That evening Celtic had had to rely on superb goalkeeping from Rab Douglas, who had been signed from Dundee late in 2000, to carry them through.

The draw for the Champions League saw Celtic share space with Juventus, Porto and Rosenborg Trondheim. It could hardly have been more difficult but confidence was brimming over at Celtic Park, as Neil Lennon commented in August 2001, 'The sense of anticipation around the club about Europe this season is infectious. There is already a huge buzz among the fans and that excitement extends all the way to the top. Martin O'Neill was in Monaco for the draw last week and he said it was the best feeling he had ever had in management, knowing his side were in the hat along with all these great European names.'

O'Neill's generally cautious approach was overturned, most surprisingly, in the game that was to be one of the most severe tests of the first two years of his managerial career at Celtic, the opening Champions League match with Juventus in the Stadio Delle Alpi. It was a match in which O'Neill gambled hugely. As he scrutinised the Juventus team sheet in the dressing-room before the match, O'Neill reached the conclusion that Juventus were going to play Alessandro del Piero in behind the front two of David Trezeguet and Marcelo Salas. As the match began, however, it was clear that Juventus were playing with all three up front, which in most instances would prompt the opposition manager to bring the two wide players back as cover. O'Neill took the audacious decision not to do so. Instead, he told Neil Lennon to sit a little bit deeper at the back of midfield, which meant that Celtic still retained five men in the midfield. It worked exceptionally well because Juventus struggled to get into a rhythm and did not play very well at all. At times, Celtic simply played them off the park and an engaging game looked to be ending in a 2–2 draw until, at the death, Juventus were given a soft penalty when Joos Valgaeren was adjudged to have manhandled Nicola Amoruso in the penalty area. The Italian stepped up to send the penalty into the net himself and Celtic had suffered a 3–2 setback just at the point when it had looked like turning into a terrific triumph. O'Neill was so perturbed at the penalty award, which he described afterwards as 'extraordinary', that the referee made his way to the touchline to send a fuming O'Neill to the stand.

Celtic's next Champions League fixture, against Porto, found O'Neill watching from the Celtic Park South Stand after he had been served with a UEFA ban from the touchline as punishment for his vociferous protests at the Amoruso penalty. Celtic won 1–0 with a goal from Henrik Larsson and O'Neill looked in danger of doing himself a severe injury when he refused to allow the sedate surroundings of the directors' box to check his habitually exuberant goal celebrations. A broken ankle or leg looked a serious prospect as O'Neill jumped up and down in the gangway. It was strange that night for the Celtic support to look down at the dugout and see John Robertson running affairs. After only a year, O'Neill's presence had become so reassuring to the support that it seemed unnatural not to see him hovering in his usual position inside the technical area. Defeats away from home to Porto and Rosenborg saw O'Neill's back three stretched to breaking point but another home win, over Rosenborg, sent Celtic into their final match, at home to Juventus on Halloween, needing a win to make it into the second group stage. Even then, they would have to rely on the result of the match between Porto and Rosenborg going in their favour.

Lubo Moravcik provides a clue as to how O'Neill manages to obtain results as and when they are required, both in Europe and in the Scottish competitions. 'He used the players at the right moments in the right place and the team never played on the day before or the day after. They always played at their very best on the day it was needed, you know. For example, if a hard game came along and we won the game, we would have been good at exactly the right moment. We would never win a game 7–0 one day and then lose in the next match. A very good win for us would be 2–0 or 3–0. If we didn't play well we would still win the game. The preparation was good.' Moravcik was used only sparingly by O'Neill in the 2001–02 season and even that was used to best effect by O'Neill. Lubo explains, 'In the game against Juventus he saw I would like to play but he never said anything to me about whether or not I would play in the days before the match. He never said, "Lubo, you will play" or something like that. I was working hard and feeling good about playing in the match and he saw that. He knew he needed to win the game and he gave me the chance. He didn't give me the chance against Kilmarnock or someone because he knew this was the right moment for me, for him, for everybody, and we did well. This was one example.

'I was feeling that this was my game because it was the last game in the Champions League and Martin knew that I had stayed with Celtic for this competition and I showed my desire to play in this game. I knew one hour before the game that I was in the team: always this is what Martin does, the team is named one hour before the game. Personally, I don't like that. I would prefer to know earlier but for this game it was not important because I was so keen to play, really play with pleasure, and give it everything. Sometimes in a League game you will be missing a little bit of motivation because, you know, when you play many games like that, the small games in the season, you need to know a little bit earlier that you are in the team. That way you can work on your motivation for the game. But for the big game you are always ready.

'Although I knew I was in the team at the last minute I was really ready to play in that game. Also, I was very good physically. I was really fit and ready to play well. In football, fitness and diet and other parts of preparation are absolutely important but after that the difference comes through details like concentration and being strong mentally and once you have got confidence and fitness you have to concentrate 100 per cent. Concentration is very important and for me the harder the game is the more you need concentration because your ability is always there, it always stays the same. So Martin saw how important it was for me to play in the Juventus match and he used that for the benefit of the team. He knew I was ready for it and he knew that if he released me into that game I would do everything I could for Celtic that night.' That decision could, without exaggeration, be said to have tipped the game in Celtic's favour. Moravcik was magnificent that night, giving arguably his best of many superb performances in a Celtic shirt. His probing passes from all angles unhinged the Juventus defence time and again in an exceptional game that enthralled every watcher and that ended in a 4–3 victory for Celtic. Unfortunately it was not enough for Celtic;

Porto had done just enough against Rosenborg to qualify for the next stage of the Champions League. Third place in the group sent Celtic into the UEFA Cup, where they were given another tough draw, this time against a Valencia side who had been European Cup finalists in the spring of 2001. Another tight match against top opposition resulted in a 1–1 aggregate draw and a nerve-racking Parkhead penalty shootout that only just went the way of the Spaniards. The Celtic team was deservedly applauded off the park after a run of European matches at Celtic Park that had been almost as exciting as any in the club's history.

O'Neill had by then introduced more of his signings. Gargantuan centre-back Bobo Balde had arrived from Toulouse and he joined Valgaeren and the irrepressible, energetic Johan Mjallby in O'Neill's first-choice back three. Douglas was improving steadily as a goalkeeper and had performed reliably in the European ties. Petta, Agathe, Lambert and Lennon formed the midfield along with the young Bulgarian Stilian Petrov, whose driving runs into the opposition penalty area brought numerous goals for himself and others. Midfielder Alan Thompson provided useful cover as did new £6 million signing from Coventry City, striker John Hartson, who worked well with Larsson, especially after an injury kept Sutton out of the team for much of the rest of the season. The manager had honed the team into a hard-working unit and the results continued to flow Celtic's way in the League, with exceptional consistency.

John Barnes kept a close eye on the doings of his successor and says, 'I'm really glad for Bobby Petta and Stilian Petrov because everybody has really stuck by them and Martin O'Neill has created that, I suppose because they know they can't fool around with Martin O'Neill and that if it doesn't work out it's not because of Martin O'Neill because Martin O'Neill is a proven manager. So if it doesn't work out people aren't going to say that Martin O'Neill is a bad manager or he shouldn't be there. They are going to start looking at the players so Martin O'Neill was coming from a position of strength from day one; the players know that if they don't toe the line they are the ones who are going to be made accountable. So I'm glad for the players who were left behind, the ones who have made it, like Stilian Petrov, who was a good player but who found it difficult when he first came, and Bobby Petta, particularly because he went through a really bad time with his family and stuff like that, and I couldn't see Bobby playing for Celtic ever again. So to be rehabilitated, if that's what you want to call it, the way he has been, is really a testimony to himself and Martin O'Neill.

'I think when Martin O'Neill went, everyone thought, "Well, Rangers are the better team so it's going to be a few years and we'll stick with Martin." He is a proven manager and that's why a proven manager should go to a big club because if they go through a dodgy spell they will back him. He had a great start and has done fantastically well in his first two years, in terms of their consistency. I did not expect him to do so well in his first year. Then again, it's funny because, as well as Celtic did, Rangers lost so many matches. That's what I always felt: it is crucial how Celtic and Rangers do against each other because you're not going to lose many matches but Rangers in that first year in particular lost so many matches against teams that you would expect them to beat. So while Celtic did really well I think Rangers really stumbled. I suppose that's what it's like in Scotland, with the success of one the other team just becomes so undermined by the whole situation that you really do capitulate.'

The Treble holders had won the opening Old Firm fixture of the 2001–02 season and in late November 2001 Celtic remained very much in charge of the destination of the title after a 2–1 home victory over Rangers opened up a close-to-unchallengeable lead at the top of the Premier League. One Rangers first-team player muttered privately in the aftermath of the match that his side had played all the good football and that nobody had mentioned how Celtic killed the game and, in his opinion, made it boring before snatching what he saw as a couple of lucky goals late on. It was a charge that was often levelled at Celtic during Martin O'Neill's first two seasons at the club because of the special characteristics of his team. Celtic had a lot of hard workers who provided the platform for some excellent players and that, in early twenty-first-century football, was sure to bring results.

That November 2001 victory torpedoed Rangers' realistic remaining hopes of the title for that season. The game had had a midday kick-off so at two o'clock the Celtic support were free to celebrate in as wild a fashion as they wished. Previous Celtic managers might have been found quaffing some early-afternoon champagne after such a triumph but it is typical of Martin O'Neill, a quiet, complex individual, that later that afternoon he was to be found in a most unusual place for a manager who had just triumphed in an Old Firm match – Borders' bookshop in Buchanan Street, Glasgow. His trip to stock up on some serious reading matter saw the unassuming O'Neill mobbed at the entrance to the premises and the store had to post security guards on the door to prevent the mob entering and disturbing the manager as he made his choice of books. It was an unusual scenario but then, O'Neill is an unusual individual. Once he had picked up his purchases, Borders' management intended to usher him out through the back door but by this time it too was under siege. Eventually, a third way was found by which O'Neill could make his exit. Staff were delighted to help the manager, who behaved like a perfect gentleman throughout and who had stated that his reception by the fans was what he had come to expect.

The opening match of 2002, a 2–0 victory over Motherwell, showed to great effect the other side of O'Neill. Celtic were by then so far ahead in the title race that Rangers had changed managers in midstream, replacing Advocaat with Alex McLeish. O'Neill could still be seen driving his team on with real urgency, as if every point was absolutely vital to stay in front. With the score 0–0 until late in the game and Motherwell adopting defensive, frustrating tactics, O'Neill became increasingly agitated, making whipping gestures with his right arm at the referee at decisions he found hard to agree with and even at one point sprinting into the Motherwell dugout to try to retrieve the ball and get play going again after those on the 'Well bench had tried to hold on to it and waste a precious few extra seconds. When Henrik Larsson opened the scoring for Celtic late on in the match the atmosphere on the touchline had become so heated that O'Neill even had to restrain John Robertson when his number two appeared bent on ramming home the message to the Motherwell bench that Celtic were now ahead.

O'Neill, perhaps subliminally echoing the American pop artist Andy Warhol – who suggested in 1968 that in the future everybody would have their 15 minutes of fame – had commented just a couple of days previously that it had seemed like only 15 minutes since he had arrived at the club. With the manager by then halfway through his initial three-year contract, it panicked those Celtic supporters who feared that it might seem like only another 15 minutes before he was en route elsewhere and uncertainty might reign at Celtic Park once again. Even that early in his Celtic career, O'Neill's record was hugely impressive and the win over Motherwell was O'Neill's 51st victory in 60 Scottish Premier League matches. The club had suffered only four League defeats in his first year and a half as manager and only one of those defeats, to Rangers in November 2000, had occurred when the club was involved in a meaningful title challenge. All of the others had taken place at times when the League title had already been wrapped up. It was a hugely impressive statistic and one that had not gone unnoticed elsewhere.

Prior to Christmas 2001 Manchester United had started looking around for a successor to Sir Alex Ferguson, who had announced in summer 2001 that he would retire at the end of the 2001–02 season. The United board had begun working hard to put in place a manager for the start of the 2002–03 season. Soundings were taken by the United board as to whom might be interested in the post and various people were approached discreetly. One of the names on the United board's short list was that of Martin O'Neill and United put out feelers to discover whether O'Neill would be interested. As 2002 approached, the United board were confident they could get their choice of successor to Sir Alex and they were a fair way down the line with arranging the appointment of one unnamed person – but not yet to the point of commitment – when Sir Alex decided he would like to remain as Manchester United manager, the option that appealed more than any other to the Manchester United support. It was then easy for the United board to do what they did, which was eventually to agree with Sir Alex that he would put pen to paper for a further three years. O'Neill, for his part, appears to have a genuine affection for Celtic and it would also have been deeply uncharacteristic of him to leave Celtic Park at a time when his work with the club was unfinished – at Wycombe and Leicester he moved on only when he had taken those clubs as far as possible. O'Neill also had a solid bond with the club, having taken the option of £2 million worth of Celtic shares in the summer of 2001.

The winning ways engendered by O'Neill were on full display in the title-clinching match of the 2001–02 season, when third-placed Livingston arrived at Celtic Park in early April 2002. For once O'Neill retreated into the dugout midway through the first half to watch the match in a calm fashion rather than prowling around his technical area like a caged beast. There was no need for any promptings from him on this occasion: Celtic's football on the afternoon proved quite magnificent as they displayed their finest football of the season to take the trophy in style with a 5–1 victory. The crowd chanted for Lubo to take the field and O'Neill, with a very nice popular touch, immediately turned to tell Moravcik to prepare to enter the fray. Two days later, on 8 April, with supreme irony, O'Neill took his Celtic team south to play a friendly against Leicester City. On the day on which Celtic had been crowned Scottish champions Leicester, missing the magic touch of O'Neill, had simultaneously had their relegation from the FA Premier League finally sealed.

O'Neill's team finished the 2001–02 season with 103 points, breaking the record they had set the previous season and making it the first time since 1982 that Celtic had won League titles in successive seasons. This time they finished 18 points clear of second-placed Rangers, whose title hopes had all but perished after that November defeat. The season reached its conclusion on 4 May 2002 with a Scottish Cup final against Rangers, who had been injected with fresh urgency after the appointment of McLeish as manager. A League Cup semi-final in February had resulted in a 2–1 victory for Rangers in McLeish's first Old Firm match, spoiling O'Neill's hopes of repeating the Treble and highlighting new resolve on Rangers' part. The aftermath of that match found some delinquents entering the garden of O'Neill's property in the West End of Glasgow to plant a union flag in his soil. If his wife and family had had any doubts about relocating from the Midlands to the Glasgow goldfish bowl they would have been reinforced by that episode.

The Scottish Cup final saw Celtic twice take the lead in an enthralling game. Twice Rangers equalised. With only seconds remaining before extra-time, referee Hugh Dallas gave Rangers a questionable free-kick, which led to Peter Lovenkrands nipping in at

Celtic's back post to nod home the winning goal. On the strength of that one goal, a considerable chunk of the press decided that McLeish and Rangers were 'the masters now' as the headline writer in the sports section of *The Herald* put it, conveniently forgetting, in their excitement at Rangers' Cup final victory, that Celtic had won the League title by a considerable distance for the second successive year. O'Neill was criticised for taking a gamble on Paul Lambert in the final after Lambert, carrying an injury, was removed from the action midway through the match to make way for Jackie McNamara. McLeish, meanwhile, took a chance on his most talented player, Ronald de Boer, who was less than fully fit. After an hour, de Boer's lack of match fitness caught up with him but McLeish kept him on the field for the full 90 minutes and received not a jot of criticism for it. Both Lambert and de Boer are experienced, influential players and in both cases their managers had to rely on the player's own assessment of his fitness for the match. McLeish had the luck with de Boer; O'Neill did not with Lambert. It was as simple as that.

It was the type of black-and-white press reaction that would fluster lesser managers than O'Neill but he had shown a mature handling of the press in his first two years at Celtic. He could flatter interviewers by agreeing with a point they made in a question, telling them, 'You're absolutely right. I totally agree with you.' Such unusual, overwhelming agreement from a manager with reporters – who are more used to being berated or treated with extreme suspicion – is the type of thing that keeps the press onside. He also demonstrated a column-filling penchant for saying very little at great length, another vote-winning talent that helps pressmen to bulk out their stories. If, in a press conference, the same question is asked repeatedly to try to provoke a response from O'Neill he will simply deny it patiently and simply every time it is asked – once, twice or three times – in a way reminiscent of the eccentric British comedian Frankie Howerd and his catchphrase, 'Nay, nay and thrice nay.'

Lubo Moravcik spent that Cup final as a substitute and the press made much negative comment on O'Neill's decision not to field the Slovakian during the 90 minutes. The player backs up his manager on that decision. 'He has never been surprised by anything that has happened in a game,' says Moravcik of O'Neill. 'I think he is always prepared with the solution for any situation before the game. For example, he had a player like me and he used me very well at the right moments. Even after the Cup final against Rangers he said, "I was keeping you prepared for the extra-time. If it had gone to extra-time you would definitely have come on." I think he was right because with a guy like me, fresh in extra-time, it could be really important. Unfortunately, he was not lucky in this case because you saw in the last minute what can happen to any team. Look at Real Madrid and what luck they had in the last five minutes of the Champions League final when Leverkusen had three really good chances and none of them went in. Either of those teams could have won that game.'

At the end of the 2001–02 season O'Neill assessed the qualities of his side and came to the conclusion that the 2001–02 side was a better one than the one that had won the Treble the previous year. 'That doesn't mean winning is taken for granted,' he stated, 'far from it. We go into every single League game with a mental attitude that the games are hard.' O'Neill was pleased with the way the side had grown in stature over the 2001–02 season, stating that his 2000–01 team would have been unable to cope with prolonged absences of key players and have still won the title. The second championship-winning side was a more resilient outfit, bolstered by the confidence that had been engendered by winning the Treble and doing so well in European competition. It meant that that team was able to cope without Chris Sutton and Joos Valgaeren for lengthy periods, both of whom had been essential to the team's successes the previous season.

'You either have the ability to be a manager or you don't have it,' says Lubo Moravcik. 'Martin's preparation is good. It is good because he has experience. He knows when to introduce players into the team. For example, in the match with Motherwell away from home last season he brought on Shaun Maloney when it was 1–1, Shaun was tripped in the penalty area, Henrik scored the penalty and we won the game 2–1. I can't explain how Martin knows when to do that; when to bring the right player on. Martin seems to have the ability to feel what is going to happen and to feel when he has to change things. He maybe makes a mistake one time from ten; the other nine times he is right.

'In the last game against Rangers he knew we needed to change something because everyone was feeling, "Maybe Lubo has to come on", but Martin was thinking, "If he comes on now, during the normal playing time, then maybe if there is extra-time those 30 minutes will be hard for Lubo." He was thinking that he didn't want to change the team and that he wanted to keep the score at 2–2 and that he could then bring on fresh people in extra-time and that way we would go on to kill the game. Unfortunately, he was wrong because they scored in the last minute but this happened only once. So I would say that even when he is wrong he is right, if you know what I mean. He made the right decision but it was only luck that worked against him.

'On other occasions he would put me on as a sub and I would score to make the score 1–0, like against Hearts and against Motherwell in his first season, when we needed to do something extra to score the goal. Almost all the time he was right when he made changes. Sometimes he was lucky. A good manager is like a good player; he is not a good player in only one match. Sometimes a good player will score two or three goals, sometimes he won't, but he will always be a good player. Martin did very well at Leicester as well; he didn't come from nothing.'

Billy McNeill has watched O'Neill's progress with contentment. 'Martin is the perfect example of a fellow who has had a good, long apprenticeship and obviously has benefited from it and learned from it and has applied it all. The way the balance has altered must be great for Martin because without beating about the bush, there's only one enemy now. The rest of the teams don't count. Years ago there were other teams who were a material threat. The frustrating thing for me now, looking at that situation, is that his ambitions are not going to be capable of being fulfilled with Celtic playing in Scottish football. That is the only worrying aspect about it all. It must be a frustrating situation for him as well. It's just a pity that they are a massive fish in a pond that is too wee. It is possible to get success in Europe whilst playing in Scotland, of course it is, but I think it's going to have to be done through developing a lot of your own players. How long that takes you or how successful you are is difficult because it is a wise but foolish man that will rely entirely on youth.

It's wonderful when you get kids coming through the ranks – it's marvellous when you've got a youngster and then you see him getting steadily better and better and then he gets into the first-team. I remember the excitement of seeing Paul McStay and Nicholas and people like that, it's fabulous, but you get a helluva lot of disappointments as well. You get boys on whom you would back your house and it just doesn't happen for them. Football is like any other profession. You see people improving and then they just suddenly stop and they can't go any further. It can happen at any time. If you had a look at the Under-15 Scottish Schoolboy international teams, and that's the Blue Riband, you then see how few of them make the grade. Look at Under-21 teams and how few of them make the next stage: the failure-rate's frightening. It's very, very difficult to anticipate it and forecast it, and it's expensive now but it has got to be tried.'

The solid backing that O'Neill has had in his first two years at Celtic was solidified even further when, one week after the Scottish Cup final in May 2002, Dermot Desmond invested more than £1 million in buying Celtic shares to reinforce his position as the major shareholder in the club and as the man with the power to be the main decision-maker at Celtic. It gave him by far the greatest shareholding of any individual on the Celtic plc's board. The Irish businessman had bought 2,000,000 ordinary shares – 6.55 per cent of Celtic's shares – to take his holding up to 6,273,770 ordinary shares, more than 20 per cent of the club.

O'Neill's strong support off the field looked sure to continue and, as Lubo Moravcik enthusiastically points out, the sterling qualities that ensured solid success for Martin O'Neill during his first two years as Celtic manager are likely to bring him further successes. 'He made good choices of players and the players did a good job for him. He is a strong guy and he knows what he wants to do in every game. He has been very strong in situations at crucial moments. He really is the boss.' As the 2002–03 season got underway in positive fashion, it really did look as though Martin O'Neill could continue to be the Head Bhoy for as long as he desired.

Index